GUILTY

Hollywood's Verdict on Arabs after 9/11

Jack G. Shaheen

OLIVE
BRANCH
PRESS

An imprint of Interlink Publishing Group, Inc.
www.interlinkbooks.com

First published in 2008 by

OLIVE BRANCH PRESS
An imprint of Interlink Publishing Group, Inc.
46 Crosby Street, Northampton, Massachusetts 01060
www.interlinkbooks.com

Library of Congress Cataloging-in-Publication Data

Shaheen, Jack G.
Guilty : Hollywood's verdict on Arabs after 9/11 / by Jack G. Shaheen.
p. cm.
Includes bibliographical references.
ISBN 978-1-56656-684-1 (pbk.)
1. Arabs in motion pictures. 2. Motion pictures—United States. I. Title.
PN1995.9.A68S52 2007
791.43'6529927—dc22
2007027709

Printed and bound in the United States of America

10 9 8 7 6 5 4 3 2 1

Book design by Juliana Spear

To request our complete 40-page full-color catalog, please call us toll free at 1-800-238-LINK, visit our website at www.interlinkbooks.com, or write to Interlink Publishing, 46 Crosby Street, Northampton, MA 01060
e-mail: info@interlinkbooks.com

Heartfelt thanks to my lovely and talented wife, Bernice, who is always by my side.

CONTENTS

Acknowledgments ix
Prologue xi

PART ONE: ANALYSIS   1

One: The Impact of 9/11 3
Two: Reel Negatives 25
Three: Reel Positives 35
Four: TV's Arab-American Bogeymen 44
Five: Real Solutions 54
Six: Conclusions 85

PART TWO: THE FILMS   91

Film Categories 183
Works Cited 190

ACKNOWLEDGMENTS

I am profoundly grateful to my daughter Michele, and to Monika and Robert for their friendship, love, and inexhaustible faith. I owe much of the success of this work to the keen editing skills of my son, Michael, and to my publisher, Michel Moushabeck of Interlink. His friendship and unfailing encouragement have helped me illuminate justice by bringing this new book out when it can be useful to peacemakers the world over.

I owe much gratitude to Pam Thompson, my editor, as well as Hilary Plum; my literary agent, James C. G. Conniff; and my friend, film scholar Michael Klossner. The moral support and expertise of insightful humanitarians such as Michael, Nawar Shora, Alexander Siddig, Citrin Steven, Professor Chuck Yates, Jason T. Young, and Eyad Zahra helped me discover many post–9/11 movies cited here. I also thank Canada's Leah Bracegirdle and film student Ryan M. Fogarty for writing to me about how hurtful images damage a people.

"Dear Dr. Shaheen," wrote Ryan, "thank you for exposing people to Arab stereotypes in your *Reel Bad Arabs* (2001) book. Your example of *Gentleman's Agreement* (1947), a movie exposing anti-Semitism, serves as a perfect model for a future movie, one that would dispose of prejudices. Stereotypes wound a person for a long time. I know this because I still gasp during the *Agreement* scene when Dave Goldman (played by John Garfield) is called a 'kike.' One day, I hope to make a feature that supports your call-to-arms by humanizing Arabs."

Leah Bracegirdle wrote: "I am an undergraduate student at Mount Allison University in New Brunswick, Canada. I myself do not have Arab roots, nor do I know many Arab people here. Nonetheless, I am proud to say your *Reel Bad Arabs* book helped make this terrible injustice more public. My eyes are now open to Hollywood's misrepresentations of the Arab people, which I regrettably overlooked in the past. More people, especially educators, should write about this stereotype. The public needs a wake-up call. As your book found its way all the way to rural New Brunswick, it will certainly make its mark in more places over the years."

Thank you to Ryan and Leah and others like them for their generous comments.

Individually and in concert let us move forward, keeping in mind A.J. Liebling's dictum: A journalist's duty is "to comfort the afflicted and afflict the comfortable." The quiet power of your activism is an indispensable and effective ingredient that will help terminate injurious myths. I humbly request that when you, the reader of *Guilty*, come across any balanced/heroic and/or slanderous reel Arabs, kindly write to me at: info@interlinkbooks.com.

I am here to support your wake-up calls.

PROLOGUE

The Arab stereotype is the only vicious racial stereotype that's not only
still permitted but actively endorsed by Hollywood.
—Godfrey Cheshire, film critic

At a time when the wounds of 9/11 remain raw, some of my colleagues asked about my motivation for writing a new book about Hollywood's portrayal of Arabs. Simple: Given the conflict in Iraq and Afghanistan, the al-Qaeda threat, and the repercussions of 9/11, it seems more important than ever to remain alert to prejudicial portraits, to test our own stereotypes, and our own sense of fairness. I decided to follow Robert Frost's wisdom— "more light, more light"—by offering fresh thoughts about reel Arabs, insights intended to stimulate thought and encourage discussion leading to a corrective. Seven years have passed since the July 2001 publication of my book *Reel Bad Arabs: How Hollywood Vilifies a People*; has anything—reel-wise—improved? Have Hollywood's powerful post–9/11 images smashed stereotypes or reinforced them? And if images have solidified viewers' perceptions of the Arab as the evil "other," as someone threateningly different, what steps should be taken to resolve the problem?

Arabs remain the most maligned group in the history of Hollywood. Malevolent stereotypes equating Islam and Arabs with violence have endured for more than a century; sweeping mischaracterizations and omissions continue to impact us all. One of the first lessons children learn about this evil "other" and one of the last lessons the elderly forget is: Arab = Muslim = Godless Enemy. And the context in which these images are viewed—against a montage of real-life images and reports of terror attacks (successful and thwarted) across the globe, of videotaped beheadings and messages from al-Qaeda, of the killing of American soldiers, journalists, and civilians in Iraq—has changed drastically. Today, the stereotype's power to inflict damage on innocent people is much greater than before 9/11. During times of armed conflict, stereotyping meets the least resistance; its mendacity most convincingly masquerades as truth, and it is most vigorously defended and justified as truth. Arabs have been so demonized that it has become impossible for some world citizens to believe they are real people; they are perceived only as the enemy, as terrorists, as the "other."

The demonic "other" is especially dangerous and seductive during conflicts. Be he Arab, Asian, black, Hispanic, Jew, or Indian, he has harmed us in the past and intends to harm us even more in the future. The "other" is always outside the circle of civilization, usually threateningly exotic or dark-looking. He speaks a different language, wears different clothing, and dwells in a primitive place such as Africa's jungles and Arabia's deserts—reel hostile environments with signposts. The "other" poses a threat—economic, religious, and sexual—to our way of life. He lusts after the fair-complexioned Western woman. Fortunately, he is inept in the bedroom and on the battlefield. Unlike our noble selves, the unkempt "other" is unethical and inferior, someone who plays dirty; he worships a strange, different deity and does not value human life as much as we do. Incapable of democracy, the "other" is projected as a violent primitive mass opposing world peace and religious tolerance. Only a brave white man and a light saber can save the "other" from himself. As settlers sing in Disney's *Pocahontas* (1995), "Savages, savages... not like you and me."

During times of war, government campaigns and media systems exert an especially strong influence in helping to create and shape public attitudes about the "other." Consider World War I. In this war, the "other" was white. So Anglo-Saxon Germans ceased being celebrated as torchbearers of civilization (forget Goethe, Schiller, Beethoven, and Mozart); instead, they became ugly "Huns" contaminating Americans with narcotics and determined to destroy civilization. US propaganda posters displayed steel-helmeted "Huns" threatening to murder women and children. Belgium's war films depicted the reel Hun horde torching villages and historical churches; Huns raped young girls, old ladies, and nuns and chopped off the hands of children. The Belgian films, points out film scholar Leen Engelen, were especially effective as propaganda, presenting Belgium as "a holy land that's been nailed to the cross by German devils." Sums up director Sally Potter, when governments and imagemakers collaborate to "reduce people to a single clichéd image of who they are—they become one homogenous thing." Thus, it's easy to despise and kill the evil 'other'—he's just not quite human.

Arab = Muslim

From cinema's beginning, Hollywood's fractured mirrors of popular imagination lumped together Muslims and Arabs as one homogenous blob. Yet, Arabs represent a minority of Muslims. Only one-fifth of the world's 1.3+ billion Muslims are Arabs. These distinctions are often blurred in American popular culture. For decades news reporters, editorial cartoonists, novelists, imagemakers, and other media professionals have vilified Arab Muslims.

This enduring mythology that "Muslim" is synonymous with "Arab" has two primary deficiencies. First, it glosses over the religious diversity of the Arabs themselves. Though faith plays an important role in the Arab world, just as it does here in the United States, it's also true that much of the Arab world is quite secular. When we think of the region does Christianity come to mind? After all, there are more than 20 million Arab Christians in the Arab world—ranging from Eastern Orthodox to Roman Catholic to Protestant—who have lived side by side with Muslims for centuries. The vast majority of Arab Americans (including me) are Christian. I've attended Mass in at least twelve Arab nations, praying at an Anglican cathedral in Bahrain, as well as lighting candles in memory of departed loved ones at a Coptic monastery in Egypt. Filmmakers, however, balk at projecting reel Christian Arabs, and their absence on silver screens misleads viewers into thinking all Arabs are Muslims. The exclusion also makes it much easier for directors to paint Arab Muslims as an alien "other," with no links to Western Christians.

Second, failure to present on movie screens Muslims of other ethnic extractions also makes it easier for producers to overlook Islam's universality, thereby simplifying its denigration of Arabs. If Hollywood demonized Turks, Indonesians, Asians, and Indians, the stereotype would lose some of its appearance of credibility.

And, these ethnic groups and others would more readily mobilize against the stereotyping. Indonesia, for example, is the world's most populous Muslim country, but its residents are not projected as Hollywood's reel bad Indonesians; nor should they be.

The reality is that Muslims reside on five continents, speak dozens of different languages, and embrace diverse traditions and history. Like Christians, Jews, and others, "Muslims are as diverse as humanity itself," explains Vartan Gregorian, president of the Carnegie Corporation of New York and a specialist in Middle Eastern history. "Religious, cultural, and population centers for Muslims are not limited to far-off Asia and the Middle East," says Gregorian; "they also include Paris, Berlin, London, New York, Los Angeles, and Washington, DC. Muslims represent the majority population in more than fifty nations—one in five people in the world are Muslims."

Thankfully, most of Hollywood's more notorious portraits of other groups like Asians, blacks, Indians, and Hispanics are behind us. Lingering still, however, is the insidious Arab Muslim stereotype.

Post–9/11 Images

"Movies are part of the air we all breathe," reminds critic Michael Medved. While each of us watches films through the lenses of our own experience, my discussions here are based on decades of painstaking research and the reality of Hollywood's post–9/11's images, and not on my personal beliefs about real and/or reel Arabs.

The total number of films that defile Arabs now exceeds 1,150. In *Reel Bad Arabs* I discussed more than 950 pre–9/11 Hollywood features. Since then, I have viewed another 100+ pre–9/11 films defiling Arabs that were not included in *Reel Bad Arabs*. Plus, in this book I analyze 100 or so post–9/11 films: *Team America: World Police* (2004), *Munich* (2005), the brilliant *Babel* (2006), and others. In my detailed review of post–9/11 films I found that 22 movies (1 in 4) that otherwise have nothing whatsoever to do with Arabs or the Middle East contain gratuitous slurs and scenes that demean Arabs. Arab villains do dastardly things in 37 films (mostly gunning down or blowing up innocent people); ugly sheikhs pop up as dense, evil, over-sexed caricatures in 12 films; 3 of 5 films display unsavory Egyptian characters; 6 of 15 films project not-so-respectable images of maidens; and 6 out of 11 movies offer stereotypical portraits of Palestinians. Finally, DreamWorks studios went out its way to distort folk tales and cinema history, seemingly depriving young viewers of not seeing reel images of traditional Arab heroes like Sinbad. Their animated Arabian adventure film, *Sinbad: Legend of the Seven Seas* (2003), displays no reel good Arabs. Not one, including Sinbad himself! Not even a burnoose or a chord of Arab music. The film was so anglicized it could have been billed *Homer: Legend of the Seven Seas.*

Refreshingly, about a third of the post–9/11 films discussed here, a total of 29, projected worthy Arabs and decent Arab Americans: Arab champions—men and women—are displayed in 19 movies; Arab Americans appear as decent folk in 10 of 11 films. Though the vast majority of films discussed here were released by major Hollywood studios, I also comment on some reel positive American and British independents, and several films from France, Israel, Italy, and Spain, such as *Only Human* (2004). And, I review three first-rate Arab–Israeli co-productions, including *Syrian Bride* (2005). I also comment on two 2005 dramas where Sikhs are tragically mistaken for Arabs (*Waterborne* and *The Gold Bracelet*).

Disturbingly, I found new, vicious, violent stereotypes polluting TV screens. I came across more than 50 post-9/11 TV shows that vilify Arab Americans and Muslim Americans. Thus, I devote an entire chapter to TV's new bogeymen. In other chapters, I discuss the impact of 9/11, reel negatives and reel positives. In the real solutions chapter, I offer suggestions toward eliminating the stereotype and concluding comments. Finally, following my discussions of post–9/11 films, the reader will find lists of recommended, evenhanded, and worst films, as well as a listing of movies by their respective categories.

Reel Bad Omnipresent Arabs

Constant in their malevolency, reel Arabs have not been static, but have mutated over time, like a contaminated virus. In conjunction with current events, filmmakers have mixed and embellished new and polluted stereotypes with old, familiar ones. In the early 1900s, for example, movie-land's Arabs appeared as sex-crazed, savage, and exotic camel-riding nomads living in desert tents. When not fighting each other and Westerners, they bargained at slave markets, procuring blond women for their harems. In the late 1960s, the stereotyping of Arabs began to accelerate with the Israeli–Palestinian issue and by the 1970s—likely in connection with the 1973 Arab–Israeli war, the oil embargo, and the 1979–1981 Iranian hostage crisis—reel dark Palestinians appeared not as a real displaced people but as reel "terrorists." Other Arabs began surfacing as fanatic sheikhs: rich, vengeful, corrupt, sneaky, repulsive, and almost invariably fat.

Add to the reel mix the intersection of "news" programming—cable and network. It, too, had a profound impact on perceptions of "Arabs" and "Muslims," selectively framing them as Hollywood's evil "other"—violent ruthless people. Starting with the 1980s, especially since Israel's invasion of Lebanon (1982), Operation Desert Storm (January 1991), the military incursions into Afghanistan and Iraq (2001 and 2003), and the fighting between Hezbollah and Israel (2006), all those reel desert nomads and obese oily sheiks were suddenly dispatched to the dressing rooms to make room for the new head attraction: Arab as crazed Islamic fundamentalist bent on destruction.

Carried on the backs of the films that bear a single-minded vitriol, cinematic renderings of the Arab are infecting world viewers, from Bombay to Boston. "Cinema has been global since day one," says the noted Argentine critic Eduardo Antin, "and American studios have had distribution offices in every country since day two." In Cuba, for example, moviegoers watch more Hollywood films than movies from neighboring Latin America countries. Sums up *Variety's* Peter Bart, "Hollywood's movies influence the way people see the world." Daily, American films become even more accessible. It works like this. Not long after films first appear in theaters they are released throughout the world to about 150 nations. Months later, world viewers purchase and/or rent the movies from discount outlets such as Wal-Mart and video stores such as Blockbuster; movie buffs go online to view movies, and they also rent or purchase them from sites such as Netflix, Amazon, Sinister Cinema, and eBay. Next, cable TV and commercial TV networks telecast the films—again and again and again. Even cable outlets in small towns regularly beam into our homes, by my estimate, more than two dozen anti-Arab films every week.

Large media companies such as Time Warner, CBS, Disney, and Sony take such popular brands as Batman, Spiderman, or Superman from comic books and turn them into movies, books, clothes, toys, and TV programs, with each of those outlets generating revenues worldwide. Movies are screened in airplanes, hospitals, schools, universities, bars, prisons, even in dentists' chairs. The more successful movies are pirated online, and cloned, leading to TV series, video games, records, CDs, games, trading cards in cereals, coloring books, theme-park rides, and magazines. Record companies release soundtracks, bookstores display glossy books about how-this-movie-was-made, and on and on.

Today, overseas box-office income overtakes domestic receipts, explains author Neal Gabler. At least "sixty percent of the studios' profits come from abroad." In France, Hollywood movies account "for nearly 70 percent of box office receipts." Muslim countries, says Gabler, make up "about ten percent" of the overseas box office. A former US ambassador to Algeria and Syria, Christopher Ross points out, "the electronic media are the premiere media in the Arab and Muslim worlds today." Thus, Arab viewers are regularly exposed to reel demeaning stereotypes of themselves and their culture. Arab teenagers, especially, he says, are impacted by reel stereotypes. Politics may be worlds apart, but young Arabs and Muslims are ardent movie buffs who regularly purchase and/or rent American films, old and new, for as little as fifty cents. Our movies, says Ross, "are the truly potent examples of our cultural imperialism."

A casual visitor abroad can see Hollywood's influence in little ways, every day, just walking down the street of capital cities across the globe: posters and billboards advertising the latest releases, eateries and bars named after famous film characters, and establishments emulating all things Hollywood. For example, in the heart of Berlin you can find the Hollywood Media Hotel; this luxury facility brims with movie memorabilia and all its ornate rooms are named after famous stars and directors.

As actor Leonardo DiCaprio said, "Film is forever"—and indeed movies seem to never die, no matter how bad, dull, or poorly done; the reel Arab in all its evolutions of ugliness lives on and on. I offer you *Ashanti*, a 1979 big-budget disaster that presents Arabs as vile slavers who abuse African boys and young women. Given this abominable film's age and its poor profit showing, I had hoped it would have been tossed onto a dump heap long ago, where its trashy images could rot in their own waste. Not so. On Christmas Eve, 2004, while I was with my family in Prague, happily preparing to attend midnight Mass, *Ashanti* resurfaced in the Czech Republic. My son turned on the TV and found a German TV station beaming the 25-year-old American film into our hotel room. Before I could turn off the TV, our granddaughters had already witnessed deranged desert Arabs raping and whipping chained African youths. After Mass, I lingered inside the church and mused about cinema's pervasive powers. Is there no safe place to take refuge from these images? The words of my supportive parish priest from Pittsburgh came to mind. "Movies are so powerful," he confided to me. "Some have more influence on my parishioners than church services."

Reel Political Implications

Filmmaking is political. Movies continuously transmit selected representations of reality to world citizens from Baghdad to Boston. Dehumanizing stereotypes emerging from the cinema, TV, and other media help support government policies, enabling producers to more easily advance and solidify stereotypes. "It has been a truism for a century that media stereotypes set the tone of many public events," writes Daniel Henninger in the *Wall Street Journal.* Policies enforce stereotypes; stereotypes impact policies. It's a continuous spiral, no matter which comes first. CNN's Peter Arnett describes the linkage best: "The media elite follow US policy," he says, "and those shaping policies are influenced in part by the stereotypical pictures in their heads."

Congress has never declared war on Iraq, not in March 2003, nor during Operation Desert Storm, January 1991. "For soldiers engaged in combat, there's probably not a difference—but in a legal and constitutional sense there is," explains my friend Professor Donald Bittner, who teaches at the Marine and Staff College. "The two US operations against Iraq," writes Bittner, "were authorized by Congressional resolutions that allowed the President to use whatever military force he saw fit, with minimal accountability and no limitations." Bittner characterizes the current conflict as "intervention, to repel aggression and to force regime change."

You, dear reader, should mull over this telling political–entertainment linkage: Long before the United States launched real expeditionary operations against Iraq in March 2003, Hollywood was already launching a reel war against reel Arabs. For years, numerous pre–9/11 Arab-as-Enemy movies helped fuel misperceptions and prejudices. Pre–9/11 action films showed Captain Kit Carson unloading bombs over Baghdad's "devil-worshippers" in *Adventure in Iraq* (1943); in *Deterrence* (1999) the US president dispatches a nuclear bomb over Baghdad. Viewers saw a marine captain blow up a Saddam look-alike and Iraqis in *The Human Shield* (1992); viewers also saw Meg Ryan and her troops gunning down Iraqis in *Courage under Fire* (1996). Kill-'em-all films like *Navy SEALs* (1990), *True Lies* (1994), *Executive Decision*, (1996) and *Rules of Engagement* (2000) projected our GIs, civilians, secret agents, the American president, Israeli troops, even cowboys, terminating reel barbaric Arabs. These scenarios and others depicted us as perfectly good angels killing them perfectly evil infidels. They assured audiences that God was on our side, that we were good Clint "Make my day" Eastwood guys, sure to win easily over bad Arab guys. After seeing our reel Western heroes shoot those bad Arabs dead in their sandals, some viewers stood and applauded.

Our speedy 2003 military incursions into Iraq prompted *Los Angeles Times* critic Kenneth Turan to pose timely questions: Did pre–9/11 films help incite xenophobia and war fever? Did the Arab fiendish enemy "other" stereotype help "feed the unusual haste with which we became involved in Iraq?" Movies, explains Turan, are really "hard-wired into our psyches, shaping how we view the world." Regrettably, pre–9/11 features glossed over a needed view of Iraq—the suffering of civilians. As we may recall, the United States bears primary responsibility for the tough United Nations sanctions imposed against Iraq in 1990 following Iraq's invasion of Kuwait and continuing until the US-led 2003 invasion of Iraq. According to a UNICEF report, the UN sanctions resulted in the deaths of over a million Iraqis, most of whom were children. Turan notes this omission, writing that "It's when politics infiltrates entertainment that it is most subversive—and most effective. [Fiction films] change minds politically... Artful entertainment easily beats full-on propaganda." To support his thesis, Turan reminds us that during the 1930s, just prior to the Holocaust, the average, cinema-going Germans were watching and "being influenced *not by documentaries, but by* Leni Riefenstahl's *entertainment movies* [emphasis added]." Riefenstahl's fantasy films "permeated German popular culture, forming a background on which the nation came to judge the emerging Nazi Party and its Aryan superiority."

Some critics have tried to bamboozle us into thinking reel images, public opinion, and politics are not linked, that movies do not impact viewers that much, here and abroad. They do. Carl Sagan calls "one of the saddest lessons of history" this: "If we've been bamboozled long enough, we tend to reject any evidence of the bamboozle; the bamboozle has captured us." Hollywood bamboozles us by placing influential stereotypes into the minds of viewers. One example: *300* (2007), a blockbuster hit celebrating, as Azadeh Moaveni wrote in *Time*, "war, militarism, and battlefield carnage." The movie follows other anti-Arab and anti-Islamic features, TV shows, and video games. In *300*, the evil, dark, uncivilized Persian "beast prepares to devour tiny Greece." The Persians represent tyranny, the barbaric Muslim East, while the heroic white Spartans represent liberty, the civilized Judeo-Christian West. When watching *300*, US Marines serving at Camp Pendleton cheered the outnumbered courageous Spartans as they brought down the Persian enemy horde. In Iran, however, nearly everyone was outraged—from dentists to taxi drivers—saying the film "was secretly funded by the US government to prepare Americans for going to war against Iran." One Tehran newscast declared: "Hollywood has opened a new front in the war against Iran." Though the film does not belittle Arabs, *300*'s dark-skinned "towel-headed" soldiers may be perceived as reel menacing Arabs, because many Americans think that like Iraq, Iran is also an Arab country, and that Iranians/Persians are Arabs.

"Of all the art forms," observes film historian Annette Insdorf, "film is the one that gives the greatest illusion of authenticity, of truth." Early on, astute political leaders recognized that motion pictures could be used to manipulate public policies and the social attitudes of mass audiences. In the 1920s, long before color, widescreens, DVDs, video outlets, and TV, Russia's Lenin declared, "For us, the cinema... is the most important of all the arts." Lenin and other political leaders began using black-and-white entertainment films as effective propaganda, advancing an agenda. Concurrently, in 1922, the Mexican government banned any US movie that was offensive to Mexicans. Mexico's actions prompted President Woodrow Wilson himself to intervene by asking Hollywood's leaders to: "Please be a little kinder to the Mexicans."

Advance ten years to the early 1930s, when Germany's Goebbels put into play the timeless blueprint for effective propaganda: "[Propaganda] must always be simple and repetitious... it confines itself to just a few points [and images] and repeats them over and over." Or, as the classic Arab proverb, has it: "By repetition, even the donkey learns." At about the same time, British filmmaker Alexander Korda was about to make a movie about T. E. Lawrence (decades before the release of David Lean's classic *Lawrence of Arabia* [1962]). But the British Foreign Office objected, arguing that because of political unrest in the Middle East it would be ill advised to depict Turks as villains. Pressure from the Foreign Office prompted Korda to acquiesce; he did not make the movie. Move ahead to the 1960s. One scene in *The 7th Dawn* (1964) shows British troops torching a Malaya village, displacing hundreds of men, women, and children. British officials refused to assist the producers, saying the scene was too violent. The filmmakers turned to the government of Australia for help, and found it. About 80 troops from the 2nd Battalion of the royal Australian regiment are in the film, portraying British soldiers.

Flash forward to France, 2006. Demonstrating anew the power of one motion picture to effect political change, in September French President Jacques Chirac decided to restore full pensions to the 80,000 Arab soldiers from North Africa who fought valiantly for the country against the Germans. What prompted President Chirac to decide to correct this long-standing and obvious injustice? He watched the superb film *Indigènes* (*Days of Glory*, 2006), which depicts heroic Arab soldiers in the French army fighting to liberate France during World War II. The scene in which the North Africans are not served the same food as the French troops, though they are fighting alongside them, against the same enemy, may have helped influence Chirac. A French sergeant who commands the regiment advises his captain to resolve the problem, telling him not to tag the Arabs "natives" nor to call them "Muslims—that's just as bad." Asks his officer: "What should I call them, then?" Says the sergeant, "The men, sir; the men."

Government strategies enforce stereotypes here at home, as well. In turn, the stereotypes influence policies. During times of conflict, especially, media systems function as common carriers for government policies. During World War II, for example, Washington turned to Hollywood to produce anti-Axis films that would inspire Americans on the front lines and their families back home. The government enlisted the services of talented filmmakers such as Frank Capra (*Why We Fight*), John Huston, Alfred Hitchcock, and Walt Disney animators. Not surprisingly, as most of our major media outlets are now owned by corporations with "vested interests in Washington policy," points out Bill Moyers, "the symbiotic relationships between the political elites and the media elites have grown."

As early as 1987, Fox executives began screening their new motion pictures "in the nation's capital for Congressmen, their wives and staffers." Asked about the congressional screenings, Thomas R. Herwitz, Fox's vice president for corporate and legal affairs, said: "We make sure members of the Congress and other government officials know what we're doing; our discussions allow them to know what's on our minds and us to learn what's on theirs." According to reports from New York's International Action Center, weeks before *Black Hawk Down* (2002) was released, the Motion Picture Association of America (MPAA) held a private screening for senior White House advisors "and allowed them to make changes" in the film. Defense Secretary Donald Rumsfeld and Oliver North, along with 800 top officials and brass, attended the screening, applauding the premiere of *Black Hawk Down* in Washington.

US presidents, too, are linked with the industry. George W. Bush served from 1983 to 1992 on the board of Silver Screen Management, a company that has produced movies exclusively for TriStar, then Walt Disney. Following the August 2000 Hollywood Gala Salute to President Bill Clinton—the largest Hollywood tribute ever produced for a sitting president—the president and Mrs. Clinton attended a reception at Sony Pictures studios. In February 2007, the MPAA conducted a first one-day symposium in Washington, DC. On hand to discuss the role of entertainment in a digital age were Hollywood heavyweights such as Will Smith and Steven Soderbergh; they interacted with politicians Charles Rangel, Patrick Leahy, and Dianne Feinstein.

Best solidifying cinema's long-standing influence and linkage with American politics are these observations, made by former Republican senator, *Law & Order* actor, and 2008 presidential candidate Fred Thompson and Jack Valenti, ex-chair of the MPAA. Appearing on NBC-TV's *Tonight Show* Thompson confessed to host Jay Leno that he never intended to spend his life in Washington as a career politician, and that he had always "longed for the realism and sincerity of Hollywood." Several years before Thompson articulated his infatuation with Hollywood, Jack Valenti got it right when he emphatically remarked: "Washington and Hollywood spring from the same DNA."

No matter the country or its politics, the historical and ongoing connection between fiction film, public opinion, and public policies is real.

PART ONE

Analysis

CHAPTER ONE

The Impact of 9/11

"If there's an Arab-American family being rounded up without benefit of an attorney or due process, that threatens my civil liberties.... It's that fundamental belief—I am my brother's keeper; I am my sister's keeper—that makes this country work."
— Illinois Senator Barack Obama

Before I discuss post–9/11 movies allow me to provide you, the reader, with a synopsis of significant events after 9/11— that is, an overview of the policies and the war on terror, which have affected Americans, notably American Arabs and American Muslims, about 10 million citizens. Immediately after the deadly attacks of 9/11, President George W. Bush helped calm fears of a backlash against Arabs and Islam. Appearing at Washington, DC's Islamic Center, the president spoke eloquently and candidly about the dangers of harmful stereotypes: "America counts millions of Muslims among our citizens." They make "an incredibly valuable contribution to our country [and] need to be treated with respect." At this crucial time, Bush also assured Americans that "the face of terror is not the true faith of Islam. That's not what Islam is all about." Elaborating on the president's concerns was British Prime Minister Tony Blair. He, too, emphasized that the battle against the 9/11 terrorists was a battle "not between Christians and Muslims, but between civilized values and fanaticism." "In that battle," said Blair, "the vast majority of decent law-abiding Muslims opposed fanaticism." Blair's and Bush's candid comments were especially influential and helpful; a different tone might have had damaging repercussions.

Both leaders spoke forcefully and effectively. Yet, later on nearly everyone—preachers, journalists, producers, entertainers, and politicians—rushed forward to advance well-entrenched media stereotypes that historically have damaged an entire people. Comments by President Bush, Defense Secretary Donald Rumsfeld, Republican presidential hopeful Tom Tancredo, Representatives Virgil Goode and Peter T. King, Attorney General John Ashcroft, and Lt. General William Boykin, a deputy undersecretary of defense, and others solidified fabricated labels and images. Said the president, just five days after the tragic 9/11 attacks: "This crusade, this war on terrorism, is going to take a while." For many Arabs and Muslims the word "crusade" is emotionally charged, recalling the many Christian armies—the Crusaders—who invaded the Holy Land. Then on August 10, 2006, President Bush remarked that defeating the plot to destroy airliners over the Atlantic Ocean was a triumph in the "war against Islamic fascists." There's nothing fascist about Islam. As a result, for some, this false linkage—connecting an entire faith, Islam, with Nazism and totalitarianism—contradicted the president's earlier statements that Islam was a religion of peace.

Later, Senator Sam Brownback (R, Kansas) spoke of the threat of "Islamofascism." *New York Times* columnist Paul Krugman pointed out that this word "carries noxious undertones"; it "intimates that there is something inherently dangerous about all Muslims." But such rhetoric continues. Presidential candidate Rudy Giuliani has warned about "radical Islamic fascism." In October 2007, David Horowitz promoted an "Islamofascism Awareness Week" on college campuses, with the aim to "discredit scholars" who take exception to these racist views.

Rumsfeld wrote a memo later, published in the *Washington Post,* that contained outrageous stereotyping of Arabs and Muslims, saying that they "are against physical labor," that oil wealth has removed them from "the reality of work, effort, and investment that leads to wealth for the rest of the world." This idleness, he contends, makes them "easy to recruit to radicalism."

Colorado Representative Tom Tancredo has asserted that a terrorist attack on our homeland may be imminent. The US can best deter such an attack, he says, by threatening to "take out" Islam's holiest cities, Medina and Mecca. If Tancredo watched *National Geographic*'s excellent 2003 documentary *Inside Mecca*, which documents the annual pilgrimage to Mecca made by some two million Muslims from around the world every year, perhaps he would contemplate retracting his threat. Representative Goode complained that too many persons from the Middle East were entering the US "legally." He told his constituents: "I fear we will have many more [Arabs and] Muslims in the United States… To preserve the values and beliefs traditional to the United States of America [we must] adopt strict immigration policies." Representative King, the ranking Republican on the House Homeland Security Committee, pitched in, remarking that the vast majority of American Muslim community leaders are "an enemy living amongst us." He went on to say that 85 percent of American mosques are "ruled by extremists." Although Muslims, Jews, and Christians pray to the God of Abraham, Ashcroft said: "Islam is a religion in which God requires you to send your son to die for him. Christianity is a faith in which God sent His son to die for you." Boykin declared we should battle Islam "in the name of Jesus." Regrettably, he also implied that "Allah" was not "a real God." Boykin did not know that the word for God in Arabic is "Allah." People who speak Arabic, be they Christians, Jews, or Muslims, say "Allah" to describe God, just as God is called *Gott* in German and *Dieu* in French. In Aramaic, the language of Jesus, God is *Allaha*, just a syllable away from *Allah*.

Some authors, journalists, and conservative talk-show hosts further fueled the stereotype. Publishers released books such as *Antichrist: Islam's Awaited Messiah, Terrorist, Allah's Torch, Allah's Scorpion, Allah's Bomb*, and *Sword of Allah*. Author Robert Spencer said Muslims were threatening Catholics and that "Islam is a serious threat to the peace… of the Western world." Michael Graham, who hosts a show on Washington, DC's WMAL Radio, told listeners: "Islam is a terrorist organization." Syndicated columnist Mona Charen wrote: "Every Middle Eastern-looking truck driver should be pulled over and questioned wherever he may be in the United States." Charen went on to say: "There are thousands of Arabs in the United States at this moment on student and travel visas. They should all be asked… to go home." On Fox-TV, Bill O'Reilly said: "I'm tilted against the Muslim world." On Fox's *Beltway Boys*, Fred Barnes advocated profiling: "If people are of Middle Eastern extraction," he said, they "should be treated a little differently, just for the security of the United States." His colleague Mort Kondracke agreed, saying Arab Americans themselves should "spread the word that this is not discrimination, you know, this is necessary." On C-SPAN, Ann Coulter declared: "We need to invade their countries, kill their leaders, and convert them to Christianity." And on HBO, Bill Maher quipped that terrorism was a sexual problem, arguing that "if we really want to stop terrorism, we should hire women to infiltrate al-Qaeda cells and f— them."

Several evangelical Christians labeled Islam as "evil." Franklin Graham, Jerry Falwell, and Pat Robertson referred to Islam as a "wicked" religion, tagged the prophet Mohammed a "terrorist," and said Muslims were "worse than Nazis." Jerry Vines said the Prophet Mohammed was "a demon-possessed pedophile." Speaking at the 2006 Missouri Baptist Convention, Reverend David Clippard told delegates: "Islam has a strategic plan to defeat and occupy America." "The Muslims," he said, "are after your sons and daughters… If you don't convert, your head comes off." Atlanta's syndicated radio talk-show host Neal Boortz told a Muslim caller that Islam was "a cult, not even a religion," and warned that Muslims had better "straighten up or we're gonna eradicate your beetles from the face of the earth." Comedian Jackie Mason tossed in a few slurs, calling "the whole Muslim religion" a "murderous organization" that teaches "hate, terrorism, and murder."

When it comes to Arab-bashing, a double standard persists. Had these slurs been directed at blacks, Jews, gays, or others, public outrage would trigger extensive media coverage; folks would be fired, as were MSNBC's Don Imus and *Grey's Anatomy*'s Isaiah Washington.

Uncontested, rancorous rhetoric gives prejudice a free pass. One primary reason the stereotype persists is that many journalists, religious leaders, and politicians fail to speak out in public to condemn repulsive rhetoric. Regrettably, when prominent Arab and Muslim Americans speak out, major media outlets fail to report their comments. Another reason the stereotype persists is ignorance. Only two percent of Americans say they are "very knowledgeable" about Islam. Sixty percent say they "are not very knowledgeable" or "not at all knowledgeable." This lack of knowledge, combined with a steady flow of hate speech and Hollywood's insidious images, helps explain Islamophobia and Arabophobia (irrational fears and/or prejudices toward Arabs, Muslims, and Islam that stir symptoms of loathing). As a result, some of us may view our neighbors apprehensively. "It is to some extent understandable that we are more suspicious of those we take to be Arabs," explains Homeland Security's inspector general, Clark Kent Ervin, "but it is also morally repugnant and unjust to slap such a noxious label on a whole group of people on account of the misdeeds of a few."

Hate rhetoric, the war on terror, the conflicts in Afghanistan, Iraq, and the Middle East have generated damaging new media stereotypes and new government law enforcement policies. Congress approved the PATRIOT Act; the Department of Homeland Security launched multicolored "Security Level Alerts," profoundly affecting citizens worldwide. Whether they lived in the US or in the 25-nation European Union, after 9/11, bearded, dark-looking men and women wearing headscarves were perceived as menacing threats to world security. Even Europe's Arabs and Muslims routinely suffer acts ranging from physical attacks to discrimination in the job and housing markets, reports the European Monitoring Center on Racism and Xenophobia. In the US, too, "the increased [governmental] monitoring of Arab and Muslim Americans" has helped advance discriminatory attacks. Though it's not fair to lump all community members into one polluted stream, some US government officials began viewing American Arabs and Muslims as "a suspicious and dangerous group to whom constitutional rights and liberties do not apply." Federal agents were given the green light to infiltrate American Muslim organizations, notes scholar Randa Kayyali.

Fortunately, we are not incarcerating any ethnic or racial groups nowadays, but one wonders how much opposition the government would encounter if officials ever did decide to round up Arab Americans and Muslim Americans, using "in the interests of national security," and "it's for their own protection" as excuses. Lamentably, nearly one in three Americans approves of the government engaging in racial profiling. As a result, "Arab-Americans have reported an increasing sense of victimization, suspicion of government and law enforcement, fear of surveillance, and concerns about protecting their civil liberties," reveals a two-year Vera Institute study, which was funded by a research agency of the US

Department of Justice. Some post–9/11 policies have sown "the deepest fear among Arab Americans, including unease about the Patriot Act, voluntary interviews of thousands of Arab Americans by federal agents, and an initiative known as Special Registration, in which more than 80,000 immigrant men were fingerprinted, photographed and questioned by authorities."

Increased civil liberties violations have resulted not only in racial profiling, but employment discrimination and arrests and imprisonments without due process. According to a May 2007 Pew Research Center poll, one in four American Muslims say they have been victims of discrimination since the 9/11 attacks. Such harassment, contends the Vera report, helps explain why some Muslim and Arab Americans are just as concerned about vicious stereotypes and about "being victimized by federal policies and practices, as they are by individual acts of harassment or violence." To cite one example of racial profiling impacting a US citizen: Abe Dabdoub manages a Cleveland plant that provides steel to automobile companies, and he regularly travels to Canada to be with family members. He often is singled out for rude profiling. On each of Dabdoub's fourteen trips to visit family, for example, Michigan's Customs and Border Patrol "agents have sent him through a security gantlet." Reports journalist Neil MacFarquhar: He "has been fingerprinted fourteen times, his body searched nine times, been handcuffed four times and isolated in a separate detention room thirteen times." And, patrol agents are "subjecting his wife to similar scrutiny."

Real Islamophobia was in vogue long before 9/11 and the Iraq war. Back in 1994 a Louis Harris poll revealed that 43 percent of Americans agreed with this declaration: "Muslims belong to a religion that condones or supports terrorism"; 47 percent concurred with the announcement that "Muslims are anti-Western and anti-American." One year later: A 1995 poll revealed that 45 percent of Americans agreed with this statement: "Muslims tend to be fanatics." Present-day polls as well as those from the mid-1990s illustrate why some of the 6 to 9 million Muslims in our nation—the vast majority of whom are citizens—continue to feel increasing isolation and hostility. The defamation of Islam, Arabs, and Muslims has even compromised justice in some courtrooms. Explains

California attorney Stephen B. Mashney: Jurors' judgments cannot help but be influenced by a "media portrayal that Arab Muslims are [our] enemies and culturally backward." The facts of the vast majority of Arab and Muslim Americans' lives, however, could not be more diametrically opposite.

"If you want to see what American Muslims truly represent, go to the University Muslim Medical Association's (UMAA) clinic in South Central Los Angeles," said Congresswoman Maxine Waters to members of the US House of Representatives, "and you'll see it there." The students who founded the clinic in 1992 "were inspired by their Islamic faith," said Waters, "a faith which told them to help their neighbors." Today, UMAA serves as a primary health care source that offers free medical services to more than 15,000 people, many of whom would otherwise have no health care at all. Some 70 percent of the patients are Latinos; fewer than 5 percent are Muslims. Better understanding and improved visibility of America's Muslims and Arabs and their commitment to assisting fellow Americans is long overdue. "Their patriotism has been grossly underreported," says David Benjamin, a former National Security Council official. "They have been our first line of defense." Since 9/11, for example, more than 200 Arabic linguists have joined the FBI. Like most Americans, they are open to values and ideals that our nation has propagated from the beginning, especially liberty, justice, and democratic governance.

Fictional TV shows like *Criminal Minds* (2007) depict a radical imam recruiting terrorists to kill Americans and terminate FBI members. In reality, Virginia's Imam Mohamed Magid and other full-time imams across the country are working closely with the FBI in battling and speaking out publicly against terrorism. In fact, on September 10, 2005, four years after 9/11, Magid presided at the funeral of two young Muslims who perished in the attack on the North Tower. It wasn't until August 2005 that medical examiners were able to finally identify enough of the two youngsters' charred tissue for the parents to hold a funeral. Magid, who was surrounded by grieving family members, had this to say: "The terrorists who kill in the name of Islam claim they are the martyrs... But the victims are the martyrs. The terrorists are the murderers, and God will deal with them on Judgment Day."

Magid and 600-plus American imams serve an estimated 1,500 mosques. They function pretty much like most devout American Christian and Jewish leaders. Muslim clerics are as a rule deeply religious men of God, exactly the opposite of reel images that project the horrible deeds of a few—unkempt, bearded, robed clerics screaming *fatwas*. Yet because members of the lunatic fringe abuse Islam by declaring that Allah approves of their heinous crimes, some of us may believe that it's a hateful faith, and that "all those Arabs and Muslims"—those here at home and those overseas—are our enemies. The acceptance of this mythology persists despite the conclusions found in the 9/11 Commission Report, which state: "Islam is not the enemy... It is not synonymous with terror. Nor does Islam teach terror." The commission's findings notwithstanding, consider these startling numbers. Two 2006 polls reveal that one in four of Americans surveyed have "extreme" anti-Muslim views; 46 percent have a negative perception of Muslims, a crude proxy for Arabs. And, nearly 50 percent of the American public approves of curtailing the civil liberties of American Muslims.

Anti-Arab and anti-Muslim stereotypes help support the views of those who believe that Arab Muslims are a violent people. As a result, the mythology—Islam is synonymous with terror; Arab Muslims worship a Moon God; they launch suicide attacks because 79 virgins await them in heaven—persists. The mythology does not exist in a vacuum. Throughout Europe and the US, some mosques are perceived as terrorist hotbeds, and they continue to be targeted, burned, and vandalized. "GO HOME" graffiti and Nazi swastikas are splashed on their walls; citizens disrupt evening prayers. In Copenhagen, Denmark, residents drenched the construction site of a new mosque with pig's blood. As Muslims consider pigs to be unclean, they could not build a mosque on pig-infested soil. A man in Katy, Texas, tried a similar tactic: he threatened to hold Friday pig races near the property. And in Portland, Maine, a frozen pig's head was tossed inside the local mosque. To illustrate how broad and damaging the stereotype has become, even some Hindu temples, community centers, and churches have been vandalized and destroyed. In April 2002, in Los Altos, California, the 17-year-old Antiochian Orthodox Church of the

Redeemer, the spiritual home where more than 200 Christians worshiped, and where American Jews and American Arabs met bi-monthly for interfaith dialogue, was targeted by arsonists. The church was burned to the ground; all the religious icons were destroyed. Five years later, in April 2007, vandals defaced the outside of Warren, Michigan's new Holy Apostolic Catholic Assyrian Church. Though its members are non-Arabs and Catholics, hooligans sprayed hateful anti-Arab threats—"Arabs Die" and "Die 2wice"—on the building.

The stereotype's virus also infects leading citizens and educational systems. One example: Every year New York creates a few new public schools, adding to the 1,000 or so already in existence. One new school, the Khalil Gibran International Academy, named after the Lebanese-American author of *The Prophet*, became the city's first public school dedicated to instruction in Arab culture and the Arabic language. Though the academy managed to open its doors to 81 sixth graders on September 4, 2007, the school's principal, Debbie Almontaser, had been hounded into resigning in the weeks preceding its opening. Critical conservatives and the *New York Sun* newspaper called her "a secret sympathizer with radical Islam." The new school was "pro-Arab" and would "accommodate and perhaps groom future radicals… using the Koran to justify the cult of death." The conservative website *Political Dishonesty* carried this commentary on February 14, 2007: "Just think, instead of jocks, cheerleaders, and nerds, there's going to be the Taliban hanging out on the history hall, Al Qaeda hanging out by the gym… Maybe in gym they'll learn how to wire their bomb vests and they'll convert the football field to a terrorist training camp." Rabbi Michael Feinberg of the Greater New York Labor-Religion Coalition called for protests against the attacks, calling them "all about insinuation and innuendo and this formula of Arab equals Muslim equals terrorist. The viciousness and the vileness of this case surpass anything I've seen before." Almontaser later called the attacks against her "part of a larger campaign to intimidate and silence marginalized communities."

Arab and Muslim Americans continue to experience verbal and physical violence, loss of jobs, and imprisonment in violation of their civil rights. The stereotype impacted prominent Arab

Americans like Osama Siblani, the successful publisher of Dearborn, Michigan's *Arab American News*. Siblani confessed to Paul M. Barrett, author of *American Islam*: "Since 9/11, I have felt choked. I can't breathe, like the Atlantic Ocean is right under my nose and rising. The world has really closed in on me." Even dark-looking youngsters are roughed up in schools and taunted in shopping malls. Muslim teens selling Girl Scout cookies are harassed. At a Virginia grocery store, the scouts were displaying a sign, "Cookies for Sale." Suddenly, a man rushed up to their table and screamed: "Terrorists!" In Seattle, two of Steve Saleh's deli customers unleashed a tirade of anti-Arab slurs, and then attacked Saleh and a co-worker shouting, "Go back to your country." To paraphrase Native American actor Chief Dan George, "When you talk to people, you get to know them. When you don't talk to them, you don't get to know them, and the thing that you don't know strikes you with fear."

Devout imams praying on airplanes are sometimes perceived as terrorists. On November 21, 2006, for example, six law-abiding imams were handcuffed and escorted off a passenger jet. Frightened passengers had found them "suspicious" because they were praying in Arabic and praying "very loud[ly]." Before releasing them, the FBI and government officials questioned the religious leaders at length. Ironically, the imams were returning from a conference on religious tolerance. Though imams regularly condemn acts of terror, more unified religious voices are needed to shatter entrenched myths. Today, religious leaders from around the world are acknowledging past sins: Roman Catholics have apologized for abusing children and for their silence during the Holocaust, United Methodists for their massacre of American Indians during the Civil War, and Southern Baptists for their support of slavery. A united group of religious leaders should take the lead in apologizing for acts of terror committed by Islamic militants. Together, they should speak out, and repeatedly sign and send to world leaders and local and international news organizations universal declarations condemning radical Islam. Included in this steady stream of unified voices that condemns those who abuse a religion should be this observation of Thomas Friedman's: "Islam teaches that you show reverence to God by showing reverence for his creations, not just his words."

When a group of people is tagged the enemy "other," reminds film director Sally Potter, "they become easily victimized by malicious harassment, crimes, physical attack, and profiling. In reality," says Potter, "almost everyone I know is very complex with interweaving identities and histories." We shouldn't try "to stereotype much of humanity under one dark complexion or one dress code," notes Saifulloh Amath, a San Jose resident who is Cham, an ethnic group native to Vietnam and Cambodia. Amath, whose family is Muslim, says: "In the Vietnamese jungle people speak Arabic, but people think we are devout Buddhists." Amath's neighbor, Redwood City native Wendy Chang, also defies the stereotype of Muslim women as a passive, meek woman—just watch her judo chop a chunk of wood. Chang, who hails from China, has a second-degree black belt in the martial arts. And there's Army Private Jimmy Wong-Soto, who is seldom perceived as a Muslim. Wong-Soto, one of the thousands of American Muslims who serve in the US military, told journalist Ahmed M. Soliman: "I feel privileged to be helping… to fight against insurgents." Given the broad range of features found in the world, the terms "Muslim-looking" and "Arab-looking," are misleading and virtually meaningless. Arabs and Muslims come in all shapes, sizes, colors, and descriptions.

Since September 11, 2001, more than 3,000 hate crimes have been reported and several innocent Americans have died. According to studies by the American Arab Anti-Discrimination Committee (ADC) and the Council on American–Islamic Relations (CAIR), our government has seized and held in custody, without trial, at least 1,500 Arabs and Muslims. Rounding up large numbers of US residents who may look like "the enemy" and detaining and/or shipping them off in the interests of security brings to mind a shameful 1942 historical incident: Executive Order 9066, which led to the displacement and incarceration of 110,000 Americans of Japanese ancestry; they were forced to leave their homes and imprisoned behind barbed wire. And there's Deer Island, in Boston Harbor. "Here, during King Philip's War between English colonists and Algonquian Indians in 1675–76, Indians who had converted to Christianity were rounded up and incarcerated. When the war was over," reminds Earlham Professor Chuck Yates, "most of the survivors were sold into slavery and shipped out of the country."

The historical lesson here is this: When journalists, imagemakers, and government leaders think a group of people might be linked to the enemy-of-the-day, even though the people singled out are law-abiding, loyal American citizens, some of us begin to mistrust "those people." After a group is labeled and feared as the enemy "other," the government might exploit public anxieties and go on to violate their civil rights, with minimal or too easily ignored public protests. Regrettably, post–9/11's reel stereotypes and government policies have silenced Arabs and Muslims in the US, making it even more difficult for them to become an integral part of our country's politics and entertainment. Some tell me they prefer to be passive, silent citizens. If they are too critical of policies, they say, government agencies may secretly monitor their movements. Or, if another act of terrorism befalls us, they worry about being imprisoned, even interned in concentration camps. Continued silence, however, advances rather than curtails suspicions. The best way to quell anxieties about civil rights abuses is for ordinary citizens and community members to speak out, to become civil rights activists.

Attacks on the civil liberties of America's Arabs and Muslims continue, covert and overt, says Professor Paul Silverstein because "law enforcement measures, politicians, religious leaders and Hollywood imagemakers have contributed to stereotyping Arab Muslims as a race." Comments Zbigniew Brzezinski, President Jimmy Carter's national security advisor: The "war on terror… has created a culture of fear in America." The result are "TV serials and films [displaying] evil characters with recognizable Arab features, sometimes highlighted by religious gestures that exploit public anxiety and stimulate Islamophobia. Arab facial stereotypes," says Brzezinki, "have at times been rendered in a manner sadly reminiscent of Nazi anti-Semitic campaigns." Silverstein, who studies the intersection of race and immigration at Oregon's Reed College, points out: Arabs are "the new Jews. They're the object of a series of stereotypes, caricatures and fears which are not based on a reality." Rabbi Eric Yoffie, the president of the Union for Reform Judaism, which represents 900 congregations and 1.5 million Jews, "accused American media, politicians and religious groups of demonizing Islam" and turning Arab Muslims into "satanic figures." Films like *Pretty Persuasion* (2005) and *Call Me:*

The Rise and Fall of Heidi Fleiss (2004) that pit Jewish Americans against Arabs don't help. Reminds author William Greider: "Jews were [once] despised as exemplars of modernism"; today's Arabs are depicted as "carriers of primitivism—[both] threatening to upset our modern cozy world with their strange habits and desires." Not so long ago, reports Mark Penn in his *Microtrends* (2007), a 1939 Roper poll found that 53 percent of Americans believed that "Jews are different and should be deported." At about the same time, Germany's dark, exotic-looking Jews were also suffering from such Judeophobia. They were perceived as "a threat to Civilization," points out scholar Amos Elon, "a horde of people... who multiply like locusts." Today, writes journalist Oriana Fallaci, "Muslim immigrants—the sons of Allah—breed like rats."

Fortunately, constructive religious gatherings between Jews and Arabs, such as the Second World Congress for Imams and Rabbis for Peace, held in Seville on March 19, 2006, are helping to shatter phobias by focusing on commonalities. Participating at the four-day gathering were some 250 people from 31 countries. During their meetings, "Imams and rabbis called on each other and the world to respect each other's religions." Said one delegate: "Contrary to widespread misinterpretation, there is no inherent conflict between Islam and Judaism." Sums up Canada's Chaim Steinmetz, "Most of the imams have never seen this many rabbis. Most of the rabbis have never seen this many imams." So, in the end, many bonded.

During the Middle Ages Pope Gregory VII noted the similarities between Christianity, Islam, Judaism, writing to an Algerian prince: "There is a charity, which we owe to each other... because we recognize and confess one sole God, although in different ways, and we praise and worship Him every day as creator and ruler of the world." A decade or so ago, Pope John Paul II elaborated on Gregory's insights. Speaking to thousands of devout Muslims at the Umayyad Mosque in Damascus, Syria, the Pope stressed our common humanity, saying: "I ardently hope that Muslim and Christian religious leaders and teachers will present our two great religious communities as communities in respectful dialogue, never more as communities in conflict." John Paul's successor, Pope Benedict XVI, is also committed to interfaith discussions. In September 2006, he met with 20 Muslim ambassadors, affirming: "Dialogue between our two faiths is a vital necessity in which a large measure of our future depends." And in October 2007 more than 130 Muslim scholars called for peace and understanding between Islam and Christianity, saying "the very survival of the world itself is perhaps at stake." In their letter to Pope Benedict and other Christian leaders, Muslim scholars from around the world used quotations from the Bible and the Quran to support their peace message, writing: "Let us respect each other, be fair, just and kind to [one] another and live in sincere peace, harmony, and mutual goodwill."

Despite the efforts of some religious leaders to shatter this stereotype, Hollywood's demonic, century-old Arab "other" continues to inscribe itself over practically any character that meets the minimal requirements of similarity: Foreign accent, black hair, dark skin, and/or a cloth draped over the head. It's not just Arabs, Jews, or Muslims, it's all those tanned unshaven males perceived to be such. Across the country, hate crimes continue to ensnare brown-skinned people—blacks, Latinos, Hindus, Iranians, Mexicans, Sikhs, and others—with violence. In 2006, hate crimes against Muslims in the US increased 22 percent, according to the FBI. Suspicion and slurs persist. For example, Harpreet, a male Sikh high-school student wears a turban to school. During Christmas holidays he and his fellow students entertain the homeless by dressing up and playing different characters. As he always wears a turban, Harpreet's teacher insisted he play Jafar, the Arab villain from Disney's *Aladdin*. "The teacher ignored the turban's religious significance to Sikhs, and she also conflated it with an Arab cultural emblem," explains journalist Khyati Y. Joshi.

The stereotype delivers a double whammy to African-American Muslims. They are labeled with the DWB label—driving while black—and with the FWM tag—flying while Muslim. Also targeted are Sikhs. Sikh men don't cut their hair, so Sikhs (like some Arabs) have beards. Some people think Arabs, Sikhs, and Indians are one and the same. My friend's granddaughter is married to a man from India, and his life has changed dramatically since 9/11. People make snide remarks, thinking he is an Arab; he is anguished and confounded by this unexpected development in his life. Consider, also: New York comedian Dean Obeidallah told an admirer wanting his autograph that he was an Arab American, and that his father was born in Palestine. Exclaimed the excited fan: "Oh, you're Arab. I love Indian food."

Sikhs, who practice a 500-year-old monotheistic faith indigenous to India, wear turbans in public—a kind of headgear apparently easily confused with Arab *kufiyas*. Since 9/11, several Sikhs have been attacked and several killed. Journalist Matthai Chakko Kuruvila reports that in July 2006 a Santa Clara man stabbed a Sikh grandfather—because the man "wanted to seek revenge for September 11 and attack a member of the Taliban." In March 2007, Kuldip Singh Nag, a Sikh American who was awarded the Bronze Star for his military service, was assaulted by a Joliet, Illinois police officer. While hitting Nag with his baton the policeman reportedly was yelling: "You fucking Arab! Go back to your fucking country before I kill you!"

Reel Sikhs surface as reel Arabs in *The Da Vinci Code* (2006), *Waterborne* (2005), *The Gold Bracelet* (2005), and *The Inside Man* (2006). In *Man*, a policeman confronts a freed bank hostage, a Sikh man wearing a turban, and screams: "A fucking Arab!" When *Code*'s Tom Hanks feels threatened, the camera cuts to a man wearing a Sikh-looking headscarf and sitting inside a sleek expensive car. Should viewers think anything at all about this scene, they'll likely think Arab Oil Sheikh. In *Bracelet*, the likeable Sikh protagonists are beaten and murdered for one reason: Their attackers tag and view them as Arabs. And, in the first-rate thriller, *Waterborne*, Los Angeles's water supply has been poisoned by terrorists; some residents die. Immediately, Arab "sand niggers" are blamed for dumping a deadly biological agent into the water supply. Screams a National Guardsman: "We should drop a bomb on their country and turn it into a parking lot." Chimes in a TV reporter: "This is the work of a vicious terrorist network like al-Qaeda." Abruptly, two men spot a Sikh wearing a blue turban. One man shouts, "Osama! Get on your fuckin' camel and go back to where you came from." Another man torches a Sikh convenience store, seriously injuring the protagonist's mother. The reel victims here are, as in some real-life cases, American Sikhs. Still, one film critic referred to *Waterborne* as being about an "Arab-American family."

The film's closing frames are especially poignant. Police nab the villain; he's a homegrown terrorist. A TV reporter declares: "What is so shocking is that Federal officials here fear domestic terrorists may be the next weapon of mass destruction this country faces. It's terrifying to think they are right here in our own back yard." This telling scene reminds us that evildoers—from Oklahoma City bomber Timothy McVeigh to priests who abuse children—come from all creeds and cultures, and are not all dark-complexioned foreigners.

Government PR Campaigns and the War on Terror

Given the US military occupation of Iraq, America's efforts in Afghanistan, US military support of Israel during Israel's incursions into Lebanon and Gaza, and growing anti-American sentiment in Arab and Muslim nations, the government's role in the struggle for world public opinion cannot be cavalierly dismissed. A new battle of ideas has emerged—"a battle for the hearts and minds of [Arab and] Muslim communities." This battle is taking place "not only in Iraq but also throughout the world," explains David M. Abshire, of the Center for the Study of the Presidency.

Weeks after 9/11, the Bush administration launched several public relations campaigns designed to enhance the image of the US abroad. Undersecretary of State for Public Diplomacy and Public Affairs Charlotte Beers put into motion a $15 million public diplomacy program to help reinvent the US for the world's 280 million Arabs. (Here, a personal note: Several times, I contacted Beers's office, offering my services gratis to help with our diplomacy efforts; no one responded.) While Beers was implementing her overseas PR campaigns, here at home senior advisor Karl Rove and other White House officials decided Hollywood's features had a role beyond merely entertainment. Rove and other advisors and diplomats formed a political lobbying group and rushed off to the West Coast. On a trip organized by then MPAA chief Jack Valenti, Rove and members of his "Hollywood 9/11 Coalition" flew off to Hollywood and met with about 50 executives, asking them to help the Bush administration to "win the war on evil." Immediately after Rove and his group returned to Washington, I again volunteered to assist. This time I traveled to the capitol and met personally with two members of his Hollywood team, offering my expertise to help us win the "hearts and minds" struggle. I never heard back.

Return to Washington, DC, May 2006: Beer's replacement, Karen Hughes, takes charge of formulating and coordinating all "strategic communication" for the Department of State, the Department of Defense, the National Security Council, the White House, and other executive-branch entities. Hughes, too, intends to reach people of all faiths and cultures, telling the *Atlantic Monthly's* Ilana Ozernoy that her new job is to be "the conductor of the big orchestra of the federal government." To help improve the US image in the Arab world, Hughes followed in the footsteps of Rove; she sent letters to "prominent folks in entertainment and media, asking if they'd be interested in going to the Middle East and speaking on any topic they want to: No replies yet." Hughes also sought to "persuade Hollywood to develop a soap opera that follows the lives of an Arab-American family in the US." It remains a mystery as to why Hughes proposed an Arab-American soap opera (which was never produced) instead of a prime-time drama or comedy series, one which could easily be syndicated and telecast abroad, over and over again.

When it comes to shaping the message our country wants to convey abroad, missteps have been the rule. The projects implemented by Beers, Hughes, and other officials have not met with much success. From 2003 to 2006, our actions or inactions in the region have driven the United States's favorable ratings in most Arab countries down to single digits. Though Hughes has stressed that "Islam is a part of America," the results of our government's well-intentioned efforts are unimpressive. State Department officials, reports *Parade*, cite lack of funding as one reason; officials say the State Department has "less than $500 million (about one tenth of one percent of our nation's official defense budget) to devote to its efforts at building better global relations." Perhaps the primary reason for our failed efforts, however, is that both the government and Hollywood have failed to offer and implement long-term innovative ideas. Look at the unfunny box-office disaster *Looking for Comedy in the Muslim World*, a dull-witted movie reflecting our real PR efforts. In this offensive 2005 movie, government officials dispatch Albert Brooks not to the Arab world, but to India and Pakistan. His assignment: To "better understand the world's Muslims." Declares the reel US president, the best way to understand somebody "is to see what makes them laugh." Yet viewers overseas, notably Arabs and Muslims, who paid to watch Brooks's film, did not find anything to laugh about. Nor did they see respectful images of Islam. Instead, they were subjected to crude, stale stereotypes, and probably rushed out of movie theaters thinking that Hollywood, like the US government, didn't care a whit about them, their religion, or their image.

Anti-American sentiment continues to escalate overseas, and here at home anti-Arab sentiment continues, as well. To date, since the US-led invasion in 2003, insurgents have seriously injured nearly 30,000 American troops in Iraq. More than 3,800 of our soldiers have perished and more than 900 civilians under contract to the Pentagon have also lost their lives. According to the UN refugee agency, about 1 million Iraqi families have fled their homes. In August 2007, the Associated Press reported that Iraqi civilian deaths are estimated at more than 70,000. There seems to be no agreement on the number of Iraqi casualties; the Pentagon's figure is 150,000; according to the Johns Hopkins/*Lancet* study more than 655,000 Iraqis have died in the violence.

Daily, the war on terror dominates headlines. TV news reports show images of courageous US troops in Afghanistan and Iraq, fighting real Arab and Muslim insurgents. News reports focus on suicide bombers and insurgents holding Westerners hostage and slaughtering our soldiers and Iraqi civilians, even those praying in mosques. TV screens reveal stark images of violence directed at innocent people worldwide, such as terrorists murdering scores of schoolchildren in Grozny, Chechnya in December 2002. In May 2003, radicals killed dozens of people in Riyadh, Saudi Arabia, and Casablanca, Morocco. In March 2004, al-Qaeda terrorists blew up a Madrid train, killing 191 passengers. On July 7, 2005, several radicals—East Africans, a Jamaican, some British natives of Pakistani descent and others—set off several explosions in London, killing 52 people. That same month another group of terrorists launched an attack in Sharm el-Sheikh, Egypt—more than 130 people perished.

American and Arab TV networks have also transmitted to international viewers reports on Lebanese civilians being bombed and security guards employed by such firms as Blackwater USA mistakenly killing Iraqi civilians, as well as marines gunning down civilians in Haditha. Four of the marines in the Haditha incident have been charged with murder, four others with lesser charges. We have witnessed stark pictures of American and British soldiers placing hoods over the faces of chained, naked Arab and Afghan prisoners. The prisoners—abused at Abu Ghraib prison and at other detention centers in Iraq, Afghanistan, and Guantanamo Bay (Gitmo), Cuba—were forced to take sexually humiliating positions. One detainee compared his detention to *The Siege*, a 1998 movie showing Arab Americans being rounded up and put in a New York City detention camp. "I was shocked, thinking that I am in this Hollywood movie," said the detainee. "Is this really happening? I laugh at myself and ask when does this movie end?" In making the connection between *The Siege* and Abu Ghraib, I ask you to ponder this question: Do films such as *The Siege* and TV shows such as *24* lead to real-life violence, contributing to the abuses at Abu Ghraib?

Misperceptions—on both sides—abound.

Our soldiers arrive in the region with a rifle in one hand and portable DVD systems in their rucksacks. So, when reporter Evan Wright began asking American Special Forces in Iraq their opinions about the ground conflict, not surprisingly, some service men and women equated real combat with Hollywood's reel wars. "The occupation," said one GI, "is a lot like *Mad Max* (1979) on camels meeting *Apocalypse Now* (1979)."

Though GIs serving in Vietnam were somewhat impacted by Hollywood's war movies, today's generation of soldiers in Iraq are much "more movie-literate than any that has come before." Reel shoot-em-ups like *True Lies* and *Rules of Engagement*, which depict gung-ho Americans gunning down vicious Arabs, help pump today's troops up. Consider *Jarhead* (2005), which is based on former Marine Anthony Swofford's best-selling book about his pre-Desert Storm experiences in the Arabian Gulf. One scene shows marines watching the Vietnam film *Apocalypse Now*. Cut to reel US helicopters launching dozens of rockets, blowing up gobs of reel

Vietnamese—the marines stand and cheer enthusiastically. The scene faithfully reflects Swofford's thesis: "Filmic images of death and carnage [in movies like *Apocalypse Now, Platoon* (1986), and *Full Metal Jacket* (1987)] are pornography for the military man." Swofford says his fellow marines "rent all the war movies they can get their hands on." Adding, the magic brutality of these "pro-war" films celebrates our fighting skills; "we are excited by them."

Given the preponderance and popularity of Hollywood's war films, do our troops in Iraq think Arabs are ordinary, hospitable, and peaceful men, women, and children who cherish life and liberty as much as we Americans and others do? Or have bang-bang movies encouraged them to view Arabs in general, and Iraqis in particular, as the evil, sinister "other"? Consider the actions of just one real marine, Corporal Joshua Belile. Soon after leaving Iraq he wrote and performed in a violent four-minute video titled "Hadji Girl." Soon after the video was posted to an internet site, it became a huge success online; thousands watched. In the video, Belile shows an Iraqi family killing their young daughter. Next, Belile strums his guitar and sings about the violent killings he's about to commit, as a marine: "I grab her little sister and put her in front of me... As the bullets begin to fly, the blood sprayed from between her eyes and then I laughed maniacally... Then I hid behind the TV and I locked and loaded my M-16, I blew those little [Iraqi] fuckers to eternity." Belile came up with the idea for his song, he said, after watching *Team America: World Police*, a movie with "some catchy lines in it." Though Belile's video was strongly criticized, he couldn't understand why, telling reporters that his marine buddies really enjoyed watching "Hadji Girl."

Hollywood's reel images are impacting soldiers' experiences of war. On the ground in Iraq, reel propaganda wars are taking place. Our GIs, explains reporter Wright, "are photographing, rhyming and recording their experiences at a prodigious rate. GIs have made dozens, if not hundreds, of Iraq movies." It works like this, says Wright. The soldiers film and edit "images of death and carnage. Next, death-metal music is dubbed over gory death and destruction battle footage, followed by fight, rape, war, pillage, burned, filmic images of dead and maimed Iraqis." Affirms journalist Louise Roug: GIs "also collect and trade the footage that depicts mutilation like baseball cards." One soldier justified the gory video productions, comparing them to the insurgents' videos showing brutal beheadings. "It's no different than watching a [Hollywood war] movie" glorifying violence, the GI told Roug. And, "it's not more graphic than *Saving Private Ryan* (1998)."

US journalists and military leaders stationed in Iraq acknowledge that al-Qaeda leaders, insurgents, and other extremists are utilizing Hollywood's Arab-bashing movies and American video games, twisting them into anti-US video games and posting them on insurgent websites, complete with splashy high-tech advertisements. The goal of these re-edited video games, report Jake Tapper and Audrey Taylor, "is to attract new, young terrorists and condition them to kill US soldiers." Pentagon officials say this is exactly what happened with a video game called "Battlefield 2: Armored Fury." Pentagon officials told a House Intelligence Committee that terrorists are increasingly using the video games "to help recruit and indoctrinate young Arabs, to pit them against US troops." Sums up one concerned American officer: "Our enemies are propagating the false notion that our military members are barbaric warmongers." Insurgents are releasing thousands of online violent videos contending that the US is at war with Islam. Journalist Steve Negus finds that "they are popping up on websites such as YouTube and MySpace."

According to Negus, insurgents take, rearrange, and then intercut selected scenes from Hollywood movies such as *Black Hawk Down* and *The Siege*. Next, insurgents edit and inter-mix film footage with Arab news broadcasts. Consider: The film *300* depicts dark Persians as "deranged savages" invading and attacking civilized Greeks, but insurgents could easily reverse the protagonist/antagonist roles. They could rearrange scenes that imply the film's heroes are the *300* insurgents, who oppose attacking Western "savages." Next, to give their edited propaganda film credibility, the insurgents toss in actual Iraqi combat footage, which depicts "infidel beheadings and suicide bombings." They blend footage of real war and reel fiction in these gory manipulative videos, called "mujahideen films," sums up Negus, to brainwash "Arab and Muslim teens too young to realize that the 'war' footage they're looking at was not shot by insurgents."

Washington may be winning the military battles, reports the Pew Global Attitudes Project (GAP), but it's losing the larger war for "hearts and minds." Since the United States has failed to effectively communicate with the Arab people, says journalist Greg Barker, the US is now "more isolated and less influential than we've been in decades." *New York Times* columnist Thomas Friedman believes that our efforts to win the war are hampered by a failure to distinguish between the brutality of radicals and the vast majority of peace-loving Arabs. Yes, he writes, there are "violent religious extremists steeped in hatred for all America, [but] we need to make perfectly clear that their actions represent a minority of a minority... What jihadist terrorists are doing in Iraq and Afghanistan do not represent the vast majority of peace loving, devout Muslims. Blowing up innocent Muslims struggling to build an alternative society to dictatorship surely destroys the Quran. They are the real enemies of Islam," he says, "because they are depriving Muslims of a better future." The fact is, time and time again, Arabs and Muslims unequivocally condemn terrorism.

In November 2005 some "real enemies of Islam," al-Qaeda terrorists, blew up three American hotels in Amman, Jordan. More than 60 people perished. Among the dead: my friend, filmmaker Moustapha Akkad, the first and only Arab-American director to speak out against Hollywood's Arab stereotypes. He was also the first to project humane images of Muslims and Islam in *Lion of the Desert* (1981) and *The Message* (1976). The killings in Jordan and elsewhere reflect harsh, tragic realities. Yes, there are violent extremists out there who abuse their faith and are intent on killing us. Yet, we should not blame Akkad's death, or the deaths of others who have perished from this tragic conflict, on 1.3+ billion people. History teaches us that from time immemorial extremists of all beliefs have abused religion. To help crush the lunatic fringe, we should cease demonizing a whole people and a whole religion, and focus on uniting freedom-loving people of all backgrounds and faiths.

CHAPTER TWO

Reel Negatives

Enemies: We first kill people with our minds, before we kill them with weapons. Whatever the conflict... we're on God's side; they're barbaric. We're good, they're evil.
—Sam Keen

More than a century of reel injurious Arab stereotypes, including the majority of post–9/11 movies, have helped us "kill people with our minds." Instead of mainstream studios projecting Arabs as regular folks—family men, women, and children—films continued defaming them as the unkempt, unscrupulous enemy "other." Here, I offer detailed discussions of those films that display Arabs as Villains, Terrorists, Maidens, Sheikhs, and Cameos (those films where producers inject unexpected, malicious slurs and scenes demeaning Arabs when the movie is about something else altogether). All these categories are noted in the film listings in the second half of the book. I also discuss some films featuring immoral Arab Americans. My explanations are not intended to exhaust you, dear reader; rather my intent is to guide and enlighten by referring to selected scenes from representative films that help damage a people.

Villains & Terrorists

A consistent pattern of reel dehumanization emerges here. Little has changed since the reel US Ambassador in *Hostage* (1986) quipped, "I can't tell one from another—wrapped in those bed sheets they all look the same to me." No matter when or where the action occurs, Hollywood presents reel look-alike Arab religious radicals lurking behind every sand dune and skyscraper, terrorizing Christians and Jews.

Hollywood's most violent movie since 9/11 is *The Kingdom* (2007). In this Rambo-in-Arabia shoot-'em-up, viewers applaud the heroics of four FBI agents who fly off to Saudi Arabia and kill Arabs. Before FBI investigators put their "boots on Saudi soil," one agent describes Saudi Arabia as being "a bit like Mars." In fact, it's much worse. Reel Saudi Arabia is a sinister desert, where evil, machine-gun-toting Arabs lurk in the shadows, waiting to kill Americans. The audience is led to believe that we had better kill the Arabs—even the women and children—quick, before they kill us. Yes, the film shows two "good" Saudis, but their presence is mere tokenism. The director could have quoted the Saudi grand mufti, who actually said four days after 9/11: "Hijacking planes, terrorizing innocent people, and shedding blood constitute a form of injustice that cannot be tolerated by Islam, which views them as gross crimes and sinful acts." He could have quoted Crown Prince Abdullah: "Terrorists are criminals and murderers with total disregard for any Islamic and human values or decency." And he could have cited the respected scholar Yusuf al-Qaradawi, who immediately after 9/11 denounced al-Qaeda, saying "Our hearts bleed because of the attacks that have targeted the World Trade Center...." The cleric is widely listened to and read by a huge Muslim audience. Instead, Berg chose to use the broadest, bloodiest brush possible.

This jingoistic film is a setback for efforts to improve relations between the United States and the Arab world. In a time that calls for cultural understanding, we get crude antagonism. In a time that calls for nuance and clarity, we get dangerous simplifications and gross distortions.

In September 2002, one year after 9/11, the historical epic *Four Feathers*, the seventh film version of A.E.W. Mason's book, arrived on movie screens. It's a familiar tale: One white, civilized British Christian "cowboy" crushes scores of dark uncivilized Arab Muslim "Indians." This one scene pretty much sums up the religious divide: As the British prepare to invade Sudan's "godforsaken desert," the camera cuts to a soldier reading a military pamphlet: "Above all," it says, "remember you're a Christian soldier."

Reel Arab terrorists show up everywhere—on land and in the air—in Europe, Hollywood, New York City, Somalia, and Israel. The made-in-Israel film *The Point Men* (2001), shows good Israelis killing bad Palestinians. The key "terrorist" brutally murders Israelis, Americans, his nurse, even a kind blond woman. In the end, the Israeli hero shoots the Palestinian dead. The Israeli film *Promised Land* (2004) shows ruthless Arab sex slavers selling off Eastern European women. In another Israeli-connected film, *Air Marshal* (2003), an insensitive, crude film that shamelessly exploits 9/11's victims, producers Avi (Danny) Lerner, Boaz Davidson, and Alain Jakibowicz show vicious, stereotypical Arabs on a commercial jet terminating passengers.

Ridley Scott's action-loaded, based-on-a-true-story *Black Hawk Down* (2002) shows valiant American troops shooting dead dozens of dark-skinned Somali Muslims. *The Deal* (2005) shows the US in turmoil: the economy's a mess and gasoline costs $6.50 a gallon. A radio commentator explains why: "The war with the Corporation of Arab States today entered its third year." Stock footage reveals enflamed Arab oil fields.

Arabic-speaking terrorists pop up nearly everywhere in the popular puppet film *Team America: World Police*, and they want to destroy America. Not to fret. Our team heroes fly off to France and gun down all those Osama bin Laden look-alikes and stop the bad guys from launching a worldwide attack that will be "9/11 times 200." Some adults may perceive *Team America* for what it is—a satire on President's Bush's war on terror. But other viewers, especially youngsters, will walk away with violent images of fervent anti-Arabism.

We also see Arab terrorists in the intelligent, compelling *United 93*, which effectively displays heroic, ordinary airline passengers and flight attendants sacrificing their lives to save countless others on the ground. Post–9/11's most disturbing movie, *The Stone Merchant* (2006), shows some reel bad Arab terrorists killing civilians at Rome's airport; the villains and their cohorts also explode a dirty bomb with radioactive material, killing scores of civilians aboard a ferry in Dover Harbor. The protagonist, a handicapped professor, preaches throughout the film that Muslims are "in a religious war to conquer the world," adding only "an army of Christians can thwart the Muslim invasion."

There's also *Red Mercury*, a fiction film set in London and released soon after real Muslims killed more than 30 Londoners,

July 7, 2005. Most of the reel scenes are set inside the Olympus Grill restaurant. Here, three nasty terrorists hold brave patrons hostage, constantly threatening them and the Grill's owner. In the end, the police act decisively, preventing the villains from unleashing their dirty bomb.

Cut to Hollywood! *American Dreamz* (2006), too, projects Arabs armed with weapons of mass destruction. Al-Qaeda terrorists decide to blow up the US president, and their chosen assassin is a naïve, peace-loving Arab named Omer. Before Omer can summon the genie from Aladdin's lamp, his wish—to appear on a top-rated TV show such as *American Idol*—is granted. But then three members of a reel Orange County terrorist cell surface, and these al-Qaeda thugs give Omer a direct order: When the commander in chief appears on the show, you must set off a bomb, blowing up the US president and yourself as well. Or else!

Or, hitch a ride to New York City! Most Arab cab drivers in New York are the same as other cabbies: Honest, helpful, and multilingual. Not so in *Fatwa* (2006) and *Crank* (2006). *Crank's* bull-headed cabbie refuses to allow the soaking-wet protagonist back into his cab. So, the hero throws the driver onto the sidewalk, and yells "Al-Qaeda!" Three people charge, beating up the cabbie. In *Fatwa*, a crazed Arab cab driver from Libya, Samir al-Faridi, brutally kills several Americans, a young Israeli girl, and reel US Senator Maggie Davidson. *Fatwa's* closing frames show reel Arab brutality: Samir entraps and forces Davidson to look at a video that shows the senator exactly how he went about murdering her daughter.

Perhaps *Fatwa* and *Crank's* reel bad cabbies helped prompt Republican Senator Conrad Burns of Montana to say that the terrorists "live among us; [they] drive taxi cabs in the daytime and kill at night." No one made a fuss over the senator's anti-Arab comment. Thus, his words advanced the stereotype, adversely affecting real Arab-American cab drivers. Had Senator Burns viewed Alex Gibney's *Taxi to the Darkside*, selected Best Documentary at the 2007 Tribeca Film Festival, he might have altered his statement. *Taxi* documents real violence—the fatal beating of an Afghan taxi driver by American guards in 2002.

Two Degrees (2001) and three 2005 films—*The War Within, Love + Hate,* and *Crash*—target Arab-American convenience store operators and their dark-complexioned look-alikes. The portraits vary. *Crash's* Iranian women appear as compassionate, respectful, and hard-working Americans. *Love + Hate* presents, for the first time ever, likeable Sikh-American characters. But *The War Within* falls back on damaging stereotypes, projecting a cartoon cutout of a reel terrorist: A Pakistani-American university graduate functioning as an evil sociopath. Though he pretends to be friendly with everyone, he rejects the Quran's message of peace—"To forbid the wrong [and] commend the good"—and joins a New York–based sleeper cell, becoming a reel suicide bomber. He walks into Grand Central Station and sets off a huge explosion, killing scores of commuters.

The most detestable post–9/11 film is *Two Degrees*. This vile movie pits crude Arab-American brothers Faisal and Reza against their African-American neighbors. The ugly, lecherous brothers operate a neighborhood store. One customer, Angela, a down-and-out African-American woman, needs some food; she begs Faisal for groceries, he agrees to help—provided she has sex with him, which she very reluctantly does. Brother Reza, too, tries to force himself onto Angela. In time, Angela's boyfriend enters the room. Furious, he shoots both men dead. The brothers are called "towelhead mother-fuckers," "your camel-eating ass," and "you Ayrabs ain't shit." Should you, dear reader, be interested in seeing more realistic images of Arab-American store owners, without the vile stereotypes, I recommend Rola Nashef's short film, *Detroit Unleaded* (2007); here the protagonists happily interact with their African-American customers, and vice versa.

Two films show vile Arabs killing, abusing, and/or lusting after the protagonists. In Disney's *Young Black Stallion* (2003), a desert bandit leader leers threateningly at an Arab teenage girl, but before he can capture her, she mounts her camel and rushes off to safety. And in *The Mummy's Kiss* (2002), homegrown female college students are seduced and terrorized by a kinky reincarnated sorceress. The sorceress also kills a college professor and a security guard. Finally, the X-rated *Mummy Raider* (2001) presents the reel stale Arab–Nazi connection: A revived rampaging Egyptian mummy tries to bring back "Hitler's Legions" from the dead.

Maidens

Hollywood's reel Arab women surface in several films, the most offensive being *Pretty Persuasion* (2005). Here, producers frame a Palestinian Muslim teenager, Randa, differently from her all-American classmates—as a shy, unwelcome, undesirable outsider. As soon as Randa enrolls at a posh Beverly Hills high school, the film's protagonist, Kimberly, points to Randa's hijab and quips: "What's that thing on your head? You haven't tried to bomb anybody, have you?" At the end of a series of humiliations, Randa kills herself. Her tragic death should have been meaningful and elicited viewers' heartfelt sympathy, but since she was portrayed all along as a cardboard cutout of a character, this is never really possible. If only *Persuasion's* producers had adhered to the wisdom of Rome's Archbishop John Foley: Young viewers, especially, writes Foley, "learn from fiction films how dangerous hatred is [and] how destructive religious ignorance is."

White-hat versus black-hat desert dramas present this stale theme: Arab Princesses prefer reel civilized Western heroes to buffoonish Arab potentates. In Disney's *Hidalgo* (2004), for example, Princess Jazira, the sheikh's bright, veiled daughter, willingly betrays fellow Arabs by helping Hopkins, the protagonist, win the death-defying desert race. Why? Because if an Arab prince wins, he will take her as "his fifth wife." Sighs the princess: "[I will become] the youngest in his harem, no more than a slave in his house." In *Secondhand Lions* (2003), when the lovely Princess Yasmine tries to escape the lecherous potentate's slimy grasp, he catches her and imprisons her in his harem. The princess places a knife to her throat—she would rather die than wed the sheikh. But in time, the American she truly loves, a reel good Texan, rides to her rescue.

Sheikhs

Uncivilized desert sheikhs with too much money and too many harem maidens surface in several films. In *Secondhand Lions* and *Hidalgo*, Arabs oppose Western protagonists and enslave young Africans. The action in *Lions* is projected in a swashbuckling comic-book style, in far-off Arabia, circa 1915. Clichéd images of the sheikh's villainous sidekicks—the dark-skinned "Arab horde"— fill the screen. Cut to a young boy's great uncles from Texas, who shoot dead dozens of the sheikh's slavers. As Uncle Hub cuts down the ruler's mustached villains—I stopped counting after 30—the sheikh's veiled harem maidens cheer him on.

Lions's producers did not necessarily have to vilify Arabs. They could have offered a more factual, realistic storyline based on the following scenario. During World War I Arabs trying to free themselves from Ottoman rule joined the Allies. Throughout the real conflict they fought side-by-side against the Turks and Germans. Given this historically accurate information, the producers might easily have depicted the two uncles from Texas befriending and fighting alongside freedom-fighting Arabs, contesting Ottoman troops.

Like *Lions*, Disney's $100-million-dollar Arabian cowboy epic *Hidalgo* replenishes stale stereotypes: Arab versus American, Arab versus Arab, Arab versus Africans, Arab woman versus Arab man. The action in *Hidalgo* takes place in 1890s desert Arabia. On screen: Movieland's first half-cowboy, half-Indian protagonist, Hopkins. Every 15 or 20 minutes Hopkins beats up or or guns down ugly Bedouin "bandits." Ruling Sheikh Riyadh's nephew, especially, wants to kill Hopkins. Here, too, Arab slavers abuse young, chained Africans. And like *Lions*'s Uncle Hub, the Western hero intervenes: Hopkins saves a black youth from being auctioned off. The angry sheikh corners Hopkins and orders a gloating Arab to sharpen his blade—to castrate the American. "You are an impure unbeliever," barks the sheikh. "You will be gelded, like a stallion not worthy of breeding."

Malevolent Arabs kidnap the sheikh's daughter, demanding she wed a fellow Arab, or else. In time, Hopkins snatches her from danger. Outnumbered 25 to one, he shoots the abductors dead. In the end, despite impossible odds, Hopkins wins the Arabs' desert race, leaving a hundred Bedouin riders in the dust. No surprise here. Ninety-nine percent of the time Western protagonists cross the finish line ahead of Arabs. Check out Disney's *Dreamer: Inspired by a True Story* (2005), Cannon's *Sahara* (1983), and Francis Ford Coppola's *The Black Stallion* (1979), and *The Black Stallion Returns* (1983).

In *The Majestic* (2001) and *Spartan* (2004) lecherous Arabs lust after blondes, again! Opening frames of *The Majestic* reveal a 1950s movie audience watching a black-and-white film called "Sand Pirates of the Sahara." The screen displays a dark desert temple, home of "HORUS, the Falcon-Headed God." Cut to the robed Prince Khalid about to rape the blond heroine. The dashing Western hero rushes into the frame. Sword in hand he declares: "Taste my steel, you dog!" Khalid pulls his sword. Blades clash! The American kills the Arab, and embraces his "desert dove." Dubai's desert sheikhs operate an international slavery ring in *Spartan* (2004), and they, too, are obsessed with ensnaring blondes. The slavers and their cohorts kidnap and whisk off to the Arabian Gulf "blond [American] girls," including the American president's daughter. One Arab sex slaver tells the American protagonist: "When we reach Dubai, I will give you many nice and smooth girls... not women, girls, all young, all blondes."

Cameos

Gratuitous slurs and scenes and dialogue targeting especially sheikhs and villains are injected into 24 Cameo movies—a quarter of post–9/11's 100+ films. Though most scenarios have nothing whatsoever to do with the Middle East, insidious Arabs pop up nearly everywhere, from the Arab desert to the US, and in every kind of tale imaginable, from sci-fi thrillers to contemporary comedies and dramas. Here's a sampling.

—Closing frames in Jackie Chan's *Gen-Y Cops* (2003) show power-mad Achmed and his uncouth henchmen moving to purchase and turn loose on civilians an awesome, destructive robot. In time the protagonists arrive; they pull their guns and open fire—BANG—BANG—BANG—the burnoosed Achmed and Arab henchmen are shot dead.

—Faisal and his "plain mad" Iraqi thugs aim to buy weapons of mass destruction in *Time Lapse* (2001). Before they can run off with the "nuclear suitcase," a US agent kills them.

—All the action in *The Marine* (2006) takes place in the US—except the opening frames. An al-Qaeda leader and some despicable Iraqi insurgents move to behead three captured US soldiers. The leader links Islam with terror, screaming: "*Allahu akbar*" (God is great). Abruptly, the marine hero enters the frame. He guns down the can't-shoot-straight Iraqis and rescues the prisoners.

—*Spymate* (2006) presents a special super-spy hero—Minkey the Chimp! Opening frames reveal the clad-in-Arab-garb Minkey performing heroics in the desert. He prevents Arab villains from launching a powerful missile that would kill the "world leaders attending a peace summit."

Minkey was not the first reel chimp to wear a burnoose and terminate and ridicule Arabs. In *Paradise* (1984), for example, Doc the Chimp topples reel bad Bedouins. And in *Cannonball Run II* (1981), a burnoosed primate kisses an Arab sheikh—full on the lips. The sheikh smiles, telling his son: "If only your mother could kiss like that."

—Reel sheikhs are sexual perverts and white slavers in *Out of Reach* (2004). Two Arabic-speaking bad guys run an Eastern European human trafficking network; the men kidnap, hold hostage, and sell young girls to the highest bidders.

—*Click* (2006) displays, for about 99 seconds, the no-class Prince Habeeboo and his five bearded sidekicks wearing robes. The prince barks orders at his classy American architect, demanding he scrap his classic, well-designed "Arabian Palace." What the Prince wants is not class, but trash—an estate that resembles an "Arabian hoochie house." He thinks a hoochie palace will make it easier for him and his silent Arabs to have sex orgies with "hoochies." The dense Arabs also insist on a much "longer bar," and demand a water drain be placed in the center of the main room—for "wet-T-shirt contests."

—Reel rich Arabs buy up chunks of the US, again. In Disney's *Dreamer: Inspired by a True Story* (2005), robed moguls invade the US and acquire racehorses and lush Kentucky farms. In *What's the Worst that Can Happen?* (2001), the two American protagonists convince a realtor they have more than enough money to buy anything, including a posh building in Washington, DC. Why does the realtor fall for their ruse? Because they are dressed like reel wealthy Arabs. Boasts one bogus Arab: "For right amount of money, camel can dance up a pyramid!"

—And in the Academy Award–winning epic, *Lord of the Rings: Return of the King* (2003), the climactic battle scene features bad guys in black head scarves. Unlike the film's otherworldly villains, these Bedouin clones possess human features.

Taken together, reel negative movies impact and demoralize viewers, especially American Arabs and American Muslims. One example: Consider clean-shaven Bay Area resident Sam Hachem, who has sandy-brown hair and gray-green eyes. Because Hachem is usually thought to be Eastern European, he's seldom harassed. But when folks find out that he's actually a Lebanese immigrant, and that his first name is really Hussein, he's suddenly perceived as a threat. Once at a bar, a patron joked, asking Hachem if he was going to blow up the place. When *United 93* (2006) was shown at a Phoenix, Arizona movie theater, two angry people confronted several young Arab-American women, telling them: "Take off your f— burqas and get the f— out of this country. We don't want you in this country. Go home." Some people fail to realize that wearing a veil or headdress does not make one less American; nor does wearing a yarmulke or a Mennonite bonnet.

Some youngsters are humiliated because vicious slurs are sometimes used to justify harassment and exclusion. Stereotypes prompt other teens to deny their roots, dye their hair blond, and tell their friends that they're Italian or Spanish—not Arab. Though one's name and faith are points of pride and dignity, some anxious youngsters trying to fit in change their names. Suha becomes Susan, Jihad goes for Jay, and Hussein opts for Harry.

The pervasive power of reel negative stereotypes impact the political and moral values of viewers worldwide. Yet imagemakers continue pitching to the studios Middle East action films riddled with clichés. Future bang-bang films, says *Variety's* editor-in-chief Peter Bart, should be: "The classic good-versus-bad guy story; the sort of yarn that stamped the Western as a studio staple." Only this time around the "bad guys would be al-Qaeda; they are all mad at the US." But is it really in our best interests to draw on post–9/11 fears and resentments, and to project the Arab people, or any other people for that matter, as being evil all the time? Yes, al-Qaeda is our enemy, but as *Chicago Tribune* critic Roger Ebert reminds us: "Every individual is somebody's child, and some hope to have children of their own. Movies fueled by hate… are not part of the solution." Fortunately, some imagemakers concur with Ebert, believing that instead of a bunch of "bad guy versus good guy" movies, more evenhanded films should rule the moment.

CHAPTER THREE

Reel Positives

The fractured post–9/11 world we are now living in has made xeno-
phobia and racism [acceptable]… But my film [Babel] is about
compassion… people sharing pain, sharing love.
—Alejandro Gonzáles Iñárritu

When I began researching this book I sensed that post–9/11 images of Arabs would be the same as pre–9/11 ones. They're not. Even though the majority of post–9/11 films do, in fact, vilify a people, I am somewhat encouraged to report that since 9/11, silver screens have displayed, at times, more complex, evenhanded Arab portraits than I have seen in the past. Some producers did not dehumanize Arabs, and instead presented decent, heroic characters—champions, even, in several films. Not all women were displayed as submissive clad-in-black objects. Nor were all Palestinians and Egyptians uniformly depicted as crazed radicals.

Hollywood's not a monolithic place; it's a diverse community with lots of different opinions about people and politics running in different directions. Several filmmakers projected Arab Americans as normal, everyday Americans: Government agents, entrepreneurs, teachers, computer specialists, victims of prejudice. For example, *Flightplan* (2005), starring Jodie Foster, begins with Foster's six-year-old daughter disappearing aboard a passenger jet en route to New York. Instantly, Foster points accusing fingers at the dark-complexioned Ahmed and his two Arab-American companions. She tells the pilot: Those Arab passengers "have my daughter. I don't give a shit about being politically correct." Concluding frames, however, show Foster bringing down the non-Arab kidnappers, and being happily reunited with her daughter. Unexpectedly, the harassed Ahmed enters the frame; he walks over to

Foster and hands her a bag that she'd mistakenly left behind. There is silence. Foster contemplates the man she wrongly accused. Acknowledging her mistake, she offers Ahmed a grateful smile.

In the futuristic film *The Final Cut* (2004), the protagonist's (Robin Williams) best friend is Hasan (Thom Bishops), an Arab-American specialist. Only Hasan has the necessary expertise to help Williams cope with his scary childhood memories, and he does.

In *Enough* (2002), an Arab-American diner owner named Phil is the best friend and primary protector of the heroine, Slim. Phil stops Slim's abusive husband from harming her and her baby daughter. When Phil learns that Slim's husband is beating her, brutally and regularly, he and his friends barge into their home. Phil fights with the husband, rescuing Slim and her child. He then whisks them off to a safe place, to be with his Arab-American friends in Michigan.

An intelligent Arab-American, Layla, surfaces as the female protagonist in the CIA spy thriller, *The Recruit* (2002). Layla's heroics save her lover's life, and she also brings down a corrupt agent. In *The Sentinel* (2006), Aziz Hassad performs like any other dedicated US Secret Service agent. Aziz is a vigilant Arab-American agent who tracks down extremists. One scene shows would-be assassins attacking the commander in chief; Aziz and his colleagues draw their weapons and open fire, protecting the president.

Refreshingly, the compelling movie *Rendition* (2007) presents an Egyptian-born American engineer as a victim of torture, and *Sorry Haters* (2006) features a compassionate Syrian Muslim cab driver, a likeable, refined, religious, hard-working man. *Esquire* editor Lisa Hintelmann was so impressed at seeing a reel Arab cabbie with integrity that she told her fellow critics: "Never—I've never seen such a positive image [of an Arab immigrant] in an American film." Director Gavin Hood's *Rendition* presents not only fair and balanced images of Arabs, but also features as protagonist an Egyptian immigrant, Anwar. Anwar is on his way home from South Africa to be with his American wife and family in Chicago. Suddenly, he is kidnapped, taken to a foreign country, stipped naked and brutally beaten. The film's theme—torture doesn't work; torture breeds more violence—reminds viewers that since 9/11 fear and civil rights abuses have changed us, and not for the better.

Disney's film *Young Black Stallion* appeared and then soon vanished from theater screens. True, the 45-minute movie is boring, poorly written, and shabbily produced. Yet its protagonists are a loveable Arab teenager, Neera and her wise, benevolent grandfather, Ben Ishak. Final frames reveal a movie first: Neera rides her horse to victory, besting the Arab male riders.

Imagemakers have often injected the Arab "other" into remakes, or tossed them into films based on books where the original text had nothing to do with them. Not the producers of *Sahara* (2005) and *Flight of the Phoenix* (2004). They avoided gratuitous stereotypes. For example, in the original *Phoenix* (1966), Bedouin desert bandits slice the Western protagonists' throats (off-screen, but still). There are no Arab villains in the 2004 version. In *Sahara*, viewers see heroic robed freedom fighters rescuing the endangered protagonists. But in Clive Cussler's book of the same name, the heroes are UN troops and Westerners. Why the switch? Director Breck Eisner explains: "I didn't want to it to be that Americans come in and simply save the day."

Brilliantly revealing our common humanity and meriting special attention is director Gonzáles Iñárritu's *Babel* (2006), Golden Globe winner for Best Picture. *Babel's* Moroccan characters—portrayed by real Moroccan villagers—appear as regular folk: Doctors, elderly nurses, husbands, wives, and children—just like us. In the opening frames, a stray bullet accidentally wounds an American tourist, Susan Jones (Cate Blanchett). Cut to several Moroccans providing needed care. One passenger on the bus, Abdullah (Mustapha Rachidi), takes the heavily bleeding Susan and her husband Richard (Brad Pitt) to his remote village; Abdullah finds a doctor who tends her wound, and has an elderly woman care for Susan.

Several memorable, heart-wrenching scenes reflect irrational post–9/11 paranoia. US Embassy officials wrongly assume that Arab terrorists shot Susan, and they believe the assassins are somewhere out there, lurking behind every olive tree. Thus, the ambulance that was en route to assist the critically ill Susan is "cancelled." The embassy's overzealous security behavior, combined with a barrage of false media reports about "terrorism," also affects the behavior of Moroccan policemen. When they find the two brothers responsible for mistakenly shooting Susan, they panic. Refusing to ask questions first, the police fire away, killing the older teen.

At the movie's end, real mutual respect exists between the Moroccan and American characters. Such respect was also carried over to the local Moroccans who appear in *Babel.* Director Iñárritu was so appreciative of their fine performances that he invited them to attend the world premiere screening. Before a packed house, he personally thanked the Moroccans, each and every one of them.

Sally Potter's radiant and remarkable *Yes* (2005) illustrates that although differences in cultures may cause clashes, love and mutual respect between an American and an Arab can triumph. This excellent film projects, for the first time in contemporary cinema history, a reel adult love story: an Arab man romances an American woman—or vice-versa, for it's the talented American scientist who pursues the Lebanese ex-surgeon. When the two make love, they do so joyously. The Arab protagonist could be Muslim or Christian. No matter; he reveres both Islam and Christianity. The dialogue, spoken in rhymed iambic pentameter, expresses sharp, controversial views about American involvement in the Middle East, notably the war in Iraq. Though this overlooked film has received limited distribution, Potter's poignant message—despite differences cultures can successfully connect—reminds us that besides the history of conflict, there's also the history of multicultural friendship. See also Ken Loach's heartwarming film *A Fond Kiss* (2004), a love story between a young, dark-complexioned Pakistani Muslim and a fair, young Irish woman, set in Glasgow.

Writer-director Stephen Gaghan effectively projects *Syriana's* Arabs, Pakistanis, and Americans as compelling characters complete with conflicting motives. (Full disclosure: I did some consulting on this film.) During *Syriana's* clash of modernity and radicalism, Gaghan eschews stereotypes. He does not vilify the region, its people, religion, or culture. For example, two unemployed Pakistani-Muslim oil refinery workers appear not as hateful suicide bombers, but as innocent victims easily seduced by an Islamic fundamentalist. *Syriana* warns us to be wary of moguls, of merciless men who consider the deaths of innocent people acceptable. Everyone is expendable: Educated Arabs seeking democracy, unemployed Pakistani immigrants desperate to find jobs and a meaningful purpose to their lives, covert CIA operatives pursuing justice, even Arab and American children. Power and money matter most. This lucid geopolitical thriller explores what happens when corrupt, influential corporate officers and American government officials mix greed, oil, and terrorism in order to maintain their monopoly on Arab oil.

As for *Munich*, I approached it with caution. In Spielberg's films, reel Arabs have tended to be nefarious. Arab terrorists try to machine-gun Michael J. Fox in *Back to the Future* (1985). Dr. Moriarty's murderous "Egyptian cult" abducts young girls from London streets and torches them alive in *Young Sherlock Holmes* (1985). In his Indiana Jones film *Raiders of the Lost Ark* (1981), Egyptians appear as Nazi sympathizers, and in *Indiana Jones and the Last Crusade* (1989), we see trigger-happy Egyptian Christian fanatics trying to gun down the heroic archeologist. And perhaps most disappointingly, Spielberg missed a golden opportunity to humanize Muslims in *The Terminal* (2004), a film based on a true story about Merhan Karimi Nasseri, an Iranian Muslim stranded at Charles de Gaulle airport terminal, when the filmmaker opted to make the protagonist a loveable Eastern European.

But in *Munich* Spielberg makes a genuine attempt to offer balanced images. Most Palestinians are not tarred in black and most Israelis are not white knights. Both have a conscience, both articulate thoughtful arguments about what it means to be a displaced people. Following a somewhat tedious opening, *Munich* goes on to capture the varied motives and emotions of an Israeli hit team as they proceed to kill, one by one, Palestinians responsible for the deaths of eleven Israeli athletes during the 1972 summer Olympics. At times, watching Israelis shoot Palestinians is as painful and heart-wrenching as watching the assassins shoot Israelis. The lives of Munich's reel Palestinians are worth almost as much as the lives of reel Israelis.

As did Spielberg's, Ridley Scott's early films painted Arabs with a sinister brush: a corrupt, obese Egyptian pops up in his sci-fi epic *Blade Runner* (1982); war-mongering Libyans are inept, disposable bad guys in *GI Jane* (1997). In *Kingdom of Heaven* (2005), however, Scott projects evenhanded images of Christians and Muslims. The Christian knight Balian and the Arab leader Saladin are both models of chivalry; they are devout, merciful, and compassionate.

Though Scott's Crusades drama makes an eloquent plea for peace and tolerance, it was not a huge box-office success here at home. Yet, the film did well overseas, especially in the Arab world. When *Heaven* opened in Beirut, journalist Robert Fisk was there to see it. "Most of [the Lebanese Muslims and Christians in the Dunes theater] were in their 20s," says Fisk; "the scene showing Saladin sending his own doctors to look after the leprous Christian King of Jerusalem prompted from the audience in Beirut a round of spontaneous applause," he writes. "The Lebanese admired this act of mercy; they wanted Saladin to show kindness to a Christian."

Near the end, observes Fisk, "After Balian has surrendered Jerusalem, Saladin enters the city. He sees a crucifix lying on the church floor, knocked off the altar during the three-day siege. He carefully picks up the cross and places it reverently back on the altar." At this point, "the audience rose to their feet and clapped and shouted their appreciation. They loved that gesture of honor. They wanted Islam to be merciful as well as strong." Fisk left the Dunes cinema in Beirut uplifted by the extraordinary performance, of the audience as much as the film. "See it if you haven't," he urges. "And remember how the Muslims [and Christians] of Beirut came to realize that even Hollywood can be fair."

Hood's *Rendition*, Gonzáles Iñárritu's *Babel*, Potter's *Yes*, Scott's *Kingdom of Heaven*, Gaghan's *Syriana*, and Spielberg's *Munich* help offset old clichés by creating decent characters and compelling scenarios as only cinema can. The films demand our attention. Forcefully and eloquently, they illustrate that cultural stereotypes, along with unabated power and unconstrained violence, are a barrier to coexistence and therefore expedite terrorism. The dramas also pose incisive questions relevant to today's quest for peace in the region: Are political objectives achieved by acts of revenge, by an unending cycle of violence that continues to the present day? What has the use of force—from the Crusades to the present—accomplished? Advises Spielberg, "There has to be a prayer for peace... because the biggest enemy is not the Palestinians or the Israelis; the biggest enemy in the region is intransigence."

Though not widely distributed, five positive, non-mainstream features present humane Arab protagonists: Roberto Benigni's Italian antiwar film, *The Tiger and the Snow* (2005); *Satin Rouge* (2002), a Tunisian movie written and directed by Raja Amari; and three Arab–Israeli co-productions: *Paradise Now* (2005), *Rana's Wedding* (2002), and *The Syrian Bride* (2004).

Benigni's *Tiger and the Snow,* not yet available in th US, offers telling, memorable images of the war's devastating effect on Baghdad's ordinary citizens: Doctors, patients, the elderly, a shoe salesman, a young girl, a brilliant pharmacist. Most impressive are scenes that focus on the friendship between two great poets caught up in the Iraq war, an Iraqi and an Italian.

Bride, Wedding, and *Paradise Now* effectively examine current realities of the Israeli–Palestinian conflict on the ground, revealing how the Israeli occupation injures and disrupts the lives of Arabs, young and old alike. Winner of the Golden Globe Award for Best Foreign Film, *Paradise Now* reveals the tragic humanity of Palestinians who live under Israeli occupation, and who are trapped in a vicious cycle of violence. Instead of advancing Hollywood's "demon" stereotypes of Palestinians, Israeli-born Palestinian director Abu-Assad illuminates the darkness by offering political realities and three-dimensional characters. His Palestinian protagonists are different from each other. They are not one-dimensional bad guys; nor are they freedom fighters, pacifists, or terrorists. They are human beings, with all the faults, excesses, ideals, and sorrows of being human. The director does not ask us to choose sides, but to choose humanity.

Abu-Assad's warm, romantic comedy *Rana's Wedding* also addresses the occupation and the border—the one separating Palestinians from Israelis and from each other. In this film, young Rana has less than 24 hours to determine the whereabouts of her beau and convince him to marry her. Even if Rana does find him, will he, given such short notice, agree to wed her? And if so, will they manage to get through several Israeli roadblocks separating Jerusalem and Ramallah, all before the 4 o'clock wedding? Can Rana track down a registrar? Can she find and purchase the necessary wedding garb, get dolled up, and finally locate and bring together all her friends and family? Can she pull it off? Best summarizing *Wedding*'s heart-warming scenario is critic Roger Ebert: This film "gives a more complete visual picture of the borders, the Palestinian settlements and the streets of Jerusalem than we ever see on the news... And we understand that the Palestinians... in many cases are middle-class people like Rana and her circle, sharing the same abilities and aspirations as their neighbors."

A bevy of delightfully fresh images of Arab women are found in the entertaining *Satin Rouge*. The story concerns a bright but bored 40-something Tunisian widow. She is lonely, has nothing to do, and nowhere to go. Suddenly, her life begins to change. She becomes a confident, successful dancer. Throughout, frames reveal her and other attractive, exuberant, middle-aged women dancing joyously. Rhythmic Arab music celebrates their classic movements. Scenes inside a local cabaret display Arab women performing. An assortment of Arab men, young and old, embrace and applaud the graceful women, especially the widow's newfound dancing skills.

The Syrian Bride, winner of the 2004 Montreal Film Festival, boasts a crew and cast of Israelis and Arabs. The director, Eran Riklis, is Israeli; Palestinian Suja Arraf wrote the screenplay. Most of the action takes place at a Golan Heights village and at remote border crossings. The reel key question: Can the protagonist Mona, a spirited Druze bride-to-be from the Golan manage to outwit Israeli and Syrian bureaucrats? In order to marry a likeable Syrian TV star, Mona must find a way to cross from her home—the Israeli-occupied Golan border—into Syria. It's Catch-22 in the Middle East: Syrian officials tell Mona she is already in Syria; Israeli guards argue she's in Israel. Again and again, Mona tries to cross from a place that one side says does not exist to a place the other side says does not exist. Even if Mona does manage to get across the border, as a Syrian citizen she can never return to her village on the Golan. The Israelis won't let her back in; she will never see her family again. At the end, the determined Mona contests the bureaucrats. She starts walking across the border to meet her intended husband. Will she make it?

Finally, Hollywood's reel positive scenarios demonstrate that movies do not have to perpetuate harmful stereotypes to be successful. Imagemakers should keep in mind that their motion pictures continue playing an important role in world politics; constantly repeated, reel evenhanded images may help advance peace. The five independent films cited here, especially the Arab–Israeli co-productions, remind us that films that humanize a people are not merely entertainment; such films may help bring people closer together off-screen as well. As *Syrian Bride*'s co-star, Hiam Abbass, points out: "Political borders dropped down on our cinema set. This film shows how we—Arabs and Israelis—can work together, and create something humanly possible that reaches people all over the world." Israeli actor Yigal Naor, who was in *Rendition*, told journalist Bob Strauss that his Arab and Muslim costars are "my best friends, my brothers. I wish our leaders would come and see how easily this can be done."

CHAPTER FOUR

TV's Arab-American Bogeymen

Τhe white man, the Negro, the oriental, the protestant, the catholic, the Jew, they've all shared the spotlight on this stage," said Danny Thomas. "Well, Danny," remarked Milton Berle, "that's the way show business operates. There's no room for prejudice in our profession."

Berle and Thomas's lofty thoughts were expressed on the *Texaco Star Theater* in 1951 during the pioneering days of television, more than 55 years ago, when only about one in ten American families owned a TV set. Today, on any given evening, says author Edward Jay Epstein, "over 90 percent of the population is at home watching something on a television set." Today, it's much easier for cinema's insidious Arab stereotypes to be reinforced and made more dangerous by TV's poisonous cocktail of fiction, facts, half-truths, and distortion. The fiction comes in the form of new TV shows, which slide in nicely with the hundreds of pre–9/11 shows lush with stereotypical Arabs: Cartoons, made-for-TV movies, TV reruns, and reruns of Hollywood films. The facts include news programs reporting on the Middle East, invariably focusing on violence: on soldiers' deaths and suicide bombings, the latest al-Qaeda tapes, hostage beheadings, bloodshed in Gaza and the West Bank, missiles crashing into Israel, and the bombardment and invasion of Lebanon. The half-truths and distortions include news programs and radio and TV talk-show hosts who use the terrible and unhappy events in such a biased way as to reinforce fearful and offensive views of Arabs and Islam.

In historical and political terms, the messages contained in all types of TV shows inexorably help shape the views and motives of vast numbers of viewers. As a cocktail it envenoms both heart and mind and plays a major role in the name-calling, hurtful discrimination, and hate crimes increasingly aimed at Arabs, Muslims, and Americans of Middle Eastern extraction.

Daily, TV's pre–9/11 stereotypes are regurgitated, thanks to cable systems and a seemingly insatiable need to find programming—quality or content be damned. Many harmful cartoons that I witnessed as a child in the 1940s are resurfacing today. My grandchildren, too, may see Heckle and Jeckle trouncing "Ali Boo-Boo, the Desert Rat," Batman beating up Egyptian baddies, Popeye trashing the forty thieves and Sinbad, Porky Pig and his camel trouncing desert Bedouin, and Bugs Bunny flooring "Ali Baba Mad Dog of the Desert."

Post–9/11 TV productions, with the exception of ABC-TV's *Lost*'s Iraqi character, Sayeed, offer up more of the same damaging Arab stereotypes that I discussed in my 1984 book, *The TV Arab*. Even HBO-TV's *Rome* (2005) demeans Arabs. In the episode "Caesarion," Caesar kills creepy and nasty Egyptians, all despicable reel TV characters, except for Cleopatra, who is nastily seductive. Little has changed since I wrote: "Television tends to perpetuate four basic myths about Arabs. They are all fabulously wealthy; they are barbaric and uncultured; they are sex maniacs with a penchant for white slavery; and they revel in acts of terrorism"

Series like Aaron Sorkin's *West Wing* and others have embellished the derogatory images that I cited in *The TV Arab*, transmitting even more disgust, fear, and hatred of Muslims and Arabs to new generations of viewers. Soon after 9/11, Sorkin helped set the tone by telling colleagues in attendance at the Norman Lear Center's symposium entitled "We Hate You (But Please Send Us More Austin Powers)" that Arab Muslim characters would be featured in his one-hour award-winning dramas "and you're not going to like them." Sorkin kept his word. Arab villains surfaced in his award-winning *West Wing* series, even kidnapping the president's daughter.

Not to be left behind are TV's repeats of yesteryear's movies like *The Siege* (1998) and *Return of the Mummy* (2001). They and at least twenty or so other feature films keep showing up every week on cable and TV movie channels, which gives them a much larger audience than their short-lived movie theater runs. Producers of made-for-TV movies also look to the Middle East for their villains, probably because it allows them to do so without tapping into any deeper veins of creativity or thought, and because they receive few if any complaints. Examples include the Sci-Fi's channel *Raptor Island* (2004), where Arabs are gunned down by Navy SEALs or snapped up as snacks by man-eating raptors; *Manticore* (2005), where Iraqi villains let loose a 2,000-year-old monster that wipes out Iraqis and US soldiers; *Legion of the Dead* (2005), where a sexy, nude Egyptian princess prowls about terminating students; *The Fallen Ones* (2005), where a rampaging 20-ton, 42-foot-tall Egyptian mummy crushes archaeologists and a benevolent rabbi and his father tries to rape the blond heroine; and finally *Sands of Oblivion* (2007), where an ancient Egyptian demon, a huge man-eating jackal-like mummy with a voracious appetite, is reawakened. Amazingly, Egypt's baddies from *Oblivion*, *Fallen*, and *Legion* pop up in, of all places, the US Southwest.

More insidious still than all these hackneyed old stereotypes, however, are TV's post–9/11 depictions of American Arabs and American Muslims as perfidious and traitorous citizens.

From TV's inception until 9/11, Americans of Arab ancestry were basically invisible on TV screens. Only two of yesteryear's TV programs, *The Danny Thomas Show* and *M*A*S*H*, boasted characters—both men—of Arab heritage: Just two. Only two male actors had ever appeared in a TV series as Arab Americans: Danny Thomas (whose show was also known as *Make Room for Daddy* [1953–64]), and Jamie Farr in *M*A*S*H* (1972–83).

No TV series—not one—has ever featured an Arab-American female character. (Arab-American actress Kathy Najimy did portray Olive Massery in NBC-TV's *Veronica's Closet* [1997–2000], but Olive's heritage was not made visible.)

The invisibility of Arab Americans on TV was bad enough, but after 9/11 scores of acclaimed TV shows began showcasing fear-provoking stereotypes of Arab Americans. Granted, from 2002–06 TV's crime shows displayed plenty of non-Arab bad guys (and good guys), but the programs did not castigate their faith. Rightly so. Across the board, there's still a great deal of work to be done before minorities and women are fairly represented in mainstream media. But why are TV producers repeatedly vilifying American Arabs in particular? Look at all the shows that feature decent characters of other ethnicities—Irish, Jewish, Asian and African, to name but a few. Where are the reel Arab-American good guys and gals?

Beginning with the 2002–03 TV season, network producers introduced a new, threatening stereotype: the Arab-American Neighbor as Terrorist (ANT). TV shows warned viewers that America's own Arabs and Muslims (not to mention Arab foreigners) were intent on waging a holy war against the US. Since 2002, more than 50 programs have drilled this mythology into our living rooms. TV's colorful, flickering images also said that regardless of our roots, faith, or skin color we ran shadowy terrorist sleeper cells inside mosques and shacks, from Los Angeles to Washington, DC. These damaging TV shows have helped generate a serious backlash against Arab Americans and Muslim Americans, punishing communities from Los Angeles to New York City.

TV dramas on all the major networks—from CBS to Fox to NBC to Showtime—have projected Arab Americans and Muslim Americans as anti-American villains who relish in blowing up people and buildings, killing their fellow Americans. These TV shows pummel home the myth that Arab Americans, along with recent immigrants from the region, pose a threat to the US. They present Arab Americans as backward religious radicals who merit profiling, imprisonment, torture, and death. Series such as *The Practice*, *Judging Amy*, *The District*, *Sleeper Cell*, *The Agency*, *Threat Matrix*, *Sue Thomas F B Eye* and Dick Wolf's *Law & Order*—have displayed stock caricatures and repeated these negative images over and over. Significantly, producers make few, if any, distinctions between Arabs and American Arabs, between Muslims and American Muslims. The bad guys are almost always blended together. Given this jumbled blend of evildoers, is it any wonder some viewers may perceive American citizens who are Muslims and Arabs as a threat?

Arab-American women remain invisible. They almost never appear on TV, and when they do they are usually silent and submissive. Or they surface briefly as wild, repressed women, such as in the series *Las Vegas*. We never see Arab-American women and men doing what other normal Americans do in successful shows such as *My Name is Earl*—going out on picnics, dating, reading the newspaper, having coffee, rushing off to work, embracing one another, being in families.

47

TV's systematic onslaught on Arab Americans began with the CBS movie *The President's Man: A Line in the Sand* (2002), starring Chuck "Delta Force" Norris. In it, Arab Americans and Arab immigrants team up to make radioactive bombs. Why? To nuke Texas. *The President's Man* is an updated version of NBC's movie *Under Siege* (1968). In *Siege*, Arab-American and Arab terrorists scheme to blow up shoppers in Dearborn, Michigan's mall. The TV movie's FBI director tells a colleague: "It's a whole different ball game. I mean the East and the Middle East. They have their own notion of what's right and what's wrong, what's worth living for and dying for. But we insist on dealing with them as if they're the same as us. We'd better wake up!" NBC's choice of venue was particularly offensive, since Dearborn boasts the largest Arab-American community in the US.

Even UPN-TV's World Wrestling Entertainment (WWE) has contributed to this stereotype. "Good guy" wrestlers began tossing onto arena mats a reel Arab-American "bad guy," Muhammad Hassan. Fans hated Hassan; they called him "terrorist" and chanted and flaunted "Go Home" signs. Unknown to most viewers, Muhammad Hassan's real name is Mark Copani.

CBS-TV's shows are especially damaging. During the 2006–07 season CBS projected homegrown Arab and Muslim Americans as a threat to our country in four popular series: *Navy NCIS*, *Numb3rs*, *Criminal Minds*, and *The Unit*. Producer Donald P. Bellisario's two hit CBS-TV shows, *JAG* (now in syndication) and *Navy NCIS*, and Joel Surnow's critically acclaimed Fox-TV series *24* began denigrating a people and their faith. Taking reel big sledgehammers, they started pounding into viewers' psyches the same dangerous lies spread by *President's Man*: Arab Americans—from Walla Walla to Washington, DC—are bombing their fellow Americans. To help crush Arab Americans—BOOM! BOOM! BANG!—Bellisario injected into his weekly *Navy NCIS* segments an attractive, intelligent Israeli Mossad agent, Ziva David. The capable David helps her fellow US agents bring down Arab and Muslim terrorists, both at home and overseas. Episodes often refer to her training with the Mossad. Watching an Israeli protagonist crush Arabs on US soil in *Navy NCIS*—a popular, prime-time American TV drama—gives added credibility to Jack Valenti's comment about Hollywood and Washington enforcing each other's ideologies. Does Bellisario insert his personal political beliefs into his TV shows? If not, perhaps in the name of fairness, he'll soon replace David, and bring into *Navy NCIS*... say, Laila Haddad, a bright Palestinian agent.

Fox denies their hit series *24* has singled out "any ethnic or religious group" for blame, saying in a January 2007 press release that *24*'s villains have included shadowy Western businessmen, Mexicans, Baltic Europeans, Germans, Russians, even the "Anglo-American president of the United States." What the Fox statement did not say is this: In three out of six seasons—2002–03, 2004–05, and 2006–07—about half of the shows focused on super agent Jack Bauer bringing down Arab, Arab-American, and Muslim-American villains, including suicide bombers and nuclear terrorists. During three of *24*'s seasons, we heard US government officials spewing out anti-Arab and anti-Muslim slurs, which were uncontested, and we watched Bauer's violent actions justify the torturing and the killing of numerous Muslim and Arab "fanatics." I stopped counting after 100 or so dead bodies. Fox has failed to weave into its *24* series the truth: There are Arab-American Jack Bauer heroes out there.

24, *Navy NCIS*, and dozens of other TV programs are frighteningly reminiscent of those 1980s and 1990s kill-'em-all action flicks, starring Chuck Norris, Arnold Schwarzenegger, and Brendan Fraser. Incredibly, government officials, TV network spokespersons, and TV stars have not publicly contested Hollywood's damaging images of Arab Americans and American Muslims. Yet, these fantasy TV programs continue to reinforce anti-Arab public opinion. Today, about half of all Americans are apparently reluctant to have Arabs or Muslims as their neighbors. TV's stereotypes have helped advance a dangerous anti-Arab/Muslim culture, in which violence against innocent people is not only imaginable but acceptable. As I mentioned earlier, since 9/11, more than 2,000 hate crimes have been committed. One such crime took place during the second telecast of *24*: three Guilford College (NC) students were arrested in connection with a group assault against three Palestinian students, whom they called "terrorists" and "sand niggers."

Some political leaders, such as Vice President Dick Cheney and Homeland Security's Michael Chertoff, say *24* is their favorite TV series; they have applauded co-creator Surnow, who jokingly describes himself as a "right-wing nut job." Senator John McCain had a cameo appearance in one show. Chertoff visited the set of *24* and met with producers and cast members; he also participated in the 2006 Heritage Foundation panel on *24*. Conservatives such as Rush Limbaugh have enthusiastically endorsed the show, saying it's patriotic, apolitical, and harmless. Humbug. Remember, this is a Fox-TV series; it's no accident that Bauer and other of the show's protagonists watch only Fox-TV. Nor is it an accident that the series exploits fear, and that it justifies the use of torture against locals and "foreigners." Characters on *24* who question the use of torture and violence are usually projected as "soft-hearted dupes." One example: An Anglo-American neighbor stops thugs from beating up an Arab-American teenager. But, it turns out the teen is not a reel good American student, rather a reel bad Arab-American terrorist intent on blowing up Los Angeles; he terrorizes the neighbor's wife and son and eventually causes the neighbor's death.

Some say the show's torture scenes have impacted members of the US military, adversely affecting "the training and performance of real American soldiers." A former US military interrogator in Iraq, US Army Specialist Tony Lagouranis, has said that he and other servicemen were encouraged to mimic torture techniques that they had seen in movies and on TV—particularly *24*, saying, "We turned to TV and movies to look for ways of interrogating." Army Brigadier General Patrick Finnegan, dean of the US Military Academy at West Point, affirmed Lagouranis's comments, telling the New Yorker that 24's grossly graphic torture scenes did in fact encourage US military personnel in Iraq to act illegally. "They are damaging the image of the US around the world," he said; "I'd like them to stop." General Finnegan and "three of our country's most experienced military and FBI interrogators" flew to Los Angeles to meet with 24's creative team, advising them to "do a show where torture backfires." They explained that in real life torture techniques never work.

Make no mistake. This political drama's unrelenting, vicious images of loathsome Muslim Americans as well as Americans with

Arab roots may be with us for some time, thanks to TV re-runs, DVDs, new TV movies, and an upcoming motion picture. Fox plans to expand its ANT message. In January 2007, the studio announced that moviegoers may soon see a feature-length version of *24*. The movie scenario pits agent Jack Bauer against a reel "bad guy" who is portrayed by Fahim Fazil, a young actor born in Afghanistan. A few months later, Sony Pictures Television announced it will develop John Updike's *Terrorist* (2006) into a TV movie. Updike's novel amplifies the Arab Americans as terrorists theme. The book is about an Arab-American high-school student, Ahmad. Though he regularly attends mosque, he takes part in a terrorist plot to blow up New York's Lincoln Tunnel.

Apparently, some imagemakers have learned little from history. Flashback to 1945: Hollywood releases *Samurai*, a reel bad movie demonizing Japanese Americans. At the time *Samurai* was released, innocent Japanese-American families were still imprisoned in camps, while in Europe their heroic sons fought the Germans. The film ignores these realities. Instead, *Samurai* depicts a Japanese orphan who, after being raised in the United States, becomes a traitor, helping to plan a Japanese invasion of California.

How much longer will TV networks continue to manipulate viewers into fear and hatred of all things Arab and Muslim? Don't they have a moral responsibility to cease propagating negative stereotypes that fuel the flames of racism, injuring real people in their everyday lives? How difficult can it be to replace outrageous stereotypes with evenhanded portraits, those reflecting commonalities? The reality is that Arab Americans love their country just as much as any other group. An Arab American is no more likely to turn his back on his country than a German, Italian, or Japanese American during World War II or a Russian American during the Cold War, or a Korean or Vietnamese American during the conflicts in Asia, or a Cuban American during the Cuban missile crisis, or any time thereafter.

As of 2007, there are about 3 million Arab Americans; four of five were born in the US. Though the vast majority of Arab Americans are Christians, TV programs present us as evil Muslims and link the Islamic faith, a religion of peace, with violence. Besides being dangerous, post–9/11 TV shows continue ignoring real

Arab-American accomplishments. Arab Americans, like their African American brothers and others, died in combat serving their country. Yet, Hollywood continues to ignore their military sacrifices and heroics. To my knowledge, despite the fact that we Arab Americans have served our nation in every war and conflict since the American Civil War—more than 30,000 served during World War II—no TV show or feature film has ever shown us fighting valiantly alongside our fellow Americans in any reel war drama. Not one TV show, not one movie, has ever projected captivating, entertaining stories that are based on our rich history, and the numerous contributions we have made and continue making, to our country. Not one TV show, not one feature film, has ever shown a devout Arab-American family worshipping in a mosque or church, attending Sunday school, religious retreats.

Our numbers include the grande dame of the White House press corps, Helen Thomas; the father of modern cardiovascular surgery, Michael DeBakey; actor Danny Thomas, the founder of St. Jude's Children's Hospital; the founder of Mothers against Drunk Driving (MADD), Candy Lightner; presidential candidate Ralph Nader; Farouk el-Baz, who helped plan the Apollo moon landings; Senate Majority Leader George Mitchell; US Generals George Joulwan of NATO and John Abizaid of Central Command in Iraq; fashion designers Joseph Abboud and Gerry "Couture Bridal Line" Maalouf; radio's Casey Kasem; novelist Diana Abu-Jaber; US women's chess champion Jennifer Shahade; teacher/astronaut Christa McAuliffe, who perished aboard the space shuttle *Challenger* in 1986; and the effervescent Robert George, who served for more than 50 years as the White House Santa Claus.

TV producers can squash TV's devastating stereotypes. Just present Arab Americans as they are: Caring fathers and mothers, military veterans, teachers, lawyers, and doctors, teens catching fly balls, families walking on the beach. The time is now to discard fixed Arab stereotypes, and this new, deeply insidious stereotype of Arab Americans, as well. Failure to do so places producers on the wrong side of editing tables—on the side of promulgating misunderstanding and hate. To their credit, a few producers have debunked this new, harmful mythology, showing viewers that the vilification of some Americans may injure us all. Young Arab Americans and Muslim Americans surface as victims of harassment and prejudice in episodes of *E-Ring, Boston Public, 7th Heaven, The Education of Max Bickford, Jack and Bobby,* and *Strong Medicine.* The positive steps taken by these producers reflect the wisdom of Senator Hillary Clinton who, early on, stressed the importance of making Arab-American contributions visible. Speaking at a 1986 White House prayer breakfast, Clinton said: "The vast majority of Arabs and Muslims in the United States are loyal citizens. [Their] daily lives revolve around work, family, and community…. It's not fair to apply a negative stereotype to all [Arabs and] Muslims." Not fair, indeed.

CHAPTER FIVE

Real Solutions

*Each of us in Hollywood has the opportunity to assume individual
responsibility for creating films that elevate, that shed light rather than
dwell in darkness, that aim for the highest common denominator,
rather than the lowest.*
—Jeffrey Katzenberg, DreamWorks

Misperceptions and misunderstandings persist. President
George W. Bush has blamed the Arab media for the
region's anti-American sentiments. Arab media, he
said in January 2006, "often give a false impression of the United
States—they don't do our country justice. You can't figure out
America when you're looking at some of these [Arab] TV stations... They sometimes put out propaganda that just isn't right,
it isn't fair, and it doesn't give people the impression of what we're
about."

In Iraq, a well-educated engineer named Sheikh Ahmad
Ghazi echoed Bush's concerns. Ghazi, however, pointed at the
American media. He accused us of putting out "propaganda,"
telling an AP reporter that the information the US media trans-
mits about Arabs "isn't right. It isn't fair, and it doesn't do Arab
nations justice." Ghazi's other complaint: US commanders in Iraq
were getting "many of their [false] ideas about the Arab people
from Hollywood."

Georgetown University's Michael Hudson summarizes this
dilemma: We Americans continue perceiving "Arabs in a generally
simplistic, monochromatic, and unfavorable light," he writes.
"And, in the Arab world America's image is distinctly unfavorable
and different from what we think it should be." As a result, says

Hudson, "Americans and Arabs are caught in a dangerously reinforcing cycle of stereotypes. Arabs respond in anger to what they perceive as our denigration of their faiths and cultures. To this Arab response Americans react with bewilderment and resentment, provoking a further negative response from Arabs." Given Hudson's telling, concise thesis, how much longer will we continue viewing each other in terms of simplistic and hostile caricatures? Are we spinning out of control inside a movie reel, gaping at one another through cracked prisms, each unable to recognize the true face of the other? If so, what should we do about these reel "cultivated images"?

The greatest civility we can show "to win the war of ideas," writes Thomas Friedman, "is to take them [Arabs] seriously." Hollywood can take Arabs "seriously" by contemplating the fresh solutions proposed here, some of which may help eradicate reel images of demagoguery, bigotry, and hate.

Presence

We can't wait around for the stereotype to fade into the sunset. That's not what stereotypes do. Instead, victims need to hunt the stereotypes down and eradicate them. Other groups—gays, women, Italians—have done it. Remember, not so many years ago Hollywood's evil "others" were Asians, blacks, and Latinos. For decades, movies ridiculed and demeaned Native Americans and African Americans. Few voices spoke out to contest stereotypes that depicted these groups and others as pimps, prostitutes, jive artists, jocks, junkies, and savages. Not any more. Organizations like the National Association for the Advancement for Colored People (NAACP) and others got together and acted aggressively against discriminatory images, lobbying the industry. Their coordinated efforts prompted filmmakers to cast aside many racial stereotypes.

But it wasn't easy; it took a lot of work and a great deal of time and effort. Eventually, women and minorities began breaking into the industry, becoming a key part of Hollywood's work force. As performers, producers, writers, and directors, they started replacing old stereotypes with more humane, evenhanded images. One example: Beginning in the late 1970s Latino filmmakers, "without almost any support from the industry," created plenty of hit films. Boasts film historian Chon Noriega: "They managed to make as many feature films about Latinos as the industry made in the previous 70 years." Noting Latino accomplishments, today's producers seek out, employ, and reveal down-to-earth images of most minorities. Though the majority of writers and producers are still white men, today's movies reflect the American rainbow with colorful and diverse portraits of Asians, blacks, Latinos, and other minorities. Now, the studios should enhance their reel radiant rainbow's glow: Include Americans with Arab roots.

In Goethe's words, "Knowing is not enough; we must reply. Willing is not enough; we must do." The fragmented Arab-American community is steadily growing in number and visibility. Yet, Arab Americans need to try harder, and make the necessary moves to activate needed visibility in Hollywood. Individuals and organizations should encourage and support a core of fully prepared and well-qualified Arab Americans in the industry.

Do not expect Hollywood to accommodate any minority. They won't. "If you're a minority group," says director Luis Valdez, "you have to push; you have to fight and climb mountains. You have to be aggressive; you have to be positive and you have to compete." Certainly, Arab-American imagemakers, be they Christians or Muslims, want to compete and contribute to the industry. But, still lacking from the community—individuals and organizations—are the real commitments needed to assist these up-and-coming young people. Lacking, also, are efforts to duplicate the success of reel workshops, like those sponsored by Act One, a Los Angeles program for aspiring Christian screenwriters. During the summer of 2005, Act One held an intensive four-week screenwriting seminar for 34 up-and-coming film students. Afterward, Hollywood studio executives began calling, requesting the participants' top five scripts.

In order for Arab-American organizations to duplicate the success of Act One, which has scores of alumni in various positions within the industry, they need financial support to expand their reach. No one group has sufficient staff to conduct research and take charge of structured media monitoring systems. Nor has any Arab-American organization come to the table with long-term plans to meet and establish an ongoing dialogue with the nation's top film critics, production companies, and filmmakers. A give-and-take dialogue would alert them to cinema's damaging Arab portraits. They might consider writing about and producing feature films that reveal and contest the stereotypes, just as they did when blacks, Latinos, and others were demonized. But the sad reality is this: As a Hollywood pressure group Arab Americans don't exist.

The majority of organizations are not entirely at fault, but some groups have only themselves to blame. Many American Muslims have found my *Reel Bad Arabs* (RBA) documentary to be useful, educational, inspiring, and a needed catalyst for change. But organizers of the 2007 Islamic Film Festival did not. They refused to screen RBA or make DVDs available for purchase at the 44th Annual Islamic Society of North America's (ISNA) Convention, because of the "sexual and violent scenes." Of course, such scenes are the essence of RBA; its purpose is to expose Hollywood's stereotypical images of Arab Muslims as sexual and violent beings. ISNA's organizers could have screened RBA, alerting participants by placing notices on doors stating that some scenes may be offensive. If important groups such as ISNA turn a blind eye by refusing to reveal and discuss the stereotype, how can it be eradicated? ISNA also failed to screen Anisa Mehdi's compelling *National Geographic* documentary, *Inside Mecca* (2003), about three individuals who travel to Mecca to perform the hajj.

To help transform Hollywood, to ensure that stereotypes cease, that depictions reflect the community's true achievements, and that humane portraits begin shaping the hearts and minds of people around the world, activists need to step forward, creating a constructive dialogue with imagemakers. Individuals and community leaders, especially those with deep pockets who consistently criticize the organizations, have mostly themselves to blame for status-quo stereotypes. As actor Heshem Issawi points out, "The community doesn't believe in the powers of the media." Community members should stop complaining and begin providing the groups and young filmmakers with the financial support needed to succeed in the Hollywood arena. If activists remain mum, and if well-established, highly visible, and successful Arab Americans don't care about or look after their own interests, how do they expect somebody else to do it? They should follow the lead of Shakira, the popular Colombian–Lebanese singer. Soon after 9/11, she was told that her album sales would suffer unless she eliminated all things Arab from her music, especially the Arabic riffs and belly dancing. She refused: "I would have to rip out my heart...in order to please them." She went on to speak out against bigotry, criticizing all the "hate crimes against everything that's Arab, or seems Arab." Which brings to mind an Arab proverb: "Your rights will not be lost, as long as you continue asking for them."

Hollywood, too, shares the blame. TV executives and producers have treated the solutions I put forth for their consideration in my 1984 book *The TV Arab* with yawns of indifference. Over the years, TV's Arab and Arab-American portraits have only become worse. Reel bad Arab TV and movie scenarios that demean Arabs, Arab Americans, and their culture have escalated.

From the start, Hollywood placed Arab-American actors at the back of the bus. Beginning with early silent films and over a span of 50 years, pioneer performers such as John George from Syria and Frank Lackteen from Lebanon were typecast as reel bad Arabs. In more than 100 films, George and Lackteen were relegated to portraying stereotypical Arab villains: sneaky spies, shifty bargainers, even Nazi sympathizers.

Not much has changed. Like George and Lackteen, today's Arab American actors also have a tough time. Unlike other performers, they rarely are given opportunities to play humane, diverse characters, roles that would contest the stereotype. Some directors contend that there's a demand for young Arab-American actors. Sure, a demand to play billionaires, bombers, bundles in black, and belly dancers. Casting directors toss them stereotypical scraps and bones. Explains Judi Brown-Marmel, an executive producer with Levity Productions: "What I find really intriguing is that people aren't quite ready to confront Middle East stereotypes... it's the last stereotype to be broken down." Actor Khalid Abdalla, who has portrayed reel Arab terrorists in films like *United 93*, calls it "an incredibly hurtful stereotype." Sums up *Munich's* Karim Saleh: "I'm stuck playing terrorists."

Other actors—Ahmed Ahmed (*Looking for Comedy in the Muslim World*), Jay "Jihad" Harik (*American Dreamz*), Nicholas

Kadi (*Soldier of God*), Sayed Badreya (*Soul Plane*), and Lewis Alsamari (*United 93*)—say Arab-American characters are invisible in multicultural films and plays such as *A Chorus Line* (1985), featuring performers portraying Asian, black, Jewish, Puerto Rican, and gay dancers. They are stuck in a stereotypical time warp, they say, one which unfairly profiles them and impacts their personal lives, as well, even when traveling. Look at what happened to Alsamari when he tried to enter the United States. Hollywood had no problem casting him as one of *United*'s four terrorists. But he could not attend the New York premiere of the movie, because the US government refused to grant him a visa.

Bashar Da'as said that he's been offered many villain roles but virtually nothing else. "The only roles open to Arab-American actors are terrorist parts. And, if it's not a terrorist," he said, "then it's a role that dehumanizes us and that's even worse." Da'as told me about one such role: "When I auditioned for a *CSI Miami* segment, they actually liked me," he said. "But the character conspires with the Nazi groups, which is nonsense. I mean an Arab extremist working with Nazis to kidnap schoolchildren? My role in the show was to put a gun to a little boy's head. You can imagine how harmful that image would be to Arab students who study here." Da'as rejected the part, telling me he tried giving "the producers a history lesson, but they didn't really care." In *Driving to Zigzigland* (2006), an independent film needing a distributor, Da'as portrays a Palestinian immigrant intent on becoming a Hollywood actor. But he soon finds out that his dream may not happen; only terrorist roles are available to bearded Arab men with accents, and Da'as refuses "to play a terrorist." One *Zigzigland* scene in particular, stands out: The casting director auditions Da'as for the role of an Islamic villain. "We need to see utter fury," she tells him. "You're a flinch away from beheading this guy with a sword." Da'as overacts, angrily screaming in Arabic. And the casting director is thrilled. "You're the best terrorist we've seen," she says.

Comedian Ahmed Ahmed recalls being discredited and then dismissed by a Hollywood executive who told him: "There's nothing funny about your people." Ahmed went to his agent for help, telling her he wanted to audition for parts other than "terrorist roles." She told him, bluntly: "As long as your name is Ahmed

Ahmed, you're only going to play evil Arabs." Another actor confided to reporter Ayman Mohyeldin: "My identity hurts me in this industry. Let's face it, politics play a role. There is so much tension between Arabs and Jews; they only want to hire us for stereotypical parts." Other actors tell me they really don't want to portray stereotypical Arabs, but they have to, at least until they "make it big." For the time being, those bad guy parts, they say, "help pay the bills. And that's better than being unemployed." Besides, if we refuse these roles, says Ahmed, casting directors will "employ dark-complexioned actors who look Arab." Finally, one actor who, much to the chagrin of his friends and family members, portrays scores of reel "terrorists," offers this rationale, saying: "Look, regardless of the character I portray, my presence on the set makes a difference. I constantly interact with my directors, asking them to make the Arab villain I play more complex, more humane. I talk to them about real Arabs who are like us," he said, "and our culture and traditions. Sometimes they listen," he said, "and make changes. Other times, not. Still, I keep trying; better to try than do nothing, right?"

To avoid being cast as stereotypical Arabs, some actors have changed their names. One confided, "I scrapped my Arab name for an Anglo one. I have blue eyes and I don't look Arab," he said, "and with my new identity I probably won't be typecast anymore; no one will know my roots. So, please don't say anything about my real name." Another actor who landed a prominent role in a big-studio film changed his name to sound European. The young actor told reporter Ashraf Khalil that he anticipates the day when he won't "feel the need to tell people he's Italian." He worries about "being relegated to playing Arab terrorists, the new Arab ghetto." "I am really proud of who I am," he told Khalil, "but I'm constantly having to lie about it." Such fibs and name changes are not unusual. Actor Jameel Farah changed his name to Jamie Farr; *Syriana*'s Siddig El Fadil became Alexander Siddig; and *American Pie*'s Shannon Elizabeth Fadal opted for Shannon Elizabeth. Academy Award winner for *Amadeus* (1984) F. Murray Abraham confessed that the "F" in his name stands for Farid. Early on, Abraham knew he had to drop Farid because that would typecast him "as a sour Arab out to kill everyone." Best summarizing the frustrations and feelings of most performers is actor Karim Saleh: "I want to play parts where I am not killing people," he says. "I want parts that show off qualities that are more normal. I want to play Woody Allen characters—writers and musicians."

Haven't Saleh and his co-performers waited long enough? Shouldn't producers give him and his fellow "Arab actors" a chance to pierce through the stereotype by portraying compassionate, heroic men and women in fresh TV shows and movies? Refreshingly, a few producers cast performers in more complex roles in two 2007 films. In *Extraordinary Rendition*, for example, Moroccan actor Omar Berdouni (*United 93*) gives a brilliant performance as an innocent kidnapped victim. And Palestinian actor Ashraf Barhom (*Paradise Now*) also gives a stunning performance as a heroic Saudi police officer in *The Kingdom* (2007). And in *The Kite Runner* (2007), the lead character of Amir is played by Khalid Abdalla, last seen in the role of a 9/11 hijacker in *United 93*. Abdalla's promotion from terrorist to heroic protagonist may reflect a growing depth in the depictions of Arabs and Muslims. "There does appear to have been a sea-change in more complex depictions of people from the Middle East," said Abdalla to *Variety*'s Ali Jaafar. "I definitely think there's more of a willingness to delve into the grey area."

I hope other Hollywood producers will address the industry's sins of omission and begin casting Arab and Muslim-American performers in non-stereotypical roles. In the fall of 2007, the CW TV network launched *Aliens in America*, a timely comedy series that reminds me of the Canadian Broadcasting Company's (CBC) successful 2007 show, *Little Mosque on the Prairie*. *Aliens*, which looks at Americans' post–9/11 fears and prejudices, is off to a good start; the series is mostly about teenagers, not terrorists. The opening segment features an average Wisconsin family, the Tolchucks, preparing to welcome into their home a blond, blue-eyed, Nordic exchange student. Much to their surprise, however, the exchange student turns out to be Raja, an amicable 16-year-old who just happens to be a Pakistani Muslim. Mrs. Tolchuck fears she's invited a potential terrorist into her home; she wants to ship Raja back to Pakistan. But in the end, Raja's kindness and idealism win her over. Explains producer David Guarascio, "We wanted to bring a character who has a sense of his own faith, and who has a strong relationship with God, into this family that really doesn't have one." Raja has "a spiritual sense of himself; he emerges as a moral compass and helps the family find their way."

Another good beginning: On March 8, 2007, the Comedy Central network telecast the highly entertaining one-hour *Axis of Evil Comedy Special*—the first program in TV's history to feature American comedians with Middle Eastern roots, Ahmed Ahmed, Dean Obeidallah, Aron Kader, and Maz Jobrani. Since the show was a huge success, other networks should follow Comedy Central's lead and include Arab-American characters in an ongoing comedy series.

Not so long ago critics said an Asian woman could never anchor the nightly news and that a black woman could never be a talk-show host, and along came Connie Chung and Oprah Winfrey. Reviewers also said no one would watch sitcoms about Jews or African Americans, and along came the comedy hits *Seinfeld* and *The Cosby Show*. Other critics insisted no one would ever accept a TV show about a plain-looking Latina girl, and along came *Ugly Betty*, a Golden Globe winner. Now is the time for a TV series like *Everybody Loves Abdullah*. To ensure its success, include the talented comedienne Kathy Najimi and pattern Abdullah after the current hits *Two and a Half Men* and *Everybody Loves Raymond*.

Networks should begin seeking out and bringing onto studio lots well-qualified Americans with Arab roots. Together, they could produce box-office hits, such as remakes of *In the Heat of the Night* (1967) and *The Magnificent Seven* (1960), one of my favorite films that would have been even better without its Mexican stereotypes. I recall, still, the original *Seven*'s diverse cast of heroes. A Russian-Swiss-Mongolian (Yul Brynner) portrayed the leader; a German (Horst Buchholz) was a Mexican; and a Lithuanian (Charles Bronson) had a half-Mexican, half-Irish role. A Brooklyn Jew (Eli Wallach) played the bandit chief. The new *Magnificent Seven* might star Salma Hayek and feature Saleh, Ahmed, and Badreya as three brave gunfighters who defend the Mexican village from bandits. A *Heat of the Night* remake could focus on an Arab-American detective encountering and contesting bigotry in a small town while investigating a murder. Arab-American actors could also be cast in starring roles in remakes of fine, financially successfully films such as *I Remember [Sitti] Mama* (1948) and *My Big Fat [Arab] Greek Wedding* (2002).

Presence propagates power.

Once Hollywood opens its doors, young Arab-American film-makers will succeed. They have what it takes to write, produce, and direct telling comedies and dramas about themselves. Some are already doing so, creating captivating scenarios that more honestly express them and their heritage. For example, Isa Totah's screenplay *America* has prompted Oscar-winning producer Mark Johnson (*Rain Man*) to make Hollywood's first mainstream film about Arab Americans. "We've had coming-of-age stories about Italian Americans, African Americans, even Vietnamese Americans, but never one from an Arab-American perspective," said Johnson. Young imagemakers will make a difference. Look at what aspiring innovators Sam Choula, Jackie Salloum, and Gemal Seede have accomplished. Seede, the CEO of Mumin Pictures, produced and wrote the short science-fiction film *Alliance* (2005), winner of Best Picture and Best Sci-Fi awards at several film festivals. Salloum's short film *Planet of the Arabs*, which is based on my *Reel Bad Arabs* book, was screened to sold-out houses at Park City's Sundance Film Festival. With almost no budget, Sam Choula took seven actors and within seven days he completed and released commercially his first full-length thriller, *The Trap* (2005).

College students, too, will help expedite change. For decades, I've encouraged Arab-American students to major and excel in media studies. In cooperation with Washington, DC's American Arab Anti-Discrimination Committee (ADC), I have awarded scholarships to young scholars. Others are catching on. Washington, DC's Arab American Institute (AAI) plans to offer similar awards. And, Emmy Award–winning actor Tony Shalhoub of the hit TV series *Monk* sponsored a 2006 filmmaker award competition; the winner received $20,000 and full access to Hollywood production services. These modest steps are already helping to build a media presence. Two of my scholarship winners, Eyad Zahra and Annemarie Jacir, have produced award-winning short films. Jacir's *Like Twenty Impossibles* looks at a film crew in occupied Palestine trying to navigate obstacles by the Israeli military. And her *Satellite Shooters*, a film on movie stereotypes, was telecast on PBS-TV. In 2008, Jacir plans to release her first feature, *Salt of this Sea*, about a young Palestinian-American refugee returning to

Palestine. Zahra's *Distance from the Sun* received the Best Short Film award at Dubai's first (2004) International Festival. Months later, the Directors Guild of America (DGA) invited its Hollywood members to view *Sun* at a special screening. His cousin, Ahmad Zahra, produced the must-see award-winning *On Common Grounds* (2004), a heart-warming documentary about Jews, Christians, and Muslims who construct a home for a poor family in Mexico. The inexperienced builders put aside their religious and political differences to build a house: "A house where all of us can live, this country, this world."

It should only be a matter of time before Zahra, Jacir, and others begin making a difference in Hollywood. Patience and persistence are the cornerstones. Some Arab-American actors have already given fine performances, performing as "regular" Americans in films like *Enough* and *The Final Cut*. Given the opportunity, other actors will expand their reel presence. Like other Americans they'll be just another minority looking back at the time when they couldn't even get an interview for the stockroom. Hollywood insiders Spencer Lewerenz and Barbara Nicolosi remind us of Dr. Seuss's tiny world of Whoville in his classic book *Horton Hears a Who*. Uninformed skeptics who don't believe the people of Whoville exist are about to boil them—alive. Suddenly, "all of the Whos join together and shout: 'we are here, we are here; we are here!' and are heard just in the nick of time, saving their world." Isn't time for Arab and Muslim Americans to shout—with one unified voice—gently, and firmly?

Fresh Films

"The ultimate achievement for screenwriters wanting to offer fair portrayals," observes critic Robert Greiner, is to present Arabs and Muslims "just like us." Acting on Greiner's advice, here are some just-like-us scenarios for filmmakers to consider.

—Update the classic Charlie Chan films. As a boy, I never missed a Chan movie. He was Hollywood's neatest, wisest, and kindest detective. The remakes will have similar plots but feature not Charlie Chan, but a new super sleuth, Charlie Habib, starring *Monk*'s Tony Shalhoub as Charlie. Assisting detective Habib will be his talented wife Lamia, played by Wendie Malick.

—Revisit Moss Hart's hit *You Can't Take It With You*, which enjoyed a successful run at the Los Angeles Theater Center. Like the stage play, Hart's rewritten film comedy might also feature likeable American-Muslim characters as the quirky folks down the street.

—Check out Lebanese-American playwright S. K. Hershewe's timeless, joyous Semitic comedy *An Oasis in Manhattan*. Family fireworks ignite when it's discovered that the daughter of a Lebanese Archie Bunker is engaged to marry a Jewish man. The father and mother of the respective newlyweds match stereotype for stereotype. In the mid-1960s, I saw the stage production of *Oasis* in Beverly Hills; it was almost impossible to identify the nationality of either member of the engaged couple, either by their looks or their actions. "Hershewe's telling message," said actor Vic Tayback, who starred in the show, "is that it's the kids who are going to take us away from prejudice between Arabs and Jews." Some Spanish and French imagemakers have picked up, somewhat, on Hershewe's theme. In the charming Spanish comedy *Only Human*, a TV personality brings her Palestinian fiancé home to meet her Jewish parents. Again, family fireworks dominate the scenario, putting in doubt whether love between Semites will triumph. Finally, an Arab-Jewish couple is featured in the upcoming French comedy *Mauvaise Foi* (2007).

—Thanks to affordable digital-video technology, several set-in-Iraq documentaries have captured the chaos in the country, revealing the war's complexities by probing the lives of ordinary people. Takeharu Watai's compelling *Little Birds* (2004) presents, for the first time, searing images of Iraqi children suffering unthinkable tragedies. Viewers may easily relate to the humane protagonist in Laura Poitras's *My Country, My Country* (2006), a Sunni physician named Riyadh who is a compassionate, educated caregiver. There's Usama Alshaibi's *Nice Bombs* (2007), which examines the American occupation of Iraq, and James Longley's gripping Academy Award nominee for Best Documentary, *Iraq in Fragments* (2006), and Hayder Daffar's *The Dreams of Sparrows* (2005), the first Iraqi-made documentary to come out of post-Saddam Baghdad. Sean McAllister's *The Liberace of Baghdad* (2005), focuses on an Iraqi celebrity pianist, Samir Peter. Stuck in a Baghdad hotel, Samir can't decide whether to stay home or move abroad. He is pleased to see Saddam gone, but his children argue that the US "liberation" has brought more destruction and death. Each documentary poses a relevant question: After the fall of Saddam Hussein, how are ordinary Iraqis managing? A March 2007 *USA Today* poll revealed that 50 percent of Iraqis say they are not better off today under the US occupation than they were under Saddam; only "26 percent feel 'safe' in their immediate neighborhoods."

—Daily, since the war began, Iraqi civilians are shot dead or wounded by insurgents, especially those who work with the US government and private companies that are linked with the government. More than 90 Iraqi journalists and 300-plus Iraqi interpreters have been killed, and hundreds have been seriously wounded. The proposed movie could focus on the damaged lives of those brave Iraqis working with us. Show how this war tests the bonds of love and friendship that exist between an Iraqi family and two American soldiers. Does their friendship survive after insurgents kill one of the soldiers? What happens to their relationship after some US soldiers accidentally gun down a family member? What occurs when a family friend, a young Iraqi translator who assists the marines, is shot dead? Finally, what happens when the one surviving GI proposes marriage to the surviving Iraqi daughter; will cultures and religions clash or unite? If the marriage does occur, will the Iraqi bride be able to immigrate to the US?

History shows that we Americans welcome refugees from all nations; only months after the Vietnam War, for example, we accepted more than 130,000 refugees from South Vietnam. Though immigration is as American as apple pie, when it comes to accepting Iraqi refugees, there seems to be a problem; to date, all too few Iraqis, even those who have risked their lives to assist the US government, are being allowed to enter our country.

—Set-in-the-US feature films might expose discriminatory acts against innocent Americans. One movie could focus on a wounded-in-action Arab-American veteran. During a gunfight in Iraq she saves the lives of several soldiers, but sadly her fiancé is shot dead. The disabled veteran returns home in a wheelchair to her small, western Pennsylvania steel town, filled with disgruntled out-of-work laborers. She seeks employment and acceptance, but before she can "settle in," she must cope with overt and subtle prejudices.

—Develop features based on actual events. During the 9/11 attacks, the Hamdani family lost their son Salman, an NYPD cadet, medical student, and part-time ambulance driver. Yet, because Salman failed to return home that tragic morning, the government acted hastily and irresponsibly, tagging him as a possible terrorist. Finally, months later, he was properly redeemed as a "hero," and is cited in the PATRIOT Act.

Salman's case is not unique. After 9/11, untold numbers of innocent people were secretly locked up. The vast majority of these "terror suspects," reports Human Rights Watch, may have violated some minor immigration laws but none were ever linked to terrorism. For example, the FBI arrested eight Arab-American restaurant workers in Evansville, Indiana. Labeled terrorists, the workers were shackled and hauled off to a Chicago detention facility. Eventually, they were let go, but FBI officials never told them why they were detained. How did the FBI's false accusations and their imprisonment affect the Arab Americans? Did their neighbors, young and old, accept them as victims, or view them suspiciously? Were they forced to close their Evansville restaurant, move to another city, leave the country?

—Consider using Danny Hakim's documentary *Shadya* (2005) as the basis for a feature-length film about the charismatic karate world champion Shadya Zoabi, a 17-year-old Arab Muslim living in Israel. Consider also films about young Christians, Jews, and Muslims—children with difficult pasts from the world's troubled spots trying to fit in. They attend summer camps like those hosted by Seeds of Peace, Camp IF, and the "refugee" camp in Clarkston, Georgia, where they try to fit in with strangers in a small town in the American South.

Universal Studios has already purchased the story rights about the Clarkston camp. In their upcoming film I propose that the youngsters, some of whom speak with thick foreign accents, show up at camp with preconceived ideas about each other, fixed stereotypes gleaned from their friends, families, and from reel images of occupation, war, and terrorism. Have some protagonists talk openly about past tragedies, their respective beliefs; others could be frighteningly silent. Frames could focus especially on members of the camp's soccer team, the "Fugees" (short for refugees). The

Clarkston team's real coach is Luma Mufleh, an Arab-American immigrant who grew up in Amman, Jordan. The studio might consider casting Shannon Elizabeth as the Fugee's reel coach. The movie could also reveal how and why Mufleh decided to coach the boys, and her struggles to convince local politicians to provide the youngsters with a safe soccer field in town. Some of Clarkston's longtime residents prefer baseball and football; for them soccer is a sign of unwarranted change, a foreign influence like Muslim girls wearing the hijab around town. Show also how teens and townsfolk interact prior to, during and after soccer practices and games. Viewers would discover whether the youngsters and the locals maintain or unlearn prejudices. As to who wins the match—would it matter?

Prior to seeing my *Reel Bad Arabs* (RBA) documentary, director Oliver Stone told his audience at Dubai's 2007 Operational Culture Bridge panel, that it was "unfair" that I was rebuking Hollywood for its cultural stereotypes of Arabs. Added Stone, anyone "could say the same thing about any minority." Two days later, Stone did a quick turnaround. He announced at a press conference that after watching my film, he came to realize how pervasive the Arab stereotype was. He told the press that Hollywood's imagemakers should make films that help bridge the gap between the two cultures.

Stone's quest for fairness is a needed wake-up call for other skilled directors and producers. In 2002, Francis Ford Coppola told a Moroccan audience that "For years, Hollywood has stereotyped Arabs as bad guys," and that, "You could make beautiful films about [Arab life and culture], but I don't know any [filmmaker] who knows anything about them." We must work to change that.

Shattering the Silence

We cannot remain silent. As Martin Luther King, Jr. said, "Our lives begin to end the day we become silent about things that matter." To quash the Arab stereotype we must first identify it as unacceptable and commit to its eradication by speaking out. A good place to start is in the classroom, the crucible in which we have historically challenged and broken many stereotypes before they fossilized.

Though I have discussed reel Arab images at more than 100 universities worldwide, not once did I ever come across a college film class focusing specifically on Hollywood's Arabs. Why the exclusion? College catalogues offer a wide range of cinema studies. Hundreds of classes and books deal with many reel racial and ethnic groups. Obviously, fresh courses focusing on the Arab "other" would benefit students, giving them opportunities to receive a more pivotal understanding of the context within which fair-minded people view Hollywood's stereotypes. Class readings could include—to name just a sampling—acclaimed works such as Allen Woll's *Ethnic and Racial Images in American Film and Television*, Harold Isaacs's *Scratches on Our Minds*, Daniel Leab's *From Sambo to Superspade*, Michael Renov's *Hollywood's Wartime Women*, Sam Keen's *Faces of the Enemy*, Gretchen Bataille and Charles Silet's *The Pretend Indians*, Patricia Erens's *The Jew in American Cinema*, my RBA and the present volume.

Documentaries that reveal the history and injurious impact of stereotypes would supplement the reading: on African Americans, *Ethnic Notions* (1986) and *Color Adjustment* (1991); on Asian Americans, *The Slanted Screen* (2006); on gays, *The Celluloid Closet* (1995), which is based on Vito Russo's groundbreaking book of the same name; on Jews, *Jews, Movies and the American Dream* (1998); on Latinos, *The Bronze Screen: 100 Years of the Latino Image in American Cinema* (2002); and on Native Americans, *Images of Indians, Part I: The Great Movie Massacre* (1979) and *How Hollywood Stereotyped the Native American* (2003); on Italian Americans, *World Beyond Wise Guys* (2008); and on Arabs, the 2006 *Reel Bad Arabs* documentary based on my book.

In addition to their role in the classroom, scholars will continue to make important contributions to research in the field. From my experience as an academic and film critic, I know there are superb cinema teachers out there who will begin to teach and write essays, books, and scripts that examine reel Arab characters and themes.

People of influence should speak up about the stereotypes. Diplomats who are committed to fostering peace, civil rights leaders, entertainment critics, and film stars, directors, and producers—as well as columnists and journalists. While stationed in Baghdad, journalist Ann Marlowe, who is Jewish, overheard her colleagues referring to Iraqis as "fat, sexist Arabs." Instantly, she countered the slurs. Later, Marlowe mused: Such bigoted statements "show an American inability to see Arabs as fully human. If Arabs are fat and sexist, what are they saying about Jews behind my back?" Iraqi men were "pretty cute. Many looked like my own people: They looked like Jews. We [Americans] need to rid ourselves of our perverse myths about Middle Eastern men and women," said Marlowe. Aren't slurs against Arabs "just another form of anti-Semitism?"

Breaking the silence means admitting something is wrong and bearing the embarrassment that comes with that. The effort necessary to change may be difficult for some. When a respected American Film Institute (AFI) historian was asked about reel Arabs, for example, he told my friend, a documentary TV producer, that this "is something a lot of people don't want to be talking about. I personally don't want to talk about it. It's opening up a can of worms." The hesitation is natural: we instinctively resist change. But this "can of worms" is no different than the cans we pried open to uncover other stereotypes. The worms are there. Pretending they don't exist is not the answer. Keep in mind the ancient Chinese proverb, "To know and not to do is not to know." Our work cannot be considered done until other forms of oppression have been challenged and overcome as well, including reel and real discriminatory actions directed against all things Arab.

"Many successful rights movements, the women's movement, gay rights, the American Indian Movement, and the like," points out Professor Chuck Yates, "followed the lead of the civil rights movement and rose to full vigor. Throughout the period of their greatest activity, they all benefited from each other's achievements and each other's examples." I ask you to consider why the rising tide that lifted your boats together seems to have left Arab boats anchored. And, I humbly ask with good cause to help me put an end to this most enduring, egregious social inequity. "We need to learn how to come together to be united," reminds Academy Award–winning actress Halle Berry. "We need to love each other— with all our shades and colors and textures—and know that we're all discriminated against. We're all in the same boat and we [should] take that knowledge and go forward."

Whenever a group moves to debunk stereotypes there are those who deny their existence, defending them as the real deal. Consider this example. Years ago, journalist Jawad Ali and I watched a PBS-TV special about hateful movie stereotypes hosted by the late Gene Siskel and Roger Ebert. We recall how the two critics went down the list, one by one, of Hollywood's racist and sexist offences: Blacks, Italians, women, gays, and so forth. And then, they finally got to the part we had been waiting for—Arabs and Muslims. But, recalls Ali, "Siskel brushed off Hollywood's odious Arab portrayals with a single sentence that went something like this: 'Oh well, as long as Arabs are our enemy and are blowing up innocent people, our movies will show them as terrorists.'" Ebert let the statement slide, and the critics moved on to other topics. "Siskel's hurtful remark stays with me, still," writes Ali. "I felt as if a diversity teacher had called me a sand nigger."

Some critics and screenwriters argue that there are no Arab villains in Hollywood movies. To support their thesis they cite Sean Penn's *The Interpreter* (2004), whose reel terrorists are "Africans from the little-known republic of Matobo," and Arnold Schwarzenegger's *Collateral Damage* (2002). Early drafts of *Damage* had Arab terrorists blowing up a US consulate, but writers deleted these scenes. Rick Lyman contends that moviemakers have "been handed the gift of villains in the form of Islamic terrorists, [but] the industry has opted for restraints to avoid the accusation of bias and the danger of offending audience sensibilities in an increasingly multiracial America." Supporting Lyman's views that "Hollywood... has lost its taste for xenophobic... stereotyping" was the *Atlantic Monthly*'s Mark Steyn, who writes that "Muslim terrorists have all but disappeared." Author Andrew Klaven has pitched in, as well. He wants Hollywood to "produce more gung-ho, patriotic war movies that celebrate our fight against Islamo-fascism in Afghanistan and Iraq—and in Iran as well, if and when that becomes necessary... We need war movies now, even more than in the 1940s," Klaven says.

Ratcheting up the rhetoric is the *New York Post*'s Michael Fumento, who writes: "Just how many Hollywood movies have been made in which the bad guys are Islamist terrorists... If you have to guess, guess 'none.'" Fumento blames "Tinseltown terror apologists [for] not wanting to stereotype either Arabs or Muslims." As a result, "the moguls in La La Land... are giving us the equivalent of 1943 movies equating FDR with Hitler." Other critics say that pressure groups, censorship, and greed are preventing portrayals of evil Arabs on movie screens. Declares *LA Weekly*'s Nikki Finke: The industry "doesn't have the balls to tell the truth [about Arabs and Muslims]. Hollywood has long been loath to portray any Arabs as villains, much less Muslim extremists," she writes, "because its movies make a lot of money in the Middle East." Finke goes on to say that Hollywood is "giving aid and comfort to the enemy," and that they are "getting rich doing it." Screenwriter Barbara Johnson, too, contends that Hollywood has ignored Islamic "terror on screen." She argues that producers have "bowed to the pressure of Muslim activists" and calls Arab and Islamic "special-interest groups... a threat to all that the creative community stands for."

Elaborating on this reel mythology are critics Michael Medved and Robert Sklar. They made a fuss because the bad guys in the 2004 remake of *The Manchurian Candidate* were not Arabs but capitalists. Though Arabs "are the most logical villains," they're not in the movie, says Sklar, because "it's politically incorrect to offend Muslim religious and ethnic responsibilities." Medved writes that the "movie industry has pointedly avoided harsh treatment of... Islamic radicals." Medved is upset because *The Pacifier* (2005) featured Serbians and neo-Nazis as villains, which he finds "completely unrealistic." Medved and Fumento are also distressed about *The Sum of All Fears* (2002). In Tom Clancy's book, the villains are a cadre of American Indians, former East Germans, and Arabs. But the movie's evildoers are German neo-Nazis. Director Phil Alden Robinson explained the switch, telling the Council on American–Islamic Relations (CAIR), "I hope you will be reassured that I have no intention of promoting negative images of Muslims or Arabs." "By cooperating with organizations like CAIR," Fumento wrote, "Hollywood kowtows to groups that aid and abet terrorists."

Like Fumento, Medved believes *Fear*'s bad guys most certainly should have been only Arab Muslims. "Our enemies," he preaches, "are Islamic and fascist." And, he argues, Hollywood's failure to focus on these "evil people...has become dangerous for our culture and for the strength of our republic."

Such shallow criticism bring to mind the intelligence of Stephen Hawking, who called the greatest threat to knowledge "not ignorance," but "the illusion of knowledge." Evidently Hollywood's defamation of Arabs in more than 1,150 feature films isn't enough. *Cineaste*'s editors, though, suggested that film critics who "resort to name-calling or chastising filmmakers for 'meddling' in political issues merely... demonstrate the poverty of their own arguments. This sort of vituperation, in fact, reveals far more about the commentator than either the filmmaker or the film being attacked." The insights offered by *Cineaste*'s editors are refreshingly welcome. Actor Ben Affleck, who portrayed Jack Ryan in *Fears*, applauded the producer's decision not to project Arabs as villains, and for good reason. "The Arab terrorist thing has been done a million times in the movies," he said.

I am encouraged by the fact that, unlike so many things in life, Arab caricatures in Hollywood movies are entirely within our control. Eradicating this stereotype should no longer be an insurmountable barrier. Some notables—such as critics Deborah Young (*Variety*), Howard Rosenberg (*Los Angeles Times*), and author Norman Solomon—have already taken a stand. They recognize, as does director Sally Potter, that besides the "history of conflict, there is also the history of multicultural friendship." Performers such as Puerto Rican singer Ricky Martin, actors Anna Thomson and Joshua Jackson, and Adam Yauch of the Beastie Boys have also spoken out. "Most Middle East people are not terrorists," said Yauch during the 1998 nationally telecast MTV awards. "Racism that comes from the US *toward* Muslim people and Arab people, that's something that has to stop. The United States has to start respecting the people from the Middle East in order to find the solution to the problem that's been building up over many years," Yauch said to applause from the audience.

Speaking at Morocco's 2002 International Film Festival, actress Anna Thomson echoed Yauch's concerns, telling reporters that the US media continue to project "ghastly lies about Arab people that are just not true." At the 25th annual Arab Children's Conference in Amman, Jordan (July 2005), Ricky Martin went out of his way to meet with a group of Arab teenagers. The youths were polite but despondent, complaining that Western media always projected them as "terrorists." Martin, a past victim of Latino-bashing, understood their concerns. He told the youngsters he would help them change Westerners' negative perceptions of Arabs: "I promise I will become a spokesperson if you allow me to," he said. "I will defend you and try to get rid of any stereotypes." The youths cheered. Speaking at Dubai's 2006 International Film Festival, Joshua Jackson (*Bobby*, 2006) told a nationally televised audience: "Every time I travel to any country, be it considered slightly foreign or very foreign, I am always struck by massive similarities rather than massive differences. We Americans and you Arabs," he said, "have many more things in common than we have differences."

American Arab Entertainment Summit

One of the problems the United States has in the Middle East is "its failure to effectively communicate with the Arab people," writes Graham Fuller, a former CIA analyst. "I have never felt such an extraordinary gap between two worlds. Clearly, in a region where we desperately need friends and supporters, their number is dwindling, and we are increasingly on the defensive." Many in the region, contends Fuller, mistakenly believe that the US war on terrorism is merely a cover for a war on Islam. President Bush, too, has addressed the war against Islam myth. Speaking before the United Nations General Assembly in September 2006, the president spoke directly to peoples of the Middle East, saying: "Extremists in your midst spread propaganda claiming that the West is engaged in a war against Islam. This propaganda is false. We respect Islam."

In order to change the Arab world's opinion of the United States, and vice versa, the government should act now to narrow this "extraordinary gap." Unfortunately, new commercial films released by our allies are bashing Americans and widening this gap. Look at Turkey, a country of nearly 70 million Muslims living in a secular state. For decades Turkey has been our committed partner, first in the Korean War and in confronting the Soviet Union, then in fighting terrorism. Yet, Istanbul's teenagers flocked to see, again and again, a not-so-flattering view of Americans in *Valley of the Wolves* (2006). One reason the teens enjoyed watching Turkey's $10-million Rambo-like box-office hit is that *Wolves* is based on a real event about our soldiers abusing Turkish troops. On July 4, 2003, some American GIs in Iraq made a grave mistake. Thinking eleven Turkish officers were insurgents, the GIs arrested and hand-cuffed them and pulled hoods over their heads. The film's opening frames dramatize this mistake. *Wolves* goes on to present damaging scenes and caricatures such as a stereotypical US commander "Sam" and his bible-thumping "trigger-happy" marines. Viewers witness coalition soldiers firebombing a mosque, abusing Abu Ghraib prisoners, and killing scores of Iraqi civilians, even children. The film also shows a US army surgeon taking organs from dead Iraqi prisoners and shipping them off to buyers in New York and Tel Aviv.

Wolves's success is due, in part, to Turkey's anti-American feelings. "On the Turkish street public opinion of America has been steadily declining," reports the *New York Times*. "Favorable views of America plummeted from 52 percent of Turks in 2000, to 15 percent in 2003." When questioned whether *Wolves* would hurt Turkish–American relations, specialist Egemen Bagis told *Times* reporter Sebnem Arsu: "Our alliance with the United States has very strong roots. One movie cannot destroy it."

The Turks are not alone. Egypt, another Washington ally, has also seen recent stereotypical Americans on movie screens. Egypt released a highly entertaining but wildly anti-American farce, *The Night That Baghdad Fell* (2005). The film's reel Egyptians describe Americans as "bullies, rapists and killers." They fear US troops will invade their country and destroy Cairo. And in *Night*, fantasy sex scenes demean a real US government official. In the film, a belly-dancing Egyptian actress—a "look-alike for Secretary of State Condoleezza Rice"—performs a strip tease. Reports Daniel Williams of the *Washington Post*: Before 9/11, such negative images in Egyptian cinema were rare. In the past, "Americans, if portrayed at all [in Egyptian cinema], were cast as unwitting victims of crafty Egyptian tour guides." Even contemporary Bolivian movies now "depict Americans as various sorts of demons." James McEnteer points out that films such as *Los Andes No Creen en Dios* (2005), *American Visa* (2006), and *Quien Mato a la Llamita Blanca?* (2006)

show Americans as reel "violent, gun-toting spaghetti-western thugs, heartless bureaucrats stonewalling visa seekers and drug traffickers."

These films from South America to the Middle East share a common theme: They offer "heavy-handed portrayals of Americans [that] reflect a long-term cultural distrust of US motives." Will Bolivia, Turkey, Egypt, and perhaps other countries continue this new trend, projecting Americans as diabolical villains?

What about us? Will we continue projecting Arabs as villains?

To help us improve cultural relations and win the war on terror, says David Abshire, president of the Center for the Presidency, we should take "a fresh look at our communications strategy, at what we communicate, how we communicate, and to which audiences." Abshire contends that media misperceptions lead to mutual misunderstandings, which in turn "impede dialogue and cooperation between the West and much of the Arab world." He emphasizes: "Perception" is the linchpin; "perception is as important as reality." Yet, their perceptions of us and our perceptions of them remain garbled. The 9/11 Commission's final report gave US diplomacy a "D" for its failed Middle East diplomacy efforts. Defense Secretary Donald Rumsfeld affirmed the "D" grade.

During Rumsfeld's March 2006 visit to the Army War College he said: "We probably deserve a D or D- as a country as to how well we're doing in the battle of ideas." Iraq, especially, continues to be problematic. To try to influence Iraqi opinion, in 2004 our government began broadcasting the Arabic-language program *Alhurra* (Arabic for "The Free One"). But, according to President Bush and a Zogby International poll, it turned out to be a multi-million-dollar failure; less than 1 percent of viewers in five Arab countries watched it. We shelled out millions for TV and billboard advertisements. We employed Iraqi Sunni religious scholars to help us launch information campaigns. We contributed money to several Iraqi newspapers so that they would print positive articles written by US soldiers.

Journalists like Alan Riding are critical of our failed PR campaigns. "It is too much to expect 'public diplomacy,' today's euphemism for cultural propaganda," writes Riding, "to provide a quick fix." To bridge this cultural divide, "new tactics are needed—innovative solutions to address new realities." Early on, in her

February 2003 testimony before the Senate Foreign Relations Committee, Charlotte Beers, undersecretary for Public Diplomacy and Public Affairs, addressed this "cultural divide." She warned that injurious stereotypes of Americans were impacting behavior on the Arab street: "We are talking about millions of ordinary people, a huge number of whom have gravely distorted, but carefully cultivated images of us—images so negative, so weird, so hostile that I can assure you a young generation of terrorists is being created." Months after Beers's testimony, Ambassador Marc Charles Ginsberg and his colleagues met about 30 young, gifted image-makers, some of whom had won Academy Awards and Emmys. They agreed that "the war in Iraq was not a war against Islam." They also agreed on the desperate need to contest stereotypes, and to develop new entertainment programs that "would be in Arabic with Arab actors, producers, and writers." If we work together to open lines of communication," said Ginsberg, these films will "help convince peace-loving Muslims they are not the target." Sums up 9/11 Commission chairman, Governor Thomas Kean: "We worry about bin Laden and al-Qaeda; we should worry far more about the attitudes of tens of millions of young Arabs, and hundreds of millions of young Muslims."

To alter the attitudes of these young people I propose a major American Arab Entertainment Summit, one which would be candid about differences but would also stress similarities. The summit would be designed to recognize, contest, and correct images of reel evil "others." Participants could also focus on religious commonalities and the Islam-as-the-Green-Menace stereotype. Emphasizing the need for an American-Arab dialogue are Angelina Jolie and Deepak Chopra: "Watching [movies, TV shows, and] the news, one would think that all [Arabs and] Muslims are either wildly fanatic or wildly irrational," Chopra says. "Frankly, I'm tired of seeing [more than] a billion people as one bogeyman…. To begin our process of listening and understanding," the United States should "host an international gathering that will improve communications with the Arab world." Affirms Jolie: "We're at a time in our lives where there is so much fear and there is so much anger"; it's crucial "for people to remain focused [and] to calm down enough to have a dialogue about finding solutions."

Two decades ago we set a masterful precedent for contesting Russian stereotypes, the successful 1986–87 Cold War "Entertainment Summit," sponsored by Mark Gerzon's Mediators Foundation. This summit came about because Gerzon was unsettled about reel Japanese images, the "Yellow Menace," as well as 1980s anxieties about reel Communists, the "Red Menace." Hollywood's 1980s films such as *Red Dawn, Invasion USA* and others were projecting reel "evil Soviet communists" invading the United States, killing Americans. Gerzon was equally concerned that Soviet films were stereotyping Americans as ruthless, heartless capitalists. Intent on "ending the Cold War on the big screen," Gerzon and his global bridge-building colleagues brought together at his summit, for the first time, delegations from both the Soviet and American film industries. Gerzon arranged for Hollywood producers to meet with Soviet imagemakers in four major cities: Los Angeles, New York, Moscow, and Tbilisi. For weeks, participants pondered how to best go about eradicating offensive American and Soviet images. Co-productions, they agreed, would be one way to help create deeper understanding and respect between the peoples of both nations. In the end, the major studios and entertainment guilds on both sides of the Iron Curtain moved forward, forming a partnership that helped foster more accurate portrayals.

Gerzon's successful summit helped bring about an abrupt halt to many reel depictions of Soviet Communists as bogeymen, and it also helped foster co-productions. Today, Andy Bird, president of Walt Disney International, calls Russia "a priority country"—more than 50 Russians are working in Disney's Moscow office. Disney isn't alone in tapping the market for Russian-made films. Twentieth Century Fox Film's teen comedy *Waiting for a Miracle* (2007) was "produced by a joint venture half-owned by Sony." Explains Marina Jigalova-Ozkan, managing director of Mickey & Company's Russian operation: "We want Russian families to go to the cinema to watch a Disney movie, but this movie need not be produced in Hollywood." Gerzon believes that what's happened with Russia illustrates that "when film producers, directors, and movie stars of a culture move beyond stereotypes of the 'other,' mainstream populations soon follow."

One opening summit program might be the screening and discussion of a non-Arab film, CBS-TV's *Misunderstanding China* (1972). This single documentary helped pave the way for improved Chinese–American relations. *China* shows how politics and entertainment are intentionally intertwined, and CBS moguls and political leaders used this film to eradicate fixed Chinese stereotypes and to advance the US government's foreign policies. The historic *China* was already being written, filmed, and edited months before CBS telecast the show—on the evening of President Richard Nixon's surprise trip to China. Narrated by Charles Kuralt, the documentary revealed, for the first time ever, America's long-held prejudicial attitudes toward this Communist country and its people. China's reel message supported President Nixon's real fresh policies: "Dirty commie" stereotypes in US popular culture should cease; we should see more accurate images of the Chinese and their culture; the Chinese, especially their ping-pong players, are pretty much just like us.

As *New Republic* columnist Joseph Braude pointed out: "When it comes to the struggle for hearts and minds in the Middle East, motion pictures [and TV shows] may well be a better ambassador of goodwill to Arab audiences than Washington's public diplomacy campaigns." To achieve greater mutual understanding, summit participants might include political, religious, and entertainment leaders from the US and the Arab world. Attending might be the president's public diplomacy staff, Hollywood's Guild members, MPAA executives, media moguls, and filmmakers and actors who've shown an interest in the issue, such as directors Mira Nair and Oliver Stone and actors Michael Douglas and Gary Sinise. Douglas works with Global Nomads Group, which helps children from across the world gain a better understanding of humanity's cultures and religions. One Global Nomads program gave "American students the chance to… understand more clearly Iraqis as human beings." Sinise cofounded Operation Iraqi Children (OIC), a grassroots program that collects and ships school supplies and toys to Iraq for distribution by US troops to Iraq's children.

Arab-American imagemakers would be important participants: In addition to those I've already mentioned in this chapter,

Sanaa Hamri, Hollywood's first Moroccan film director *Something New* (2006); actresses Selma Hayek and Touriya Haddad (*Five Fingers*); the young Omar Naim, who wrote and directed the science-fiction thriller *The Final Cut* (2004); Ruba Nadda, the Canadian-Arab director whose romantic feature about a Canadian-Muslim woman in love with a non-Muslim, *Sabah* (2005), delighted audiences; and Jehane Noujaim, whose award-winning documentary *Control Room* captured the 2006 TED Prize. Noujaim was also awarded $100,000 to help support her one world-changing wish: "To bring the world together for one day a year through the power of film."

Robert Inger, Disney's chief executive, and Michael Lynton, CEO of Sony Pictures Entertainment, should also participate. Lynton and Inger are innovators who are creating and expanding local-language film production businesses. Sony is currently working with "directors and actors in China, India, Mexico, Spain, and Russia to make movies for release in each of those markets and, on occasion, internationally as well." Inger has linked Disney with film companies and producers in China, India, Latin America, South Korea, and Russia. Up-and-coming Arab filmmakers, from Jordan to Dubai, should participate, to discuss with Inger, Lynton, and other executives possible co-productions in Arab nations as well. Director Nadine Labaki should attend; Lebanese audiences have applauded her heart-warming feature *Caramel* (2007). Set in present-day Beirut, the movie shows the humanity of five women, Muslim and Christian, young and old, working side by side in a beauty salon. There's Nayla Khaja, Dubai's first female producer, whose 2004 documentary, *Unveiling Dubai*, illustrates that in Dubai "women are as likely as men to be driving late-model Jaguars; and blue jeans are as common in shopping malls as the black abayas." And Jordan's Randa Ayoubi, whose new cross-cultural animated TV cartoon series, *Ben & Izzy*, follows the adventures of two 11-year-old boys, Izzy from Jordan and Ben from the US. Others attending might be American and Arab film scholars, emerging writers and directors who are interested in developing scenarios that reflect the region's cultural richness and diversity. Recently, Jordan's students, for example, began participating in writing workshops offered by the Sundance Institute, and thanks to Steven Spielberg, some are enrolled in degree programs at USC's School of Cinematic Arts. Three of Hollywood's upcoming Iraq-themed movies, *Battle for Haditha*, *Redacted*, and *The Hurt Locker*, were filmed in Jordan. Saudi Arabia's Prince al-Waleed Bin Talal could also participate. He hopes to develop a creative, independent Arab cinema, having financed the Kingdom's first feature film, *Keif al-Hal?* [How are you?]. In the works are several other films, to be shot in Saudi Arabia, Lebanon, and Tunisia.

Finally, Iraqi filmmakers such as Mohamed al-Daradji and Ismaël Ferroukhi should attend. Ferroukhi's loving French film *Le Grand Voyage* (2004) shows the evolving relationship between a devout father and his not-so-religious son as they travel 3,000 miles by car from their French home to Saudi Arabia, where the father makes his pilgrimage in Mecca. Memorable frames show the father at prayer, interacting with pilgrims, and though he has barely enough money for bread and eggs, he humbly assists those less fortunate than himself. In April 2007, Baghdad hosted al-Daradji's homegrown feature *Ahlaam*, about local Iraqis caught up in warfare. Produced in the face of physical dangers and government intervention, it's one of a few features to come out of Iraq since the US invasion, reports *Variety*'s Ali Jaafar. While filming on the streets of Baghdad, al-Daradji often wielded "a camera in one hand and an AK-47 in the other; he was kidnapped twice and shot at by both insurgents and US troops." He and his colleagues believe Arabs should tell stories about themselves. "Iraqi filmmakers," he says, "must stay here and make our films even with all the dangers... We must show the Iraqi point of view." Algerian-French filmmaker Rachid Bouchareb concurs: "We have only been in the audience while the West gave us [its version]. We need to change that. Why is the cameraman always pointing in one direction?" he asks. "We have to show the other side."

Summit sessions could take place in Hollywood, New York City, Beirut, and Cairo; they could be telecast and viewed by audiences throughout the world. Viewers could see Arab and American imagemakers engaged in purposeful dialogue, challenging and ultimately modifying clichéd views of each other. One summit session could consider the question: How can we make Arab movies more readily available to American viewers? Like most foreign movies, Arab-produced films do not reach most viewers via mainstream US movie theaters or TV or cable outlets. Instead, the films receive limited screenings, mainly at Arab film festivals in Santa Fe, Chicago, Minneapolis, Seattle, San Francisco, and Washington, DC. "Though audiences at these festivals," says film specialist John Sinno, are able to see Arab experiences that are narrated by Arabs, "it's still a limited group. But that's all right; attendance is growing so it's a kind of a win-win situation."

Throughout the summit, critics, government officials, and academics should play pivotal roles in maintaining a constructive dialogue, one which enhances the quest for peace and harmony. "Dialogue," reminds Diana Eck, professor of comparative religion at Harvard, "enables each of us—Christians, Jews, Muslims, and others—to find a means to understand ourselves, our faith, and our culture more deeply, enabling us to become instruments of creative change." Religion teacher Jamie Hamilton, for example, takes his Phillips Exeter Academy students to observe Friday prayers held on campus. One participating student wrote in his final paper, "While attending Muslim prayers, I underwent a great paradigmatic shift, discovering something that watching CNN (where Muslims are portrayed as terrorists first, humans second) for nearly my whole life had shielded from my eyes; Islam is not something to be scared of...." The student's words offer a potent reminder that by confronting our ignorance—and by working to overcome it—we have the ability to live in a pluralistic society with respect for each other.

Israeli filmmakers might also participate, engaging in an open, meaningful conversation with their Arab "cousins." Their presence could help debunk status-quo prejudices, leading to new co-productions similar to *Encounter Point* (2006), a memorable documentary that shows ordinary Israelis and Palestinians working together in Israel to achieve peace. Israel's Robi Damelin, whose son was killed in the conflict, speaks for all the film's non-violent protagonists when she says: "It's necessary to see each other as human to stop the cycle of violence." For those readers who question an Israeli presence, consider this July 22, 2006 letter from 36 Israeli filmmakers to Palestinian and Lebanese filmmakers who were attending a film festival in Paris. The letter was written when Israel was attacking Lebanon: "Allow us to tell you that your films, which we try to see and circulate among us, are extremely important in our eyes. They enable us to know and understand you better. Thanks to these films, the men, women, and children who suffer in Gaza, Beirut, and everywhere else our army exercises its violence, have names and faces. We would like to thank you and encourage you to keep on filming, despite the difficulties."

Granted, an American Arab Summit similar to Gerzon's successful Iron Curtain gathering alone can not be expected to fix all the region's problems. Public diplomacy can only be effective if it becomes a part of and helps reinforce fresh, substantive policies that can eventually bring about a just Middle East peace. In his acclaimed book *Power, Faith, and Fantasy: America in the Middle East: 1776 to the Present*, Michael Oren points out that American popular culture has impacted the region and its peoples. Oren goes on to say that peace is possible, provided the United States replace fantasies with realities. Replacing our fantasies, however, may be difficult, especially if Oren's concluding thought is true: "And producers of films about the mysterious, menacing Orient," he writes, "will never lack for audiences." David Pollock, a former State Department diplomat who studies Arab attitudes toward the US, points out that there are limitations to any public diplomacy campaign. "We cannot turn the picture upside down and make America loveable," says Pollock. "There are real differences, and no amount of fluff or clever programming will be able to change that." Still, the summit would certainly help reduce the region's increasingly negative attitudes about the United States, and vice versa. As Secretary of State Condoleezza Rice says, "We are facing a generational struggle against a new and deadly ideology... We need to do much more to dispel dangerous myths [about the United States] and get out the truth. Our interaction with the rest of the world must be a conversation, not a monologue."

Together, our voices form a global chorus, one which may curtail the stereotype's damaging impact. As Nobel Peace Prize winner Elie Wiesel reminds us, "Intolerance is the enemy of progress, the enemy of humanity." Let us resolve mutual myths by moving forward, addressing dangerous, fixed misperceptions of Islam,

Arabs, and Americans. By setting into motion a long overdue and vital dialogue, the summit could help bring about a necessary and major rethinking of how we project them and how they project us. And it might even raise the failed diplomacy D grade to a solid B.

CHAPTER SIX

Conclusions

The cinema is the tool for peace.
—Hiam Abbass, actress in *The Syrian Bride*

I have sought to reveal truth about Arab images. As a writer, I cannot make policy, but I can project light on damaging stereotypes that are impacting people and policies. The cinematic future will reveal whether the aftermath of 9/11 gives rise to a new genre of inventive portraits that humanize the Arab.

The Arab population of the Middle East is predicted to swell from its current 280 million to as high as 460 million by the year 2020. In many Arab countries 70 percent of the population is under the age of 30; an estimated 41 percent of Arabs are 14 and younger. In spite of Hollywood's reel discriminatory images, millions of Arabs from diverse regions of the world like many aspects of American culture, especially our entertainment offerings. Opinion surveys reveal that they broadly approve of American education, science, and technology. And, at least 51 percent of Arab youngsters want to emigrate to the West. Explains Tariq Ramadan, whose US visa allowing him to teach at the University of Notre Dame was revoked in fall 2004, negative and cultivated images of Americans persist "in the Arab and Islamic world." But, although "one hears a great deal of legitimate criticism of American foreign policy," says Ramadan, "this is not to be confused with a rejection of American values." In short, Arab youths may denounce US policies by day, but at night they eagerly consume Hollywood's movies.

American films and movie stars are favorites of young Arabs and Muslims—even in countries where anti-Americanism is rampant. In Iran, for example, 75 percent of filmgoers prefer Hollywood movies. There are many successful, state-of-the-art movie theaters in the Middle East, often located in posh shopping malls. Arab fan clubs embrace Hollywood stars. From Saudi Arabia, for example, the president of the *Xena: Warrior Princess* fan club wrote to actress Lucy Lawless, who portrays Xena: "There are lots of fans here [in the Kingdom] who love Xena; your series gives us passion, hope and courage; we can't wait to see the movie." Arabs also respect Oprah Winfrey and actor Ben Stiller (who is Jewish). Stiller has fans in Damascus. "I love him," says one Syrian Muslim woman who has a crush on him. The 1994 film *Forrest Gump* made an impression on Egyptian viewers, some of whom, after watching scenes that show Gump with several American presidents, took to the streets and protested the rule of President Hosni Mubarak.

In spite of our politics and stereotypes, Hollywood's popularity among Arab teens persists. Affirms the eminent Cairo-born writer Mus'ad Hegazi: "Arabs may hate American foreign policy," he says, "but they love Charles Bronson." Joseph Braude suggests that in the Arab world, "Hollywood rivals the mosque for impact on the popular imagination... can someone who loves American movies really hate America?"

We will most likely continue to see movies displaying Arab Muslims as terrorists; the fact remains that al-Qaeda is a real enemy. But film industry executives have a moral obligation to ensure that future films do not focus only on extremists. What better time than now to demonstrate the true positive impact of cinema, to project real human interest films that inspire dialogue about relevant issues?

Several soon-to-be-released films just narrowly miss making this book: *Lions for Lambs, Nothing is Private, Vantage Point,* and the Italian film *O Jerusalem.* Initial drafts of *Traitor* show Muslim terrorists preparing to attack the United States. *Iron Man,* which is based on the popular Marvel comic-book series, also displays Arab villains, including an arms merchant who kidnaps the heroine. Some press releases contend that Adam Sandler's *You Don't Mess with the Zohan,* and Brian DePalma's *Redacted* offer complex, humane portraits. *Zohan's* theme, one cast member told me, is that everyone, especially Israelis and Palestinians, gets along here in the US. Viewers will see an ex-Mossad agent bonding with a lovely Palestinian woman. The independent film *Extraordinary Rendition* is based on the true story of Canadian citizen Maher Arar, who in 2002 was arrested at New York's John F. Kennedy Airport and whisked off to Syria, where he was imprisoned and tortured. DePalma's *Redacted* dramatizes the real-life rape and killing of an Iraqi girl by US soldiers, who had also murdered her family. The movie is the director's attempt to help "stop the war" by bringing "the reality of what is happening in Iraq to the American people," he told reporters after the screening at the Venice Film Festival.

I believe thoughtful imagemakers are beginning to rollback slanderous portraits and create fuller, more complicated Arab characters and stories. Reel Arabs are merely puppets in the hands of the industry—producers, directors, writers, and actors are their masters. Without their string-pulling, the stereotype is a lifeless doll, gathering dust in an unseen corner. Should they will it to vanish, vanish it will.

Reel history is on my side. Not so long ago mainstream studios cast major stars in daring breakthrough films that contested the stereotypes of the day. Think of how *Gentlemen's Agreement* (1947) offered a new portrayal of Jews; *Go for Broke* (1951) of the Japanese; *The Defiant Ones* (1958) of African Americans; *Zorba the Greek* (1963) of Greeks; *Harry and Tonto* (1974) of the elderly; *Moscow on the Hudson* (1984) of Russians; *Stand and Deliver* (1988) of Latinos; *Dancing with Wolves* (1990) of Native Americans; *Mississippi Masala* (1991) of Indians; and *Philadelphia* (1993) of gays. These box-office hits and others help fracture entrenched stereotypes.

Change will come—one summit, one college film course, one character, one movie, one TV show, and one courageous imagemaker at a time. I am not alone in my optimism. Performers and directors such as Natalie Portman and Ari Sandel share my vision. On receiving an Oscar for his short film *West Bank Story* (2006), a musical comedy about Israelis and Palestinians that takes place between two falafel stands in the West Bank, Sandel told his worldwide TV audience, "My movie is about peace and hope... because I really do believe peace can happen." The Israeli-born actress Portman reminds us that Jews and Arabs are historically cousins. "Unless we accept the fact that we are constituents of the same family," she says, "we will blunder in believing that a loss for one 'side' is not a loss for all humankind." Our cultures and faiths, Christianity, Islam, and Judaism, reminds Portman, "are too close not to consider ourselves brothers and sisters."

We should remember that the "people of the book"—Jews, Christians, and Muslims—are all children of Abraham. All three religions emphasize an ethic of humane behavior and belief in one God who reveals his will through the sacred scriptures. Central to the three faiths is peace, which is reflected in the similarities of their greetings. *Shalom aliechem* in Hebrew, *pax vobiscum* in Latin, *salaam alaikum* in Arabic: "Peace be with you."

Decades ago, the classic 1922 film *The Young Rajah* upheld religious commonalities. The female protagonist asks Rudolph Valentino, who plays an astute Indian prince, this question: "The Bible, the Talmud, and the Quran. Which do you find is true?" Answers the prince: "There are many paths; all lead to God." The message of today's *Kingdom of Heaven*, says Ridley Scott, "lies in the subtle invitation to dialogue, and to put aside conflicts at a time when everyone should coexist for the sake of the common good and world peace." *Rajah* and *Heaven* bring to mind this historical example of religious tolerance. In 1219, when St. Francis of Assisi traveled to Egypt, he was received by the sultan Melek el-Kamel. The sultan was impressed with his Christian faith, so he allowed St. Francis to preach to his Muslim subjects. He also respectfully asked St. Francis to: "Pray for me that God may deign to reveal to me that law and faith which is most pleasing to him." Later, when St. Francis returned to the Crusaders, he was declared a heretic. Ironically, it was the Muslim sultan who prevented the Crusaders from killing him.

Civilizations need not "clash," but rather blend. In his acclaimed book, *The Prophet*, Kahlil Gibran reminds us that we are all children of the Holy Spirit, writing: "I love you when you kneel in your church, when you prostate yourself in your mosque, and when you pray in your synagogue." Mahatma Gandhi and Muhammad Ali share Gibran's vision. Their voices reflect an important resounding message: Humanitarianism is possible; cultures and faiths can coexist. "Rivers, ponds, lakes and streams; all are unique. Yet, all contain water, just as religions all contain truth," said Ali. "Each of us has the breath of God breathed into our being," observed Gandhi. "The Bible, Qur'an, Torah and other holy books" remind us that "we are all children of one and the same creator. Every human life," said Gandhi, "Muslim and non-Muslim, Christian and non-Christian, Jew and non-Jew, has exactly the same human worth."

By transmitting this "same human worth" onto cinema screens, Hollywood will have at long last constructed bridges of understanding and trust. Whether we live in Texas or Timbuktu, our voices will form a universal choir, one which maroons the stereotype. Keep the faith: New films will lead the way, illustrating that regardless of color, creed, or culture, we are bound together.

PART TWO

The Films

The majority of post–9/11 movies continue denigrating Arabs. Yet the strength and sharpness of some movies, whether mainstream (*Babel*), foreign (*Paradise Now*), or independent (*Yes*), have, in fact, projected the humane Arab in complex shades of gray, not in evil black silhouette. To reflect this, 29 movies—nearly one in three—are in my "Recommended" and "Evenhanded" lists (see pages 181–182). Here are discussions of most of the films, with examples of dialogue and images, various character types, plot details, background information, and commentary from noted film critics. I also discuss a few films featuring Arab-American characters. I cite several movies advancing common misperceptions, in which reel dark-looking Indians, Iranians, Sikhs, Turks, and Pakistanis are perceived as reel Arabs.

Note that actors listed are only those who are mentioned in the descriptions of the films or who play Arabs.

Abbreviations:
A: Actors
B: Based on the book by
COL: Columbia Pictures
D: Director
IFC: Independent Film Channel Productions
MGM: Metro Goldwyn Mayer
NS: Not seen
PAR: Paramount Pictures
SP: Screenplay by
TCF: Twentieth Century Fox
UNI: United Artists
WB: Warner Brothers

AIR MARSHAL *(2003) Nu Image; D: Alain Jakubowicz SP: James Becket, Aaron Pope A: Eli Danker, Devika Parikh* **VILLAINS, WORST LIST**
Israeli-born producers Avi [Danny] Lerner, Boaz Davidson, and Alain Jakubowicz showcase vicious Arab terrorists killing airline passengers. This shabby movie shamelessly exploits 9/11's victims and their loved ones. Regrettably, the producers failed to heed the advice given to young Peter Parker (Spider-Man): "With great power comes great responsibility." This film is a cheap rehash of two 1986 films, *Hostage and Delta Force. Marshal's* producers have also participated in several other Arab-bashing films: *Delta Force* and the US SEALs movies, *Executive Decision* (1996), *Chain of Command* (1994), and *American Ninja 4* (1992). See a complete listing of their films at www.imdb.com. Pay particular attention to their links with Israeli producers Menachem Golan and Yoram Globus. For the other Israeli-connected films check out: Golan's *Finest Hour* (1991), Tobe Hooper's *Night Terrors* (1993), *Deadly Heroes* (1994), *Delta Force One* (1999), *Operation Delta Force V* (1999), and *The Order* (2001).

AMERICAN DREAMZ *(2006) UNI; D, SP: Paul Weitz A: Hugh Grant, Dennis Quaid, Sam Golzari, Tony Yalda, Jay Harik, Shohreh Aghdashloo* **VILLAINS, EVENHANDED, ARAB AMERICAN**
Dreamz presents a satiric view of the Iraq war. It features a Bush-look-alike president, Arab terrorists, and a TV series based on *American Idol* and hosted by a smirking Brit, Martin Tweed (Grant). Opening frames: An al-Qaeda training camp. An inept recruit named Omer (Golzari) bumbles through a combat-training course; poor Omer doesn't have what it takes to be a soldier. Afterward, he confesses to the camp leader, an Osama look-alike, that instead of fighting he wants to be a performer, to sing and dance to American show tunes. That does it. Osama's clone dispatches Omer to Orange County to live with his wealthy Arab-American relatives. Cut to the family's gay teen son Iqbal (Yalda) teaching Omer how to dance. Presto! Omer becomes a finalist on the hit TV series *Dreamz.* Cut to the Arabian terrorist camp; the leader hears the good news and gives Omer a special job: During the telecast he will blow himself up, along with US President Staton (Quaid), who's a guest judge on the show. To ensure Omer does just that, three Arab

assassins pay him a visit. Two are reel silent caricatures. But the head terrorist's a reel baddie: he orders Omer to "martyr" himself. "People call me the torturer because I like to torture people."

Meanwhile, the country's experiencing "Omer-Mania"—audiences love him; he's on the front pages of all the entertainment magazines. Closing scenes take place at the *Dreamz* TV set. The three terrorists enter the studio and assemble their bomb inside the men's room. Omer finds the weapon. What to do? Does Omer want to be the next Frank Sinatra, or should he carry out the suicide mission? He muses, "I just feel confused about this country. There are so many nice people here but it does so much harm in the world... Are Americans to blame for America?"

Omer's reel question merits pondering. Should real "nice" Americans be blamed for our government's policies? Omer thinks not. He opts to perform rather than ignite the bomb. Cut to the US president saying on national TV: "The problems over there [in the Middle East] will never be solved." Counters Omer: "I deeply hope for all our sakes that you are wrong." Suddenly, a lovesick, jilted US soldier armed with the bomb rushes onto the stage. What happens next is a movie first: A young Arab and a US president work together to prevent violence. Both try to convince the soldier not to kill himself. In the final frames, the FBI nabs the three terrorists. The president survives. Although Omer comes in second place, we see him happily touring the country "with a repertory of Broadway hits." At Omer's side is his manager, cousin Iqbal.

"Arab-American activists eyeing stereotypes in Yank pop culture will have a field day with performances of Mideast characters," notes *Variety* critic Robert Koehler (21 March 2006). Affirms A. Macresarf in *Epinions*: The Orange County scenes, especially, usher in "some of the most starkly misjudged stereotypes of Arab characters in any recent Hollywood movie" (27 March 2006). But I found Omer to be a likeable reel Arab. Sure, his Arab-American cousins are somewhat stereotyped, but they are an amusing, likeable family. I laughed with them, not at them.

In some Arab nations the real *American Idol* is a smash hit; a few countries have produced similar shows. Thus, the scene that shows Osama's double and his cohorts hunkered down inside a cave watching Omer perform on *American Dreamz* "as avidly as any group of American teenagers" may be more realistic than one might think. *Dreamz* is a full-length version of the short-lived TV comedy series *That's My Bush!*, which also spoofed presidential buffoonery. If you liked the TV series as much as I did, you'll enjoy *Dreamz.*

Note: In J. Neil Schulman's low-budget feature *Lady Magdalene's* (2007), al-Qaeda villains also surface in the US, this time in a Las Vegas brothel and the Nevada desert. Schulman was kind enough to send me a screening copy (the film is still in search of a distributor) along with a note, saying, in part: "I did my best to avoid stereotyping of any sort. After all, my star and fellow executive producer Nichelle (*Star Trek*) Nichols is renowned for her breaking of stereotyping of African Americans." Yet, in spite of Schulman's and Nichols's noble intentions, *Lady Magdalene's* advances the stereotype of Arabs as reel morons, and as reel ruthless assassins.

AND NOW… LADIES AND GENTLEMEN *(2002) PAR; D,*
SP: Claude Lelouch SP: Pierre Leroux, Pierre Uytterhoeven A: Jeremy Irons, Patricia Kaas **CHAMPIONS, RECOMMENDED**

Midway into this film, the two protagonists, a European jazz singer, June (Kaas), and a jewel thief, Valentin (Irons), arrive in Fez, Morocco. Both suffer from unexpected blackouts. Warm, caring Arabs look after them: a faith healer, taxi driver, porter, surgeon, bus driver, maid, nurse, desk clerk, and at times even the police. When an unexpected robbery takes place at their posh hotel, Valentin is framed for the theft. Not for long: Thanks to two reel good Moroccans—a bright nurse and a Moroccan maid—the real thief is caught and imprisoned. Valentin is free to move on.

One imaginary scene pokes fun of Hollywood's reel Arabs. Valentin dreams he is attacked by two Moroccans with knives. But, he floors them. Jane finds his dream amusing, saying: "Like in the movies." Chuckling, they nod.

Those wishing to see real talented Moroccans should view Stephen Olsson's excellent documentary, *Sound of the Soul* (2006). Olsson's beautifully photographed film focuses on the Fez Festival of World Sacred Music; memorable performances of spiritual music from groups from Morocco to Russia to the US remind viewers of "the essential oneness at the core of all religions and faiths."

AROUND THE WORLD IN 80 DAYS *(2004) Walt Disney Pictures; D: Frank Corasi SP: David Titcher, David Benullo, David Goldstein B: Jules Verne A: Arnold Schwarzenegger* **MAIDENS, SHEIKHS, TURK-AS-ARAB**

TAKE that blonde! Beginning with the 1900 short *Rescue from a Harem*, dark-complexioned potentates almost always held hostage fair-complexioned Western maidens. Eight or so decades ago silent films displayed most "foreign" men of color as debauched curs. In *Ships of the Night* (1928), for example, the Asian Yut Sen and the Hispanic Captain Molina imperil the blond heroine's virtue. Today's potentates, like this film's Prince Hapi, still threaten the blond's virtue. Present-day California Governor Arnold Schwarzenegger stars as the lecherous egomaniac, Hapi, a Mideast potentate surrounded by red-fezzed bodyguards and exotic belly dancers. When Hapi meets the visiting French heroine he insists that she become "wife number seven." "You have seven wives?" asks the shocked heroine. Boasts Hapi: "One for each day of the week... Do Tuesdays work for you?" She tries to escape. Hapi and his guards block her path. But she eludes Hapi's lecherous grasp. Interestingly, the film's producers show the French heroine and her friends happily interacting with ordinary families in reel France, India, and China. So, why didn't we see the protagonists enjoying the company of likeable Turks in Constantinople?

Reel Turks have often been projected and perceived as reel Arabs. For example, in *The Seven-Percent Solution* (1976), an obese Turkish sheikh kidnaps the Western heroine for his harem. In the Mr. Peabody and Sherman cartoon "Lawrence of Arabia," the Turkish "Sultan" and his desert troops wear white robes and white headdresses; they look and act exactly like reel Bedouin. For a Turkish perspective, Ferzan Ozpetek's erotic and beautifully pho-tographed feature *Harem* (2003) presents a different view of harems and potentates. Here, the sultan is a benevolent ruler, and his harem functions as a safe haven, where women comfortably socialize and care for their children.

BABEL *(2006) PAR; D: Alejandro González Iñárritu SP: Guillermo Arriaga A: Brad Pitt, Cate Blanchett, Said Tarchani, Boubker Ait El Caid, Abdelkader Bara, Mohamed Akhzam* CHAMPIONS, RECOMMENDED

This compassionate, heart-wrenching film reveals universal human emotions, as well as cultural and racial identities. The Japanese, American, Mexican, and Moroccan protagonists are projected as humane, three-dimensional characters. Though unforeseen events bring them pain and suffering, they remain determined to make the right decisions. For the Moroccan scenes the director wisely used locals to portray the villagers; they bring effective, beautiful authenticity to their roles. Opening frames: A poor Moroccan home, a goatherd in the background. Cut to the family inside: husband, wife, and several children. Anwar (Akhzam) is hosting Hassan (Bara), an elderly tribesman seeking to sell him a rifle. After some good-hearted bargaining, Hassan trades his high-powered 270-caliber rifle to his host for 500 dirham and one goat. The pleased Anwar hands the rifle to his two young sons, Ahmed (Tarchani) and Yussef (El Caid), telling them to shoot the jackals that are killing their goats. Ahmed shoots and misses a jackal. Young Yussef boasts he's the better shot. The boys argue. Next, they test the rifle's range—"up to three kilometers." They fire away at rocks, even a passing car. Next, they target a tourist bus.

A bullet crashes through the bus window, accidentally going through the upper left shoulder of Susan Jones (Blanchett), a tourist from California. Her husband Richard (Pitt) moves to stop the bleeding; the bus comes to a screeching halt. The boys run off. Cut to the youths' father telling them "some terrorists have killed an American tourist... terrorists attacked a bus." The frightened boys hide the rifle. Cut to the bus: A passenger, Abdullah (Rachidi), takes Richard and the heavily bleeding Susan to his remote village. Though Susan's wound is serious, her fellow Western passengers are concerned only about themselves; they want to move on. A Moroccan doctor tends Susan's wound as best he can. An elderly woman remains at Susan's side, calming her down, enabling her to rest.

The next scene brilliantly reflects irrational post–9/11 paranoia. Richard's told that no ambulance will come to their aid. Why? "The Americans stopped the ambulance; they want to send a helicopter." US embassy officials think the shooting was not an accident, but a terrorist act. Like the US officials, Richard's fellow travelers panic, sneak back onto the bus, and drive off. They, too, fear Moroccan terrorists are lurking behind every cup of mint tea. Meanwhile, the embassy's overzealous security behavior, combined with erroneous media reports about "terrorism," prompt Moroccan policemen to use little restraint. When they locate Hassan, the rifle's original owner, the police assume he's guilty. So, they beat him, severely. Next, the boys confess to their father what actually happened. Expressing anger, then sorrow, Anwar rushes off with his sons in search of a safe place. But the police spot the family and start shooting at them. Fearing for his life, Yussef fires back, wounding a policeman. Brother Ahmed is shot dead. Father and son mourn. Flashback to the boys atop the mountain; their embraces reflect brotherly love, the fresh mountain breezes, freedom.

Babel reveals our common humanity. Unlike most stereotypical images of Arabs, the Moroccans in this film are a likeable, diverse group: Doctors, elderly nurses, friends, and family. They are real people—just like us. The title refers to the tower of Babel in the ancient city of Babylon, where residents considered themselves supreme beings who could reach heaven—on their own.

The film's rifle incident reminds me of why guns are dangerous in the hands of boys, be they Moroccan or American. When I was seven years old I went out "shooting" with my friend, Larry. For his tenth birthday, Larry had gotten a new Red Ryder BB gun. Like Yussef and Ahmed, we tested its range; we shot and missed various objects. When darkness approached we dared target a not-so-friendly neighbor's street light. But the gun jerked. Scores of pellets completely shattered their front window. Fortunately the family was not at home.; no one was hurt.

See Todd McCarthy's review in *Variety* 23 May 2006.

BELLY OF THE BEAST *(2003) GFT Entertainment; D: Siu-Tung Ching SP: James Townshend A: Steven Seagal, Kevork Malikyan* **CAMEO, VILLAINS**

Masked members of the radical Islamic group Abu Karaf kidnap and imprison two American women in Thailand. The villain providing weapons for the reel Muslim bad guys is an Algerian named Zadir (Malikyan).

BLACK HAWK DOWN *(2002) COL; D: Ridley Scott SP: Ken Nolan B: Mark Bowden A: Sam Shepard, Tom Sizemore* **VILLAINS, WORST LIST** This box-office hit was filmed in Morocco and produced in cooperation with the Department of Defense. Although Somalia is located in East Africa, it is a member of the League of Arab States and is one of 22 Arab countries. Arab or African, the movie's racial stereotypes are inexcusable. A US Army officer who was involved at a very high level in our 1993 "Black Hawk Down" operations in Somalia wrote to me: "I thought the portrayal of the Somalis was pitiful. It's hard to believe… Hollywood still perpetuates caricatures of sub-Saharans. I couldn't tell if we were fighting Aideed's [Arab Muslim] militias in south Mogadishu, or the Bloods and Crips in South Central Los Angeles." The actual fifteen-hour battle claimed more than 1,000 Somali and 18 American lives.

In the film, our soldiers are trapped. A US general accuses a Pakistani Muslim general of negligence, for delaying a much-needed rescue attempt.

What really took place, explains my army contact, is that "MG Garrison had no contact with the Pakistani commander, [and] the Pakistani commander did not drag his feet."

In the final frames of the movie, an ill-tempered Pakistani soldier denies US soldiers' access to the APCs. A battle-weary American GI tries to enter the rescue vehicle. But the gruff Pakistani soldier barks, "There's no room here—go on top." The reality is that the Pakistanis did not prevent our troops from riding in the APCs. What actually occurred, writes my contact officer, is that "the APC's were packed with the dead and wounded." In fact, says my source, "Pakistani troops offered up tanks, not APCs."

Of course key facts were omitted from the movie: "A couple of Pakistani soldiers were wounded during that mission; one Malaysian soldier was killed and several were wounded… They weren't mentioned in the film at all, an omission that prompted an official complaint from the Malaysian government after the film's release."

Note: Weeks before the film was released, according to New York's International Action Center, the MPAA held a private screening for senior White House advisors, "and allowed them to make changes. Defense Secretary Donald Rumsfeld and Oliver North, along with 800 top officials and brass attended the movie's

Washington DC premiere" (12 December 2001). Pentagon officials were pleased with the film. "Powerful," said Rumsfeld.

But I'm troubled by the omission of needed historical content
and the simplicity of its good-versus-evil story line. Film critic
Michael Massing complains that the "Americans are uniformly
dedicated, likeable and brave. The Somalis are uniformly grasping,
creepy and savage—dark-skinned anthropoids with sub-machine
guns." The movie resembles a violent video game: Rambo-like
super white soldiers mow down scores of black "skinnies." The
film never reveals Somali humanity. Viewers are never told why so
many Somalis are fighting against American soldiers; nor does the
film explain that one year earlier, in 1992, the Somalis were very
friendly to the Americans—"the 20,000 Marines who came in
December 1992 basically ended the famine."

For a more accurate view of what happened in Somali, see the
History Channel's *True Story of Black Hawk Down* and Mark Bowden's compelling best-selling book *Black Hawk Down: A Story of
Modern War*. Both offer much-needed historical perspectives, and
both give the enemy a face. Actor Josh Hartnett, who portrays one
US hero, also defers to Bowden's text. Appearing on the *Today*
show he said: "It's good to read the book; it's important."

BORAT: CULTURAL LEARNINGS OF AMERICA FOR MAKE BENEFIT GLORIOUS NATION OF KAZAKHSTAN

*(2006) TCF; D: Larry Charles SP: Sacha Baron Cohen, Anthony Hines,
Peter Baynham Dan Mazer A: Sacha Baron Cohen, Pamela Anderson*
CAMEO

This outrageous box-office hit comedy revolves around Borat
Sagdiyev (Cohen), a journalist from Kazakhstan who "brings to
America a host of prejudices so ingrained as to offend everyone he
meets," writes critic Kirk Honeycutt. One scene in particular
stands out. En route to California Borat stops off at a Texas rodeo.
Prior to singing in front of a large crowd Borat interviews an older
Texan. As the man thinks Borat is a Muslim from the Middle East,
he wants to help him to fit in with the crowd. He tells Borat to
shave his moustache and also spews racist slurs aimed squarely at
Middle Easterners. Borat lets the Texan rant; he does not attempt
to contest the slurs. Cut to Borat center stage at the "Imperial

Rodeo." He begins abusing our national anthem, and the crowd boos—though seconds earlier he'd gained the crowd's support by declaring: "We [the people of Kazakhstan] support your war on terror!" Everyone cheers. "May USA kill every single terrorist!" More cheers. "May you destroy their country—so not one single lizard will survive in the desert." Yippee! Then Borat exclaims: "May George W. Bush drink the blood of every man, woman, and child in Iraq." Cheers, galore!

Perhaps the purpose of this scene was to poke fun of Texans' overzealous patriotism. But the scene didn't make me laugh; it made me ill. There's nothing funny about watching a crowd applaud the drinking of Iraqi blood. Some viewers say the film reinforces prejudices. Other viewers and critics, however, defend Cohen, saying he uses Borat's outlandish comments such as "I have sex with my sister" and "Jews have horns" to expose, not advance, the average American's racist beliefs. For example, Borat's interviews in Washington, DC show politicians Bob Barr and Alan Keyes willingly playing along with the "joke." But this writer considers the film to be repulsive. Cohen's derogatory comments about Arabs, Jews, women, and others, especially the people of Kazakhstan (they are depicted as idiots, rapists, prostitutes, and bigots), are damaging, hurtful and unacceptable.

See Kirk Honeycutt, *Hollywood Reporter* 12 September 2006; Leslie Felperin, *Variety* 10 September 2006; John Tierney, *New York Times* 11 November 2006.

CAVITE *(2006) Gorilla Films; D, SP: Neil Dela Llana, Ian Gamazon*
VILLAINS

Cavite is an independent film showing a devout, decent Muslim being terrorized by an unseen, ruthless Islamic fanatic. The terrorist demands that the protagonist blow up a church filled with worshipers. And he does—saving the lives of his mother and sister. In the end, the protagonist's girlfriend admits to having had an abortion. Why? "I can't have a baby that's a Muslim," she tells him.

THE CHRONICLES OF RIDDICK *(2004) UNI; D, SP: David Twohy A: Keith David, Vin Diesel* **CHAMPIONS, RECOMMENDED**

Director David Twohy's *Chronicles* is an action-filled sci-fi film about whether the human race can survive. Early frames display humane Arabs, a devout Arabic-speaking Muslim cleric (David), and his wife and child. They risk their lives to assist the protagonist, Riddick (Diesel). Though invaders kill the devout cleric, his family survives. The cleric, called "Imam," also appears in Twohy and Diesel's 2000 sci-fi thriller *Pitch Black*. In *Black*, the Imam and his three young Arab companions survive an outer space crash; they and a few others are stranded on a desert planet that turns pitch black. At night, deadly alien creatures attack, killing nearly everyone; only the three Western protagonists and Imam survive. Imam refuses to drink alcohol; he and his Arabs pray, devoutly, as they bury the dead. They recite *Allahu akbar* (God is great), and "All praises to Allah for His blessings to us." When crew members complain about the lack of water, the holy man calms their fears, and the Arabs go on to find the water; naturally. When aliens brutally kill the Arab youths, Riddick caustically questions Imam's beliefs: "How much faith do you have left, father?" Imam says: "He is with us, nonetheless."

CIVIC DUTY *(2006) Landslide; D: Jeff Renfroe SP: Andrew Joiner A: Peter Krause, Kari Matchett, Richard Schiff, Khaled Abol Naga* **ARAB-AS-VICTIM?**
This psychological thriller effectively focuses on post–9/11 paranoia, asking needed questions about tolerance, prejudice, racial profiling, and personal responsibility. Color-coded terrorism warnings, escalating prices at gas pumps, the president and his Homeland Security cohorts warning citizens to watch for "evil terrorists"—taken together, these warnings prompt the film's protagonist, unemployed accountant Terry Allen (Krause), to spy on his neighbor, Gabe Hassan (Naga) the "Middle Eastern looking guy renting the apartment downstairs." Terry soon begins sinking into a media-fueled obsession with the war on terror. Screenwriter Andrew Joiner explains that the "media is essentially the devil on Terry's shoulder." Terry's wife Marla (Matchett) protests, but after Terry goes through Hassan's trash and sees him "unloading stuff" in the early morning, he's sure the young Arab's up to no good. "He

fits the profiles too well," says Terry. Next, he finds out that an Islamic group, the "Sons of Benevolence," is giving the student tuition dollars and more, and that his mostly empty apartment contains some questionable boxes, and glass beakers full of dangerous-looking chemicals. Terry follows Hassan in his car; when he spots him picking up another dark Arab, he panics and rushes home. Terry goes online and checks the site "Most Wanted Terrorists"—Hassan's not on the list. Still, convinced that "the guy downstairs is responsible for killing innocent people," Terry contacts FBI agent Hilary (Schiff). Hilary refuses to assist, telling Terry he has no evidence. Hassan is innocent—"a model student," says Hilary; "he's here working on his master's in environmental studies." (Indeed, Hassan is portrayed as a handsome, intelligent, educated Arab student; credit Egyptian actor Abol Naga for a fine performance.)

But Terry gets angry—and violent. The film's final 25 minutes occur in Hassan's apartment. Terry barges into his neighbor's kitchen, tags Hassan "a piece of shit," ties him up a chair, beats him, and points a gun at his head. The men shout at each other while debating politics, war, and racism. Terry demands that Hassan confess; Hassan insists he's innocent; he counters Terry's accusations with logical answers. All the film's characters, except for Terry, say Hassan is innocent. But, surprisingly, final frames take a turn, implying that perhaps Hassan is a terrorist, after all. This ambiguous ending troubled me. The film should have made it perfectly clear that Hassan was innocent. Suggesting that Terry's post–9/11 paranoia might be justified may encourage real-world behavior.

See Justin Chang's review in *Variety* 12 June 2006.

CLICK *(2006) COL; D: Frank Coraci SP: Steve Koren, Mark O'Keefe; A: Adam Sandler, Rob Schneider, David Hasselhoff* **CAMEO, SHEIKHS** Nine days after it opened, this highly successful movie grossed over $87 million. It's an all-American comedy about an all-American architect, Michael Newman (Sandler), who uses a special "universal remote control" to fast forward and rewind various phases of his life—from birth on. Opening frames reveal Newman as a happily married family man; his attractive wife loves him, and they have two adorable children. At work, Michael attends an office meeting that is abruptly disturbed by six uncouth, bearded, robed Arabs who are quickly shown to be perverts. Here's the scene. For 99 seconds, Michael and his boss Mr. Amman (Hasselhoff) poke fun of Prince Habeeboo's (Schneider) five silent aides, as well as Habeeboo himself. The prince is a sort of blackface. Michael and his boss keep mispronouncing the prince's name, calling him what sounds like "Ali Poo Poo." Prince Habeeboo rejects Michael's carefully planned, elegant design for his Arabian palace. "Where's the bar?" he asks. The prince insists Michael eliminate the restaurant, dump the waterfall, and scrap the atrium. He also wants a water drain installed. Why the changes? So Habeeboo can host "wet t-shirt contests" and have more space in which to consume booze. Are you asking me to design an "Arabian hoochie house?" says Michael. The prince and his entourage begin gesticulating in a vulgar manner, referring to having sex with these "hoochies." Arabs have nothing to do with this movie's plot. Why inject and project them as drunken perverts?

THE CONDEMNED *(2007) Lionsgate & World Wrestling Entertainment; D, SP: Scott Wiper SP: Rob Hedden A: Steve Austin, Robert Mammone, Dominic Brancatisano* **CAMEO, VILLAINS**

Ten condemned criminals from third-world prisons are released and whisked off to a remote island in New Guinea and forced to fight to the death—"one lives, nine die." Opening frames focus on the event's organizer, an evil reality TV producer named Breck (Mammone). On hearing one of his criminals has been killed, he fumes, saying: "They shot the Arab! We had him and they shot the fucking Arab." He rushes over to a map and tells his producers: "Look, you see here, this is the Arab world. If they don't have anybody to cheer for they don't log on [to watch our show]. I want a fucking Arab— a child-killing, Quran-raving, suicide-bombing Arab." The producers try to recruit some Arab "fundamentalists" from a prison in El Salvador. Unexpectedly, Jack Conrad (Austin) surfaces and beats up the "the Arab" (Brancatisano). Now, Breck wants Conrad! When a producer ventures, "thought you wanted an Arab," Breck barks back, "Fuck the Arab; I got this cowboy; he's perfect." Beck's slurs against Arabs are not contested.

CRADLE 2 THE GRAVE *(2003) WB; D: Andrzej Bartkowiak SP: John O'Brien A: Jet Li* **CAMEO, EGYPTIANS**
A rich, swarthy bearded Egyptian bids to acquire a new and powerful nuclear device.

CRANK *(2006) Lakeshore; D, SP: Mark Neveldine, Brian Taylor A: Yousuf Azami, Jason Statham* **CAMEO, VILLAINS, ARAB-AS-VICTIM**
This thriller's all about a hit man, Chev (Statham), whose enemies inject him with a potent Chinese death serum. Near the end, Chev dashes across Los Angeles in search of an antidote and intent on finding and killing those responsible for poisoning him. Chev flags down an Arab cab driver wearing a black stocking cap and in need of a shave (Azami). "Where we go?" the cabbie asks. "Just drive," says Chev. The cabbie listens to Arab music. When Chev tells him to change the tune, the driver switches to a swinging bebop song. He takes Chev to a convenience store, and then drops him off at a Beverly Hills penthouse where Chev goes swimming with his clothes on. When he rushes back to the cab, the driver yells, "You're not getting into my cab, wet!" Barks Chev: "I just paid you $200.00 to wait three minutes." Insists the cabbie: "You're not getting into my car. No way!" Chev curses, and then throws the cabbie to the sidewalk. Next he points at him and yells to the gathering crowd "al-Qaeda, al-Qaeda!" Three people, two of whom are women, charge the Arab driver and beat him up. Chev steals the cab and drives off.

Next, Chev calls up a friend; cut to his pal's female companion playing the slots. She pulls the lever. Three mismatched images surface on the machine, the center photo al-Qaeda terrorist, complete with blood-red Arabic writing. The terrorist wears dark glasses, grasps a machine gun, and, like the Arab cab driver, wears a black stocking cap that covers his entire face.

The way the film is constructed suggests first that Arab cab drivers are greedy and ungrateful, and then the slot machine's Arab terrorist frame gives credence to Chev's accusations that the cabbie is "al-Qaeda." Such images could easily have been avoided. The driver didn't have to be an Arab. Even so, why tune out the cab's Arab music; and why was it necessary for Chev to call him "al-Qaeda?" Why show women trouncing the driver? Why didn't Chev simply toss the driver to the ground, and drive off with the cab? And, why insert an Arab terrorist image into the slots?

CRASH *(2004) Lionsgate; D, SP: Paul Haggis A: Shaun Toub*
This well-intentioned Academy Award–winning film explores prejudices and race relations in present-day Los Angeles. Some reel groups—not Iranians—fare better than others. Several scenes display an angry, stereotypical Iranian-American shopkeeper Farhad (Toub). Early on, Farhad tries to buy a gun. The prejudiced salesman calls him "Osama" and shouts, "Get out of here—Plan a jihad on your own time!" Later, vandals wreck Farhad's shop. Plastered on the walls are the words "rag head" and "Arab." Says his shocked wife: "They think we're Arab. They think Persians become Arab." Her comments ring true: Most Americans perceive Iranians as Arabs and vice versa.

But Farhad's not a likeable person; at times his behavior is racist. When he hires an honest Latino locksmith to replace the store's lock, the man tells Farhad that his door, not the lock, needs fixing. Instead of thanking him for his honesty, Farhad screams at him: "You cheat, you fucking cheater." Later, after his store is vandalized, the raging Farhad blames not himself, but the Latino for the crime. He takes a gun, drives to the man's home, and then fires the gun at the man and his young daughter, nearly killing them. Given his violent actions, it's impossible to empathize with Farhad and his misfortunes.

The Iranian=Arab myth persists. Consider the June 7, 2006 headline of the *Houston Chronicle* about the "new quest" for an "Arab bomb." The accompanying article, written by a *Chronicle* correspondent based in Washington, DC, is all about "the threat [against the US] posed by the prospect of a nuclear-armed Iran."

DAWN OF THE DEAD *(2003) Universal; D: Zack Snyder SP: George Romero, James Gunn* **CAMEO, VILLAINS**
This remake of the 1978 classic zombie horror film *Night of the Living Dead* (1966) links Muslims with fear, violence, and death. Opening scenes display a city in chaos: There are traffic jams, speeding ambulances, scores of people screaming and taking refuge in a mega shopping mall. Cut to hundreds of Muslims praying in

a mosque, followed by pictures of American GIs in the Iraqi desert fighting Arab zombies. US news broadcasts from Iraq imply there's a world war against the flesh-hungry Iraqi undead. These Iraqi-as-zombie scenes do not appear on the DVD release. I thank Italian journalist and scholar Chiara Carella for this citation; she saw *Dawn of the Dead's* reel Iraqi zombies in a theater.

Two sci-fi TV movies, *Manticore* (2005) and *Raptor Island* (2004), similarly pit US forces against Arabs. In *Raptor*, Navy SEALs and man-eating dinosaurs terminate reel Arab terrorists. *Manticore*, which is set in present-day Iraq, shows US soldiers gunning down scores of Iraqi "lowlifes," and blowing up a 2,000-year-old invincible ancient Persian monster.

DAY ON FIRE *(2006) Lodestar Entertainment; D, SP: Jay Anania A: Carmen Chaplin, Alyssa Sutherland, Olympia Dukakis, Avi Tairy (English, Arabic dialogue)* **CHAMPIONS, PALESTINIANS, EVENHANDED**

Director-writer Jay Anania's well-intentioned independent film shows how terrorism, whether occurring in Jerusalem or New York City, harms innocent people. The story focuses on Najia, a dignified Palestinian journalist (Chaplin), and Shira, an intelligent Jewish fashion model (Sutherland). The movie shows Shira and Najia bonding and becoming friends. Opening frames display stock news footage of a Jerusalem suicide bombing and the attack's bloody aftermath. From here on, the action shifts back and forth from Israel, to occupied Palestine, to New York. Scenes in New York show Najia interviewing Dr. Mary Wade (Dukakis). Najia asks about what happens to the bodies of "suicide bombers, some of whom are just little kids." Wade offers this graphic explanation: "Well... they get blown into pieces, the top half and the bottom half, period." At a cafe, Najia meets and befriends Shira. She tells Shira that her parents and sister died in Palestine; Shira says her friend died in "one of the towers." Cut to employees abusing a homeless man, Najia defends him, saying: "Hey, no need to humiliate him."

In the end, tragedy strikes. Najia finds out that her brother (Tairy), "a good boy, a very fine boy" has killed himself and others in a suicide attack. Stock footage reveals mangled body parts. Dazed from the carnage, Najia reflects on past relationships with her brother: "I was like a mother to him. He was studying to be a teacher but he loved music best; he had a beautiful voice. He sang like an angel." Suddenly, off camera and without warning a bus hits Najia, killing her.

Cut to a dark alley; without warning a man who had been stalking Shira, attacks her, yanking out her eyes. Final frames focus on physicians harvesting Najia's corneas and giving them to—Shira.

Credit Anania for his message of peace, and for showing the tragic reality: Innocent people, be they Palestinians or Israelis, whether they live here or abroad, suffer needlessly, and perish from random acts of terror. Unfortunately, Anania does not permit us to learn much about Najia and Shira. Had he developed their characters a bit more, had he illustrated their growing friendship, he could have enhanced his theme and his poetic foundation. As it is, *Fire* drags at times; similar images and dialogue are repeated over and over again. Duets by singer Judy Kuhn and pianist John Medeski are well done. But their oft-repeated tunes and their on-camera appearances stall the action.

A DAY WITHOUT A MEXICAN *(2004) Alta Vista Films; D, SP: Sergio Arau SP: Yareli Arizmendi A: Raul A. Hinojosa* CAMEO, ARAB AMERICAN

One third of California's citizens are missing—the Latino third. Several residents express concerns about the state's Latino population, noting their many contributions. One concerned resident is Abdul Hassan (Hinojosa), an Arab-American professor. Hassan tells his fellow Californians: "This is a disaster… if we don't find those Latinos we're all in serious trouble. You know, I teach at a university and I used to work with Raul. We were a team—Abdul and Raul."

THE DEAL *(2005) Front Street; D: Harvey Kahn SP: Ruth Epstein A: Christian Slater* CAMEO, VILLAINS

This routine set-in-the-near-future political drama tells us that the US is at war with the Arabs, and that corporate heavies and the Russian mafia are engaged in a ruthless oil conspiracy. We never see any reel Arabs—not one. Credits roll: On screen, an Arab oil field's aflame; US jets swoop over Arab oil tankers; artillery shells are fired. Darkness: More burning oil fields. Cut to the streets of New York City. Gasoline costs $6.50. The economy's a mess. Explains a radio announcer: "The war with the Corporation of Arab States today entered its third year, while oil fields in the world's most oil rich region continue to burn."

DELTA FARCE *(2007) Lionsgate; D: C.B. Harding SP: Bear Aderhold, Tom Sullivan A: Dan Whitney, DJ Qualls* **CAMEO, SHEIKHS**
Larry the Cable Guy (Whitney) and two of his blue-collar buddies are mistakenly taken for army reservists and whisked off to "Fallujah, Iraq." But when their army plane encounters severe weather, they're abruptly released from the plane, and mistakenly touch down somewhere in Mexico. Here, the wannabe soldiers spot a portrait of Pancho Villa. "We're in Iraq," says Larry. Thinking Mexico's Villa is Iraq's "Butcher of Baghdad," the men swing into action to liberate a Mexican village from banditos. Malapropisms concerning Arabs and Muslims prompt sour slurs. For example, Larry's pal, trigger-happy ex-cop Everett (Qualls), is eager "to shoot somebody." "Charlie's a sneaky bastard," he says. When he accosts two Mexicans, he barks, "We need to find out whether they're terrorists, Turds, or Shit-ites." Some viewers may find this film funny; I did not. Given the rising number of casualties in Iraq and cinema's sad history of stereotyping Mexicans, I fast-forwarded through most of it. In addition to mocking Mexicans, the film also ridicules white Southerners.

DEUCE BIGALOW: EUROPEAN GIGOLO *(2005) COL; D: Mike Bigelow SP: Rob Schneider, David Garrett, Jason Ward A: Federico Dordei* **CAMEO**
This raunchy comedy focuses on man-whores of various ethnic backgrounds who are being killed, one by one, in Amsterdam. One male prostitute escaping the murderer's wrath is a dapper Arab, Mahmoud (Dordei).

A DIFFERENT LOYALTY *(2004) Forum Films; D: Marek Kanievska SP: Jim Piddock A: Sharon Stone, Rupert Everett* **CAMEO**
The Lebanese are neutral backdrops in this tedious film, in which Leo Cauffield (Everett), a communist sympathizer, defects to Russia, leaving behind in Beirut his wife (Stone) and children. Twenty minutes of the film take place in Beirut, circa 1963 and 1967. The camera presents Beirut as a pleasant place to live, with lovely beaches, respectful mourners at a funeral, well-dressed and helpful Lebanese hotel clerks, children playing in the streets, and a boy misbehaving in a bustling market place. A fun-filled evening gala features a lovely female Arab vocalist singing Arab music, backed by Arab musicians in tuxedos.

DISTRICT B13 *(2004) Magnolia Pictures; D: Pierre Morel SP: Luc Besson, Bibi Naceri A: Bibi Naceri, Samir Guesmi, David Belle, Cyril Raffaeli* **VILLAINS, WORST LIST**
Paris 2010: In a garbage-infested walled-off area outside the lovely Champs Elysées, two million undesirables and criminals reside. The main thug is a ruthless Arab, Taha Bin Mahmoud (Naceri), who terrorizes residents with his gang of heroin traffickers. Taha's accountant is Jamel (Guesmi), another Arab. The film's most offensive scenes: Taha kidnaps the hero's sister, Lola, drugs her, chains her to a short leash, and drags her around like a lap dog. When he acquires a deadly bomb, he ties Lola to the weapon, and then aims the bomb at the heart of Paris. He intends to "kill millions of innocent Parisians"— unless the government forks over "20 million Euros." In time, the film's heroes rescue Lola and stop the bomb launch. Taha's cohorts gun him down; he had it coming.

In *Escape from LA* (1996)—the criminals-in-isolation story line is somewhat similar, but without the Arab villains. Instead, an Arab-American woman assists the protagonist.

DREAMER: INSPIRED BY A TRUE STORY *(2005) Dream-Works; D, SP: John Gatins A: Dakota Fanning, Kurt Russell, Oded Fehr, Antonio Albadran, David Morse, Kris Kristofferson* **SHEIKHS, CAMEO**
This is another set-in-Kentucky horseracing family crowd-pleaser. Yet, producers toss into the bluegrass state two rich Arab brothers—Prince Tariq (Albadran) and Prince Sadir (Fehr). These

staunch rivals own some of Lexington's finest racehorses. Nine minutes into the film Prince Tariq's prize racehorse, Sanador, suffers a fatal injury. His leg is broken; he must be put down. But, no, a Kentucky working-class horse trainer, Ben Crane (Russell) and Cale, his lovely 11-year-old daughter (Fanning), intercede and save the seriously injured horse's life. Though Tariq's gruff employee, Palmer (Morse), agrees to spare Sonador (dreamer in Spanish), he tells Ben: "You're fired. Take your two Mexicans with you." The defiant Ben counters Palmer's slur, emphatically: "They're men; they have names." Conversely, later, when Ben's father asks him: "Are you going to spend the rest of your life shoveling for sheikhs?" Ben is silent. Soon, Dreamer makes an amazing comeback and he's chosen to race in the Breeders' Cup Classic. But, Ben and Cale can't afford the $120,000 entrance fee. Here's where the Arabs come in again. Remember, the two brothers are keen rivals. Sadir's prize horse was not selected; Tariq's was. Dreamer might pose a threat to Tariq's horse—he could defeat the Arab entry. So, Palmer offers to buy him back for $100,000, and he offers Ben and the Hispanics their jobs back. Cale, who now owns Dreamer, refuses the offer. Aware that Palmer's doing Tariq's dirty work, Ben and Cale pay a visit to Prince Sadir (Fehr) and ask him for the $120,000. Pause. "You look me in the eye," Sadir tells Cale, "and tell me your horse can beat my brother's horse." Cut to the race. Will Dreamer defeat Tariq's previously unbeaten black thoroughbred? Of course! The "bad" Arab horse loses to the "good" American horse. Cut to the grim-faced Tariq, alone in the owner's circle. Off in the distance, a smiling Sadir waves to Cale.

Why show Arab brothers, without wives and children, as feuding princes? Why not project them as the Americans are shown, as a caring loving family? The two rich Arabs serve no purpose—plotwise—except to sustain and advance the reel myth: US average Americans always cross the finish line ahead of THEM wealthy sheikhs. See *Hidalgo* (2004), the *Black Stallion* films (1979, 1983), and especially the closing frames of another set-in-Kentucky film, *Simpatico* (1999). Here, rich Arabs pop up again, but rather than sell them her champion horse, the protagonist (Sharon Stone) grabs a gun and shoots dead her own thoroughbred.

ENOUGH *(2002) COL; D: Michael Apted SP: Nicholas Kazan A: Jennifer Lopez, Chris Maher* **CHAMPIONS, RECOMMENDED, ARAB AMERICAN**

Credit Nicholas Kazan and Michael Apted for the first post–9/11 film to feature a courageous Arab-American character—Phil (Maher), a benevolent restaurant owner. When Phil's waitress, Slim (Lopez) marries, Phil dances with her, boasting about being her "surrogate father... who really loves her." Later, Phil is shocked to learn that Slim's husband has trapped her inside her own house, and is beating her. So, Phil and his friends launch a rescue mission. Cut to Phil crashing into the house, where he struggles with and helps bring down Slim's abusive husband. He and his pals run off with Slim and her baby girl. Phil fears she and her child may not be safe, so he buys two airplane tickets, and sends them off—to his pals in Michigan. Cut to Phil's Arab-Americans friends warmly greeting and providing shelter for Slim and her child.

FAHRENHEIT 9/11 *(2004) Miramax; D, SP: Michael Moore* **SHEIKHS**

Early on Moore targets the Saudis. These Arabs, he declares, are buying up our country, influencing President Bush's foreign policies, and helping Bush profit from oil deals. Later, Moore comments on the Iraq war. He presents stark, gripping images of the injured and mutilated bodies of American soldiers and Iraqi civilians—men, women, and children. His clips also show, albeit briefly, some US soldiers verbally and sexually abusing Iraqi prisoners. Moore's thesis: The war is wrong and immoral; as a result of Bush's policies Americans and Iraqis are much worse off. "Immoral behavior," he says, begets more immoral behavior. *Fahrenheit 9/11* was a box-office smash. Early receipts show the film grossing more than $100 million, the most ever for a documentary film. Note: Soon after the film's release, NBC-TV's Conan O'Brien spoofed *Fahrenheit 9/11*, lambasting rich Saudis (11 July 2004).

FATWA *(2006) Capital City Entertainment; D: John Carter SP: Scott Schafer A: Lauren Holly, Roger G. Smith* **VILLAINS, MAIDENS, WORST LIST**

This low-budget film shows a crazed Arab-Muslim cab driver from Libya killing Americans, including a US senator. Samir al-Faridi

(Smith), a bearded, mentally unbalanced cabbie moves to terminate Minnesota Senator Maggie Davidson (Holly), a conservative politician seeking harsher anti-terrorist laws. We see Maggie warn her lover about an Arab terrorist using "Cobalt 47 to build a radioactive weapon… he wants to construct the bomb in the trunk of his cab and then let it loose in [New York's] financial district…." Cut to the bearded Samir making a bomb; cut to bags of ammonium nitrate; cut to the suicidal Samir making a video recording, speaking Arabic as he mumbles and prays to Allah. Later, an American customer at a diner comments about Samir's behavior, telling his friend: "Those of us who were brought up in this country, we live for ourselves. [But Arab immigrants like Samir] live for God." Cut to Samir, sloppily licking apple pie crumbs off his fingers. Cut to an evil, nameless Arab woman, ordering Samir to kill the senator.

This reel terrorist is an evil fundamentalist who "dresses like a whore and seduces men to their deaths." The final fifteen minutes occur in Samir's cab. Samir locks Maggie inside the back of his cab. Next, he delivers some lethal heroin to Maggie's young pot-smoking daughter and her Israeli girlfriend; the girls inhale and die. Inside the cab, the helpless Maggie watches a live video of the girls' deaths. Cut to Samir. He shows Maggie a photo of his son, saying: "You kill my child and I kill yours… you take his life. I take your life." (Though we have not seen anyone murdering Samir's son.) Maggie screams at Samir, "You're just like the criminals who attacked the towers." Cut to an American hit man about to shoot Maggie. But, when he deduces that Samir, the Arab, wants to murder Maggie, the hit man has a change of heart. He turns into "the jingoistic John Wayne," and moves to save Maggie's life. CRUNCH! He rams his car into Samir's cab. Samir's trunk bomb explodes. The screen dissolves, slowly, into whiteness. I agree with the IMDB critic Joel Pearce, who writes that *Fatwa* "is racist propaganda, creating offensive caricatures of both Western and Middle Eastern culture. Instead of breaking down the cultural barriers, it just adds yet another layer to the already impenetrable wall."

THE FINAL CUT *(2004) Lionsgate; D, SP: Omar Naim A: Robin Williams, Thom Bishops* **ARAB AMERICAN, EVENHANDED**
This futuristic film, written and directed by Omar Naim, raises

the telling question: Are medical implants ethical or unethical? Upon request, an expensive chip is inserted into a newborn baby's brain. This chip records a person's entire life. When someone dies, professional "cutters" can—for a price—omit from the clip all the dead person's "bad" deeds. The film's most accomplished and most expensive cutter is Alan Hackman (Williams). He helps the living remember "what they want to remember about the deceased." Alan can even turn murderers into saints. Alan's friend and fellow cutter is an Arab American named Hasan (Bishops). When Alan begins experiencing scary childhood memories he turns to Hasan for assistance. Hasan successfully performs a dangerous operation on his friend, enabling Alan to finally cope with the past.

FINAL DESTINATION 3 *(2006) New Line; D, SP: James Wong SP: Glen Morgan A: Mary Elizabeth Winstead* CAMEO, VILLAINS

Threatening Arab symbols are employed as instruments of death at an amusement park and a high-school gym. Throughout, the protagonist tries to interrupt "death's" plan to murder her friends. Her supernatural digital camera gives her needed clues, showing how her friends will die. One clue shows her friend ducking under the amusement park's "Whirling Dervish" ride, the sign for which features a bearded Arab with two huge Arabian swords in each hand. The sinister-looking Arab looks nothing like an actual dervish, of course.

Another friend is working out in the school gym. The camera repeatedly shows a sign for the "Sultans," the high-school team's nickname. Two large, crossing Arabian swords—the same as those held by the park's dervish—are emblazoned on the logo along with a man wearing an Arab head dress. Her friend lifts weights underneath two massive real and dangerous Arabian swords and a plaque with this warning: "What doesn't kill you makes you stronger." Suddenly, the two swords fall down onto the gym equipment, cutting the cables that hold his weights. The weights crush his head. Taken together, the Sultans logo, the deadly Arabian swords, and the bearded Arab "dervish" subtly imply that Arab terror is responsible for the student's death.

FIRE OVER AFGHANISTAN *(2003) New Concorde; D, SP: Terence S. Winkless SP: Rady Radouloff A: Jeff Stearns, Dimitar Terziev, Jordan Bayne* **VILLAINS**

Afghanistan is not an Arab country. But this film's reel Afghans look and act like reel bad Arabs. The story concerns an upright Afghan leader and two heroic Americans. They move to defeat evil Afghans, led by a warlord named Babashan. Amazingly, it takes only two Americans, a Black Hawk helicopter pilot named Captain Walker (Stearn) and Kris (Bayne), an attractive, spunky journalist, to wipe out "that bastard Babashan" and his cronies. An Afghan Muslim calls Kris: You unworthy "Jew or Christian." This unpleasant film presents a scene depicting an ugly Afghan stripping and brutally raping Kris stands out for its grotesqueness. A similar violent scene occurs in *Afghan Knights* (2007) when an Afghan warlord rapes his young wife, forcing himself on her from behind and repeatedly shouting, "You are filth!"

FIVE FINGERS *(2006) Lionsgate; D, SP: Laurence Malkin SP: Chad Thumann A: Laurence Fishburne, Ryan Phillippe, Gina Torres Touriya Haoud, Said Taghmaoui, Colm Meaney* **ARAB IMPERSONATORS**

In the Amsterdam airport, Martijn (Phillippe), a Dutch jazz pianist, says goodbye to his Moroccan girlfriend, Saadia (Haoud). He and an Englishman, Gavin (Meaney), fly off to Morocco. Here, Martijn plans to finance a food program—or does he? Upon arrival in Rabat, the two men board an airport bus, filled with Moroccans and a squawking chicken. Abruptly, they are kidnapped, drugged, and held hostage. From here on, the film becomes a recorded stageplay; all the action takes place inside a deserted warehouse. When the men regain consciousness, they are bound, chained, and blindfolded. When their captors, Ahmat (Fishburne) and Youseff (Taghmaoui), begin interrogating them, Gavin protests. BANG! Ahmat machine-guns him and his blood spatters all over Martijn. Flashback to scenes of civilized Holland—in fact, every time Martijn's captors use violence the camera cuts back to peaceful Holland. Convinced that Martijn is not really a humanitarian, Ahmat demands to know Martijn's real objectives, his funding sources. Martijn feigns ignorance. Youseff (Taghmaoui) takes a paper cutter and chops off his pinky finger. (The Muslim nurse in *The English Patient* [1996] performs a similar act). Entering the frame is Aicha (Torres); she's dressed in white from head to toe. Aicha feigns being kind to Martijn then cuts off his thumb. Next, she heats a hacksaw and saws off another finger; Martijn screams and screams; he will never play piano again. Next, Aicha shows Martijn a box with his four removed fingers—on ice.

In the concluding frames, we get a surprise twist that does not work. Martijn confesses that he's a member of a Dutch terror cell and the goal of his so-called food program is to inject poisonous bacteria into food supplies that would eventually kill thousands of Americans. He goes on to list the names of his fellow terrorists. Suddenly, Youseff shoots Martijn dead. The three interrogators remove their Arab garb and drop their Arab accents. We discover the warehouse is actually in New York City, not Morocco. Gavin's death was faked, he is alive and well inside a recording booth documenting Martijn's confession. Gavin, Ahmat, Youseff, and Aicha are, in fact, American intelligence agents. Ahmat compliments his fellow agents, saying "nice job, nice job," boasting that torture was the only way to ascertain Martijn's true identity and uncover the terrorist cell. Torture works. When he and Aicha walk off for a drink, the Statue of Liberty is in the background.

Viewers who didn't stick around for the weak ending might have walked off thinking that the torturers were Arabs; after all, 98 percent of the film shows the interrogators in Arab garb, speaking Arabic.

See Jay Weissberg's review in *Variety* 4 May 2005.

FLAGS OF OUR FATHERS *(2006) WB; D: Clint Eastwood SP: William Broyles, Jr., Paul Haggis A: Ryan Phillippe, Jesse Bradford, Adam Beach* CAMEO

This brilliant Clint Eastwood film documents the hellish battles of Iwo Jima by following the fates back at home of the three heroic survivors who were in the famous flag-raising photograph. Fifty minutes into the film, in April 1945, a one-liner blames America's war woes on Arabs. The head of the Treasury Department tells the three heroes that our government is nearly broke and asks them to help convince Americans to buy war bonds. The official explains: "Our dollar is next to worthless; ships aren't being built; tanks aren't being built... don't be surprised if your planes don't take off the runway because fuel dumps are empty. And, our good friends the Ay-rabs are only taking [gold] bullion [for their oil]." This Arab-bashing line is out of place and historically inaccurate. Back then, the popular oil villains were Rockefeller and Standard Oil. The line also falsely implies that stingy, greedy Arab nations intentionally hurt us during WWII, which is entirely false. In 1945, Arab countries were mostly occupied by British, French, or US troops. Britain, for example, controlled the oil-producing countries of Iraq and Kuwait. In Saudi Arabia, which did require payment in bullion after America went off the gold standard, production was in its infancy. Similarly, the pejorative "Ay-rabs," with the drawling long "Ay" is an inaccurate projection of present-day prejudices on the past. No one I know recalls hearing it until the Six Day War, in 1967.

FLIGHTPLAN *(2005) Touchstone; D: Robert Schwentke SP: Peter A. Dowling, Billy Ray A: Assaf Cohen, Jodie Foster* **RECOMMENDED, ARAB AMERICAN**

Prejudices are exposed and debunked in this action flick. After a few hours in flight to New York on a jumbo jet, Kyle Pratt (Foster) discovers her six-year-old daughter, Julia, is missing. Who took the girl? The obvious suspects are three mostly silent Arab Americans, especially the bearded Ahmed. (The Israeli-American actor Assaf Cohen gives a brilliant performance as Ahmed). The frightened Kyle continuously glares at the three Arabs, who are framed to look shifty. "What's the problem," asks Ahmed. "You walked past me five times." Kyle's convinced Ahmed had planned Julia's abduction. Why? One night when she was back in her Berlin flat, Kyle spotted some dark-looking men looking out a nearby window. She believes these men were Ahmed and his pals. The frustrated Ahmed counters Kyle's accusations and blames her for Julia's disappearance: "I travel with my children. I have my eye on them all the time. I don't lose them and blame somebody else." Furious, Kyle attacks Ahmed. Cut to an American bigot screaming at the three Arab passengers. The flight crew helps contain the man and Kyle;

Ahmed asks the passengers, "Anyone else with questions?" No one speaks. "Then I guess we will have to find a few other Arabs to harass." Undaunted by Ahmed's claim of innocence, Kyle tells the pilot, Those Arabs "have my daughter. I don't give a shit about being politically correct."

In the final frames, Kyle finds and rescues her daughter. She also brings down the two non-Arab kidnappers. The last scene occurs after the plane lands, safely. Kyle happily embraces Julia. Ahmed walks over to them and gives Kyle the luggage she's forgotten. Not a word is exchanged. Instead, she looks at Ahmed and smiles in acknowledgment of her mistake.

FLIGHT OF THE PHOENIX *(2004) TCF; D: John Moore SP: Lukas Heller, Scott Frank, Edward Burns A: Dennis Quaid* **VILLAINS**
Villainous nomads attack the Western heroes. Tagged "arms merchants," these bad guys dwell in the Gobi desert, hide their faces with dark cloth, and ride camels and horses. They may be perceived as Arabs but they aren't. In the original version of *Flight of the Phoenix* (1966), Bedouin bandits sliced Westerners throats, off camera.

FOUR FEATHERS *(2002) PAR; D: Shekhar Kapur SP: Michael Schiffer, Hussein Amini B: A.E.W. Mason A: Heath Ledger, Djiman Hounsou* **VILLAINS, WORST LIST**
Just one year after 9/11, Paramount released this $100 million shot-in-Morocco rusty political drama, complete with 1,500 Moroccan extras as villains. Paramount should have called this, the seventh version of A.E.W. Mason's tale about the British hero Harry Feversham (Ledger), *Harry of Arabia*. Harry is the civilized British Christian cowboy who brings down uncivilized Sudanese Muslims.

Before the British invade Sudan's "godforsaken desert," a soldier peruses a military pamphlet that states, "Above all, remember you're a Christian soldier." The action begins around 1875, at a time when "God has endowed the British race with a worldwide empire." British soldiers are dispatched to the Sudan because "an army of Mohammaden fanatics has attacked [and slaughtered] a British regiment" there. Young Harry refuses to join his regiment.

Thus, his friends send him three white feathers—a sign of cowardice. To prove he's a true hero, Harry rushes off to the Sudan. From here on, frames show heroic Harry over there, posing successfully as an Arab and killing scores of Sudanese desert dwellers.

Viewers never ascertain why the Sudanese attacked; there's no Sudanese point of view. The stale myth that Islam is a violent faith is enforced. We see Sudanese Muslims praying, and then ambushing a British regiment and shooting dead scores of British soldiers. There's more reel Arab brutality: British soldiers are hung; inside a filthy Sudanese prison soldiers are tortured and stuffed together as sardines in rusty containers. Amazingly, Harry, who is in disguise as a really dark Arab, looks, speaks, and acts more Arab than any reel Arab. He kills the brutal prison guard and rescues his military friends. Thanks to Harry, British colonialism triumphs and British troops gun down the camel-riding Sudanese "heathens." Abou (Hounsou), the movie's token "good" Muslim, surfaces in a few scenes. Abou is "good" for one reason: He helps the Christian protagonists and betrays his fellow Muslims. For information on other *Four Feathers* films, see my *Reel Bad Arabs*.

Reel history shows that Hollywood's Muslim villains are almost always Arab Muslims, but there are some exceptions. *Tears of the Sun* (2003) projects Nigerian Muslims as religious fanatics who relish killing Christians—white and black. The set-in-India film *Flame over India* (1957) shows barbaric Indian Muslim tribesmen attacking the civilized British. The reel antagonist is a well-dressed Indian Muslim journalist—a hateful bigot out to murder a six-year-old Hindu prince. Afghans are occasionally villains in films, such as *Fire over Afghanistan* (2003). Turkish Muslims are vile beings in *Midnight Express* (1978). Iranian Muslims are heavies in films such as *Not without My Daughter* (1991), *The Hitman* (1991), and *Into the Night* (1985). Conversely, an African-American Muslim teenager, Ahmad Abdul Rahim, appears as "one of the boys" in four *Bad News Bears* baseball films.

FULL DISCLOSURE *(2001) First Look; D: John Bradshaw SP: Tony Johnston A: Fred Ward* **CAMEO, PALESTINIANS, WORST LIST**
In California, Algerian villains dispatch two UCLA Palestinian students to murder an American peace activist. Not to fret: an

attractive American blonde kills the Palestinians. Cut to the protagonist, a hard-boiled reporter (Ward). He loves a Palestinian
woman, but her past is shady. He tries to protect her from assassins,
but she is shot dead.

That Arab villains are tossed into *Disclosure* didn't surprise me.
After all, anti-Arab dialogue and/or disagreeable Arabs have been
inserted in more than 300 films that have absolutely nothing to do
with the plot or the region. For example, this from the 2004 USA-
TV movie, *Call Me: The Rise and Fall of Heidi Fleiss.* Viewers see a
nearly naked Heidi (Jamie-Lynn DiScala) enjoying herself while
bedding various clients. The really big bucks come from those "foreigners," boasts Heidi. Cut to Heidi strutting toward a hotel room
guarded by a grim-looking Arab. She groans, "If only my Hebrew
teacher could see me now." Heidi enters the Arab's room. A gruff-
looking Saudi, "Prince Hassan," greets her. The following dialogue
implies Palestine does not exist, that Palestinians are terrorists who
hate Jews; and that regardless of how much money the Arabs have,
even nice whores like Heidi shouldn't bed them.

> HASSAN: I live in London.
> HEIDI: That means we don't have to sweep for bombs.
> HASSAN: We're not in Palestine, my dear.
> HEIDI: Hello—you mean Israel.
> HASSAN: I certainly don't mean the Zionist entity.
> HEIDI: What is it with you guys, anyhow? What do you
> want, for God's sake? I mean, besides a heap of dead Jews.
> HASSAN: Out.
> HEIDI: Asshole!

GEN-Y COPS (*or* JACKIE CHAN PRESENTS GEN-Y-COPS)
(2003) UNI; D: Benny Chan SP: Felix Chong, Bey Logan A: Memo Tan-
han CAMEO, SHEIKHS

In the final minutes of this Chan film, Achmed (Tanhan) and his
Arab henchmen pop up and park their sleek, black limos.
Achmed's Arabs wear lengthy burnooses that look like pawed-over
bed sheets. Cut to rich, anxious Achmed forking over $400 million
to the primary bad guys. Why? Because Achmed wants to buy and
put into play an awesome, destructive robot. Not to fret. In time,
the Gen-Y cops arrive, shooting all the Arabs dead.

THE GOLD BRACELET *(2006) K.R. Films; D, SP: Kavi Raz A:*
Kavi Raz RECOMMENDED
This excellent film advances the theme that regardless of its
faults, America remains a land of opportunity, where the mixing
of cultures is a blessing. In this movie, the best friend of the Sikh
protagonist, Arjun (Raz), is an American Muslim. One of his
well meaning Anglo-American customers praises Arjun for fixing
his car, and at such a low price. But, he mistakenly and repeatedly
calls Arjun "Arab." No matter how many times Arjun tries to correct him, the good-natured customer still calls him "Arab."

Then, the attacks on the Twin Towers bring tragedy to Arjun
and his family. Since they are perceived to be Arabs, some of
them are harassed and beaten. The wise, benevolent Arjun and
his hard-working Sikh brother are shot dead. Explains the radio
newsman, one brother "was mistaken for an Arab by the killer."
Despite the loss of loved ones, Arjun's family proceeds with a joyous, though tearful, Sikh wedding celebration.

Bracelet reminds us that when real antagonists mistakenly view
dark-looking people as evil Arabs, Sikhs, Indians, and other non-
Arabs may become victims of real hate crimes.

HIDALGO *(2004) Touchstone; D: Joe Johnston SP: John Fusco A: Viggo*
Mortensen, Omar Sharif, Zuleikha Robinson, Said Taghmaoui, Silas Car-
son, Adoni Maropis VILLAINS, MAIDENS, SHEIKHS, WORST LIST
Bang, Bang, Bang! Welcome to Disney's reincarnated cowboys and
Indians! This $100 million shoot-'em-up was filmed in Morocco
in cooperation with Moroccan officials. Instead of gunning down
reel Indian "savages," the stalwart Frank Hopkins (Mortensen)—
who is half-cowboy and half-Indian—shoots dead Bedouin
"bandits." To attract viewers, Disney promoted the film as "a true
story," but Disney fibbed. Pure bunk, said the Long Riders' Association and other respectable equestrian organizations. Set in the
1890s, this desert drama replenishes stale stereotypes: Arab versus
American, Arab versus Arab, and Arab versus blacks. At the movie's
start, as Hopkins prepares to leave for Arabia, he stares admiringly
at the Statue of Liberty and dreams of winning the 3,000-mile
"Ocean-of-Fire" death-defying desert race. Once in Arabia, Hopkins is threatened by a swarm of cheating, unscrupulous Arabs.

The sheikh's corrupt nephew (Maropis), and the vicious Katib (Carson) intend to kill him. Arab slavers are hauling off to the auction block young Africans in chains, giving Hopkins his first chance to be a hero: he saves one youth. Cut to Hopkins trying to shake hands with Sheikh Riyadh (Sharif), the ruler. The sheikh balks: It's "an impure act to shake the hand of an infidel." Not only that: they intend to castrate him.

But of course, Hopkins is spared—he must ride the desert race. If Prince Bin Al Reeh (Taghmaoui) wins, he will take the sheikh's daughter, Princess Jazira (Robinson), as "his fifth wife." Poor Jazira; she will become "the youngest in his harem; no more than a slave in his house." So, the desperate Jazira betrays her fellow Arabs and helps Hopkins win the race. "Why do I feel you truly see me when others do not?" she purrs.

Eventually Hopkins has to rescue Jazira and kill about 20 Arabs. The heroics displayed by this cowboy/Indian against evil Arabs reminded me of old movie Westerns, when Tom Mix and Gene Autry triumphed over Indian villains. Finally, Hopkins, the first non-Arab to compete in the horse race, leaves 100 Bedouin riders behind in the dust.

In marketing Hopkins-of-Arabia, Disney's writers took the cowboy's best traits, and blended them with the Indian's noble attributes. Disney knew audiences would no longer accept cowboys gunning down Indians, and rightly so. But Disney also knew audiences would applaud a cowboy/Indian protagonist gunning down Arabs. For its first week, *Hidalgo* was #3 at the box office. A few reviewers noted the stereotypes. Wrote a *Hollywood Reporter* critic (1 March 2004): "The Bedouins are so burdened with villainy that actors can bring little dimension to such characters." *Wall Street Journal* critic Joe Morgensten said: "*Hidalgo* characterizes its Arabs as wily, oily, devious or downright dishonorable." After watching *Hidalgo,* I came up with this question for Disney's executives: What if the writers had given you a screenplay that featured a horse race showing Hopkins besting not Arabs, but evil Asians, blacks, Jews, or Hispanics. Wouldn't you relegate the screenplay to one of your theme park's dump trucks?

HIDDEN *[Caché] (2005) Les Films du Lasange; D, SP: Michael Haneke A: Juliette Binoche, Daniel Auteuil, Maurice Benichou* **ARAB-AS-VICTIM, EVENHANDED**

The subplot of this French film is the fear and loathing of the racial other, in this case Algerian Muslims. In October 1961, French rightists led a pogrom against local Arabs. When the Algerians (FLN) retaliated, the Paris chief of police ignited a bloody purge, and the bodies of 200 Algerian "jigaboos" were tossed into the Seine. Though more than 40 years have passed since this tragedy, racism in France still flourishes. Without any evidence, for example, Georges (Auteuil), the wealthy protagonist, accuses Majid (Benichou), a poor Algerian, of terrorizing him and his family. Georges goes to Majid's rundown flat and accuses Majid of placing anonymous phone calls and sending crude drawings and video surveillance tapes to his residence.

Flashback to Georges and Majid as children—forty years ago. Young Georges is upset because his parents pay attention to the "adopted" Majid, so Georges unfairly blames Majid for a crime he did not commit. His cruel lie ruins Majid's life; the hurt, confused boy is taken away from the residence and dispatched to a children's home. Obviously, Georges is directly responsible for Majid's misfortunes. Yet he denies any responsibility: "I don't feel responsible," he says. "Why should I?" Cut to Georges's living room. The TV set beams images of dying Iraqis. Does anyone "feel responsible?" No! No one pays attention; no one cares about those "other" Arabs who die—whether they are the Algerians the French drowned in the Seine or today's Iraqis, shot dead in Baghdad.

HOME OF THE BRAVE *(2006) MGM; D: Irwin Winkler SP: Mark Friedman A: Samuel L. Jackson, Amad Kamal* **VILLAINS**

The American protagonists protecting us from those evil Arabs are, as in *The Kingdom*, a black man (Jackson) and a white woman (Biel). Nearly all the action takes place in Spokane, Washington, but the first 20 minutes show US soldiers in "hot, dusty, horrible Iraq." Initial frames show happy soldiers playing basketball and football—they are going home in two weeks. The camera cuts to a herd of sheep, a few dogs, and then cuts to an ungrateful clad-in-black Iraqi woman. Though Jackson is carefully treating the woman's sick baby girl, she shouts in Arabic at him. When the soldiers receive orders to deliver "medical supplies," a gesture of "good will to the Iraqi people," one complains, "I don't like these [humanitarian missions]; we're always putting ourselves in danger." And indeed, the troops are ambushed and several die. Cut to our soldiers gunning down scores of Iraqis; they are, after all, as my friend Professor Chuck Yates says, "The Enemy—furtive, faceless, fickle, and fanatical." The message conveyed in these Iraqi scenes is clearly that when we Americans try to help "those people," they try to kill us. Yates and I found especially troubling the use of the Improvised Explosive Devise (IED) and the motif of the Arab kid as terrorist [see both *The Kingdom* and *Rules of Engagement*]: It's an Arab child with a tootsie pop who seems to detonate the bomb. Sneaky Arabs.

The Iraq war scenes were shot in Morocco.

THE HOT CHICK *(2002) Touchstone; D, SP: Tom Brady, SP: Rob Schneider A: Rob Schneider, Rachel McAdams, Shazia, Osman Soykut* **CAMEO, EGYPTIANS**

The screen says "Abyssinia, 50 BC," but opening scenes reveal Egyptian characters inside an Egyptian temple. The Pharaoh (Soykut) and Princess Nawa (Shazia) don magic earrings. Cut to the US and the American protagonists, Clive (Schneider) and Jessica (McAdams). They now wear the ancient Egyptian earrings, one each. Presto! Surprisingly, they wake up transported into each other's bodies; Clive becomes Jessica and vice versa.

INSIDE MAN *(2006) UNI; D: Spike Lee SP: Russell Gewirtz A: Denzel Washington, Willem Dafoe* **CAMEO, VILLAINS**

This Spike Lee film slurs Arabs. The action takes place in multi-ethnic New York. Inside a bank, robbers hold dozens hostage. Eventually, they release some, one at a time, placing hoods over their heads. Aggressive policemen search the released hostages for weapons, and then interrogate them. One hooded hostage exits the bank with his hands up. Three policemen with SWAT weapons surround him. The officer removes the man's white mask and hood and screams: "Aw shit, it's a fuckin' Arab!" No. The released man is actually a bearded Sikh wearing a blue turban. The angry policeman asks if his laptop is a bomb, and if he is "booby trapped." He orders a fellow officer to "take him down." And the police do. The released Sikh protests, "I'm not an Arab, I work at the bank, I'm a Sikh!" No matter. One policeman tears off his turban, which is a religious dictum. Later, he repeatedly tells other officers that he's a Sikh and not an Arab. The Sikh's protests reinforce the reel myth: Sikhs and other dark-looking persons are good; Arabs are bad. Surprisingly, midway through the film, a disturbing slur: Police Captain Darius (Dafoe) shouts this ethnic epithet: "those rag heads at Munich." Why have Darius shout "rag heads," a damaging racial epithet? *Munich* and the slur have nothing whatsoever to do with the story. No one contests Darius's comment.

JACKASS NUMBER TWO *(2006) PAR; D, SP: Jeff Tremaine SP: Spike Jonze, Johnny Knoxville A: Ehren McGhehey* **CAMEO, VILLAINS**
Viewers who enjoy watching raunchy, obnoxious skits with nudity and gross humor may like this film. Some viewers probably enjoyed seeing loony daredevils doing bizarre stunts, and delivering outrageous pranks, for laughs. But I found *Jackass* to be a crude movie that tries to push the limits of public sensitivies. Especially offensive was the film's "terror taxi" scene. Near the end, actor Ehren McGhehey prepares to frighten a taxi driver. How? By donning traditional reel bad Arab garb, including a fake beard, for a prank, called "terror taxi." This scene enforces the myth that Arab = Muslim = Terrorist. Dressed as an evil Arab, Ehren enters a cab with a fake bomb and tells the Indian driver to take him to the airport. Next, he tries out some terror humor on the cabbie, saying: "Where I'm going, I don't need luggage." Unexpectedly, the Indian cabbie stops the car, draws a gun, and scares the wits out of Ehren. The cabbie, an actor hired by the producer, is in on the joke. He and other *Jackass* cast members begin laughing. Ehren learns that his fake beard was made out of all the cast's pubic hair and he throws up in disgust.

Some Arabs and Muslims who grow beards in the tradition of the prophet Muhammad may find this to be a disturbing scene.

JARHEAD *(2005) UNI; D: Sam Mendes SP: William Broyles Jr. B: Anthony Swofford A: Jake Gyllenhaal* **BEDOUIN**
This antiwar film documents the experiences of Marine Corporal

Tony Swofford (Gyllenhaal) during the first Gulf war in 1991. Three scenes merit our attention. One: To illustrate how Hollywood's war films help pump up recruits we see the marines- in-training watching and applauding Coppola's 1979 Vietnam epic, *Apocalypse Now*. On screen, US helicopters launch rockets that kill scores of Vietnamese. The marine audience cheers enthusiastically. Two: Another scene shows the importance of speaking some Arabic. In the desert, our marines spot several Bedouins and their camels. Fearing that the Bedouin may be hiding "weapons under their robes" the squad prepares to gun them down. Tony shouts, "Don't fire!" Alone, he approaches the Bedouins and speaks to them in Arabic. He learns that they are in the area only because someone "shot three of their camels." Three: So-called friendly fire kills innocent people, marines, and Arab civilians. US pilots mistakenly "think the Arabs are Iraqis." The camera reveals charred body parts, many people are injured, as well; we see a child's burned body inside a school bus. An Iraqi soldier appears once, inside a damaged control tower. Two planes drop bombs, obliterating him.

THE KEEPER: THE LEGEND OF OMAR KHAYYAM *(2005)*

Guide Company Films; D, SP: Kayvan Mashayekh SP: Belle Avery A: Bruno Lastra, Christopher Simpson, Marie Espinosa

This magnificently photographed family film, directed, co-written, and co-produced by Kayvan Mashayekh, features an outstanding musical score, plus visually compelling location shots. The movie was filmed in 37 days in Uzbekistan, Bukhara, and Samarkand. Regrettably, the film tries to say too much about too many issues in too short a time. Poor performances by some international actors don't help. Throughout, scenes flash back and forth between Omar's (Lastra) life in 11th-century Persia and his descendants, a contemporary Iranian-American family, in Houston. The Persian scenes fail to say much about Khayyam the man or his accomplishments. Too much attention is given to the poet's on-off relationship with the sultan, his yearning for a gorgeous servant girl, Darya (Espinosa), and his on-off friendship with his childhood friend, Hassan (Simpson). Hassan believes that his own harsh, hardline interpretation of Islam is correct. Omar's interpretation differs dramatically; he contends that Muslims should embrace the sciences and the arts. The scenes worth watching are those that focus on the connections of 21st-century America to Persia's rich artistic tradition. Three-dimensional portraits of Houston's Iranian family portray immigrants who, like most immigrants, seek to preserve their heritage while making it big in their beloved new country. Sadly, the family's eldest son, Nader (Behinaein), the family's "keeper" of Omar's legend, dies of leukemia; his younger brother, Kamran (Echahly), is left to preserve the legend. Kamran flies to Europe, where he befriends a scholarly English woman who enables him to become Omar's new "keeper," and finally travels to contemporary Iran. We see the boy and his wise grandfather embracing; the emotional depths of Khayyam's legendary poems are revealed.

Although this film portrays Iranians, not Arabs, it's included here because Iranians are so often mistaken for Arabs, and vice versa (including during the Iranian Revolution, when Arab students were harassed, or in the Gulf War or post–9/11, when Iranians have been harassed as Arabs), and Omar Khayyam is often mistakenly called an Arab poet. Unfortunately, for about 10 seconds in *Rush Hour 3* (2007), actor Chris Tucker spews out sleazy prejudices that some Americans have about Iranian Muslims.

THE KINGDOM (2007) UNI; D: Peter Berg SP: Matthew Michael Carnahan A: Jamie Foxx, Ashraf Barhom, Jennifer Garner, Ali Suliman, Hezi Saddik VILLAINS, WORST LIST

The Kingdom is Hollywood's most anti-Arab post–9/11 film. My friend TV director Ahamd Zahra told me: "I saw it and wept."

Stereotypes reign in this black (bad Arab) and white (good American) drama, in which four heroic FBI agents fly off to Saudi Arabia and kill Arabs. No plot surprise, here; watching reel Arab corpses pollute silver screens has become an all-too-familiar sight, as commonplace as seeing camels roaming the desert. What did surprise me was the millions of dollars Universal spent hyping this film. Weeks before *The Kingdom* debuted, TV viewers were saturated with bang-bang commercials promoting the movie's violent scenes, mostly during football games. When the film was finally released in movie theaters worldwide, I was pleased to see an *Entertainment Weekly* blurb stating that the film's director, Peter Berg, "was determined to avoid stereotypes." Berg even referred to my *Reel Bad Arabs*, saying, "I don't think any filmmaker is in the business of turning people off." Given Berg's rhetoric, I'd hoped his film would eliminate stereotypes; instead, it embellishes them, blatantly exploiting our emotions.

I first learned about Berg's *Kingdom* while participating in Dubai's International Film Festival in December 2006. My host told me that because the script was riddled with anti-Arab scenes, Dubai's film execs wanted nothing to do with it. Universal shot the movie instead in nearby Abu Dhabi. Some of my host's friends were cast as extras, and they had reported that all the director wanted them to do was "look and act mean" and "die realistically." On returning home, I offered my services to the studio as a consultant and asked if I might view and comment on the film during post-production. My requests were turned down.

This $70 million jingoistic thriller turned off many critics, including the *Los Angeles Times*'s Kenneth Turan and the *New York Times*'s A.O. Scott, who wrote: "Just as *Rambo* offered the fantasy of do-over on Vietnam, *The Kingdom* can be seen as a wishful revisionist scenario for the American response to Islamic fundamentalist terrorism." "*The Kingdom* provides the most vivid, across-the-board portrait of malevolent Arabs it can manage," wrote Turan. "The film's theme is similar to those jingoistic World War II-era 'Yellow Peril' films." Still, Berg's phony *Kingdom* turns some people on. When I watched it, a few teenagers cheered every time Saudis were shot dead in their tracks. Perhaps the scenes reminded them of violent anti-Arab video games.

The Kingdom offers gunfights galore, explosions, suicide bombings, rocket-propelled grenades, and clearly defined heroes and villains. Berg's political message is simple: All Arab Muslims, notably the Saudis—men, women, even children—are Islamic terrorists intent on killing Americans. He presents two types of evil Saudis: heinous grenade-launching terrorists and all others, who are silent, obstructive, uninterested in justice, and fully compromised by the terrorists.

So we had better kill them before they kill us. And we do kill them—again and again!

The movie is very loosely based on the 1996 bombings of

Khobar Towers in Dhahran and the 2003 attack on an US compound in Riyadh, which killed 30 people, including 9 Americans. Berg mutates these real tragic events, cleverly manipulating viewers into thinking his movie's false scenes are what really happened.

Opening frames focus on American oil company workers and their families during a softball game at the "Rahman Compound." Saudi terrorists attack, killing scores of reel Americans. More than a hundred people—primarily women, teenagers, and children—are either mowed down or blown to pieces; an additional 200 Americans are seriously wounded. "All glory to Allah!" "Allah will give us victory," declare the terrorists.

During the attack, the Saudi ringleader's young son watches the slaughter impassively. Back in the US, the son of FBI agent Fleury (Foxx) tells his father, "There are a lot of bad people out there." Says Fleury, "Yeah, but you're not one of them." In other words, the film asserts that Arab kids may look innocent but they, too, are "bad people."

The film's State Department officials are stereotyped as pro-Arab wimps who refuse to allow FBI investigators to put their "boots on Saudi soil." To get into Saudi Arabia, Fleury sets up a secret meeting with Prince Thamer, the Saudi ambassador. Fleury threatens him, saying something like: "If we [agents] don't get clearance, then it will be brought to the press... how Saudi wives donated $3 million to an Arab-American organization outside of Baltimore, and how this money's been used to help fund terrorist groups." In reality, charitable Arab women such as those who belong to Washington, DC's Mosaic Foundation have donated millions to American hospitals and educational and charitable institutions. Berg's attack on Arab-American groups is based on prejudices, not realities. No Arab-American organization in the US has ever been truthfully linked to terrorism. Not one.

Fleury and three other FBI agents head for Saudi Arabia, which agent Mayes (Garner) describes as being "a bit like Mars." They have five days to find and bring down the villains in a place that turns out to be much worse than Mars—a sinister desert with evil machine-gun-toting Arabs lurking in the shadows, waiting to kill Americans. During the final 30 minutes, an explosive firefight takes place—I stopped counting after 35 Saudi bodies hit the sand. The camera cuts to one kidnapped agent about to be beheaded by the heartless followers of Abu Hamsa (Saddik). Our agents arrive in the nick of time, rescuing their colleague and killing the ringleader.

If Berg was truly sincere in wanting to help curtail the American-against-Arab mentality, he should have done several things. He could have followed the advice in *Reel Bad Arabs*, instead of giving lip service to it. He could have studied Ed Bradley's telling CBS-TV *The Saudis* (1980), a brilliant documentary that humanizes the Saudi people, or Todd Nimms's *Home: The Aramco Brats' Story* (2007), a wonderful film showing that since the 1940s, numerous Saudis have befriended and happily interacted with US oil employees and their families.

Finally, instead of presenting all Saudis as either terrorists or their supporters, why not present some decent, ordinary Saudi citizens? In his book *My FBI: Bringing Down the Mafia*, former FBI director Louis J. Freeh commends the Saudis for helping his agents with the investigation of the Khobar attacks—something no one watching *The Kingdom* would guess. Berg does find two "good" Saudis, Colonel Ghazi (Ashraf Barhoum) and Sergeant Haytham (Ali Suliman), willing to help Fleury investigate the horrific attack. But he might have expanded their roles, instead of just offering a token 90-second scene featuring Ghazi's loving, mostly silent, family.

Agents Fleury and Mayes, a black man and white woman, bring down the evil terrorists. In *The Siege* (1998), too, a white female CIA agent (Annette Bening) and black male FBI agent (Denzel Washington) crush Arab villains together. "I'm sure it's just pure coincidence," my colleague Chuck Yates told me, "but I think *The Kingdom*'s formula is pretty much like the one used by director George Romero in *Night of the Living Dead* and *Dawn of the Dead*: When all the living are being terminated, who's left? A black man and a white woman. In the end, there's not much difference between a reel Arab terrorist and a reel zombie, eh?"

Eventually, the FBI may use *The Kingdom* to recruit new members. Military commanders, though, should find that the movie insults the integrity and ability of our troops. Think about it: Four FBI agents fly over to Saudi Arabia and take only five days to find and efficiently shoot dead dozens of Arab villains, including Abu Hamsa, the mastermind behind the attacks, and then return safely home.

Echoing the opening frames, the final scene perpetuates the theme of Arab children as terrorists—a theme that also surfaces near the end of *Rules of Engagement* (2000). When the mastermind's innocent-looking grandchild is asked what his grandfather told him before he died, he whispers, "We're going to kill them all." The camera presents an extreme close-up of the boy's threatening eyes. This scene only makes it more likely that some Western viewers will fail to mourn the deaths of innocent Arab children who are gunned down or blown up in Iraq, Palestine, Lebanon, and elsewhere.

I wonder about the impact *The Kingdom* will have on our servicemen and women in Iraq and Afghanistan. Will it make them more likely to engage in wanton violence against civilians? And I wonder how viewers in the Middle East will react to *The Kingdom*. In any case, it has been banned in Bahrain and Kuwait due to its unflattering portrait of Arabs.

See Lisa Schwarzbaum, "Mission: Implausible," *Entertainment Weekly* 5 October 2007; A. O Scott, "FBI Agents Solve the Terrorist Problem," *New York Times* 28 September 2007; Stephen Farber, "The Kingdom," *Hollywood Reporter* 12 September 2007; Kenneth Turan, "The Kingdom," *Los Angeles Times* 28 September 2007; John Hartl, "The Kingdom: Star Power, Opulent Sets, But Little Substance," *Seattle Times* 28 September 2007; Joe Morgenstern, "Kingdom Has Oil, Guns, Sheikhs, But Little Depth," *Wall Street Journal* 28 September 2007.

KINGDOM OF HEAVEN *(2005) TCF; D: Ridley Scott SP: William Monahan A: Orlando Bloom, Ghassan Massoud* CHAMPIONS, RECOMMENDED

I did not expect Ridley Scott's antiwar epic to be critical of Europe's invasion and occupation of Jerusalem. After all, Scott featured warmongering Libyans in his *GI Jane* (1997), money-grabbing Arab kidnappers in *Gladiator* (2000), and in *Black Hawk Down* (2002) portrayed "the Arabs of Somalia as generically violent animals, as journalist Robert Fisk writes." In this bold movie, however, Scott offers evenhanded images of Christians and Muslims—and he casts Arabs to play Arabs. *Kingdom of Heaven* does more than entertain viewers; it challenges them and make an eloquent plea for tolerance and peace. Throughout, the heroic Christian knight Balian

(Bloom) strives to fulfill his father's quest, to "fashion a kingdom of heaven" where there is peace between Christian and Muslim. Balian and the Arab leader, Saladin (Massoud), are models of chivalry, devotion, and compassion. Islam is not projected as a "demonic religion of apostasy and blasphemy." When Robert Fisk saw the movie in a Beirut theater, he was "deeply moved." It was "a revelation," writes Fisk, "to sit through the film among Muslims—most of them in their 20s—who were watching historical events that took place only a couple of hundred miles from us." In the film, Saladin and his Muslim soldiers, as well as Balian and his Christian soldiers, are honorable men; they show "generosity as well as ruthlessness to their enemies." Ruthlessness to be sure: We see the Christian Knights Templar committing "their orgy of rape and head-chopping among the Muslim villagers." And, a knight murders Saladin's sister. Later, Saladin puts his sword through the murderous knight's throat. But after the honorable king of Jerusalem prevents a battle between Crusaders and Saracens and falls fatally ill, Saladin dispatches his own doctors to attend the Christian king. This scene, writes Fisk, prompted from the Muslim audience in Beirut "a round of spontaneous applause." Muslims admired this act of mercy; they wanted Saladin to show kindness to a Christian. "Unlike any other recent film, here in Lebanon *Kingdom of Heaven* has captured the admiration of Muslims," he writes. One harsh critic, however, British historian Jonathan Ridley-Smith, said the movie was "Osama bin Laden's version of history. It will fuel the Islamic fundamentalists." Fisk contends that the reason critics such as Ridley-Smith condemned this movie is that they "felt uncomfortable at the way the film portrayed 'us,' the crusaders."

The closing scene is worth noting. "After Balian has surrendered Jerusalem, Saladin enters the city. He sees a crucifix lying on the floor of a church, knocked off the altar during the three-day siege. He carefully picks up the cross and places it reverently back on the altar. At this point," writes Fisk, "the audience rose to their feet and clapped and shouted their appreciation. They loved that gesture of honor. They wanted Islam to be merciful as well as strong." Fisk left the Dunes cinema strangely uplifted by the extraordinary performance—of the audience as much as the film.

"See it if you haven't," says Fisk. "And remember how the Muslims of Beirut came to realize that even Hollywood can be fair."

The film took in only $47 million in the US, but *Kingdom of Heaven* has been a huge financial success overseas, taking in $163 million in foreign markets.

While visiting the Umayyad Mosque in Damascus, Pope John Paul II affirmed the film's message: "It is my ardent hope that Muslim and Christian religious leaders and teachers will present our two great religious communities as communities in respectful dialogue, never more as communities in conflict," he said.

For more on the same subject, I recommend the feature film *King Richard and the Crusaders* (1954) and the two-hour PBS documentary-drama *Empires* (2005).

See Robert Fisk, "Why Ridley Scott's Story of the Crusades Struck Such a Chord in a Lebanese Cinema," *Independent* 4 June 2005.

THE KITCHEN *(2001) D, SP: Andre Degas A: Jason Raize, Mark Margolis* **ARAB AMERICAN**

This independent film is the only American film to ever feature two Arab-American male lead characters. Though *The Kitchen* was telecast two or three times on PBS stations in New York and San Francisco, it never reached movie theaters; nor is it listed on the IMDB database. The film focuses on two regular New Yorkers, Farid (Margolis) and his son Jamal (Raize). Farid runs a corner grocery store; Jamal, a jazz musician, has no interest in working in or taking over the store. Throughout, Farid refuses to accept Jamal's quest to be a musician. The set-in-his-ways Farid refuses to compromise fixed old-country beliefs. Jamal tries but fails to convince his father that though their goals differ, they should find a middle ground, and get along. We see Jamal befriending and romancing a lovely woman, and watch him jam with several multicultural friends. When a few toughs direct some anti-Arab slurs at Jamal, his musician friends step forward, countering them.

LAND OF PLENTY *(2004) Emotion Films; D, SP: Wim Wenders SP: Michael Meredith A: Shaun Toub, Michelle Williams, Bernard White, John Diehl* **PALESTINIANS**

Despite Wim Wenders's noble intentions, this film fails to offer fresh insights about the 9/11 attacks. The scenes drag along, and regrettably the stereotype of the Vietnam veteran as a patriotic psycho is advanced. The protagonist, Paul (Diehl), a Vietnam vet, is a self-appointed homeland security agent who cruises along in his media-equipped van looking for potential terrorists in Los Angeles. Paul relishes hearing right-wing radio talk-show hosts bash liberals like Ralph Nader. His niece, Lara (Williams), arrives in LA from Palestine, and immediately advances the Palestinian stereotype with a one-liner about how she saw crowds of "ordinary" Palestinians "cheering out in the streets..." after 9/11, "cheering because they hate us... they hate America." The fact is that hours after the 9/11 attack more than 200 Palestinians went to the American consulate in Jerusalem to offer their sympathy; they placed a memorial wreath in front of the consulate, lit candles, and prayed. Americans never saw this reality—on the news or in a film.

Later on, the film reveals harsh realities. Lara goes to her computer and watches Palestinians and Israelis mourning at funerals. In the background, a large banner proclaims, "Better to have the pains of peace than the agonies of war." The brief funeral frames enable us to empathize, equally, with both Palestinians and Israelis. The film also dispels the myth that America's dark-complexioned Arabs and Pakistanis are terrorists. Early on, Paul witnesses a drive-by shooting: Some "bad white kids on drugs" drive by and shoot dead Hassan (Toub), a homeless man wearing a turban who "had no possessions, nothing to eat."

Paul mistakenly thinks Hassan was an Arab terrorist; he believes Hassan was mixing chemicals to make a dirty bomb, targeting the people of Los Angeles. Later, thanks to Lara, he finds out that Hassan and his brother, a hospitable, soft-spoken man named Youssef (White), were not terrorists, but poor, harmless men from Pakistan, trying to survive in the US.

LARRY THE CABLE GUY: HEALTH INSPECTOR (2006)
PAR; D: Trent Cooper SP: Jonathan Bernstein, James Greere A: Iris Bahr
CAMEO, VILLAINS
This bland comedy features Larry as the city's health inspector. He collars culprits who are poisoning the fine cuisine being served in local restaurants. Near the end, cut to Larry's assistant Amy (Bahr)

inside a noted restaurant's kitchen, where she hears the French chef yelling at the mayor, "You're asking me to poison the food that it took me so long prepare!" Before the mayor responds, he spots the spying Amy. Frightened, she calls Larry for help. Immediately, Larry barges into the kitchen in reel bad Arab garb. A large red-and-white tablecloth covers his head and he speaks with a thick Arab accent. As he rescues Amy, he shouts: "You have brought shame to our family, flaunting yourself in front of the imperialist swine [and] leaving me to fend for myself in the house with nothing but a goat for company." This one line covers a wide range of stereotypes: Arab women belong at home; Arabs are violent; Arabs dislike Americans; Arabs and animals live together. The producers could at least have had Larry performing like a reel romantic Arab, entering the kitchen posing as a Valentino-like sheikh, who uses his wit, good looks, and charm to rescue Amy. Note that when Larry poses as a bearded rabbi, he nabs the villains.

THE LAST KING OF SCOTLAND (2006) Fox Searchlight; D: Kevin Macdonald SP: Peter Morgan, Jeremy Brock B: Giles Foden A: Forest Whitaker CAMEO, PALESTINIANS

The action in this historical fiction film occurs in 1970s Uganda, during the rule of General Idi Amin Dada (Whitaker). He and his brutal regime are responsible for the deaths of "300,000 Ugandans." Just before the movie ends, the producers unexpectedly inject Palestinians terrorists. Wearing checkered *kufiyas*, they hold airline passengers hostage at the Entebbe airport. This news appears on screen: "48 hours later Israeli forces stormed Entebbe and liberated all but one of the hostages." The Entebbe hijacking did occur during Amin's regime, a major incident that drew media attention worldwide. But concluding with the raid scene seems abrupt and may lead some viewers to lump the horrific actions of reel Palestinians together with those of the ruthless dictator, Amin.

For viewers interested in the Entebbe rescue, there are three TV movies: *Victory at Entebbe* (1976), *Raid on Entebbe* (1977), and *Operation Thunderbolt Entebbe* (2000).

THE LAST SHOT *(2004) Touchstone; D, SP: Jeff Nathanson A: Alec Baldwin, Joan Cusack* **CAMEO**

This Disney film is all about the FBI using a phony movie as a sting operation to nab mobsters. Agent Joe Devine (Baldwin) goes to Hollywood seeking advice from Fannie (Cusack), a well-established production executive. Devine waits in Fannie's office; she's on the phone shouting, "Stop it, Arnie... You tell me where my fucking script is. You wanna eat lunch off my ass?... Arnie, I'll make you a deal. You deliver that script and lunch is on me, you Lebanese piece of shit! Love to Bernice and the baby." Fannie slams down the phone. Her slur has no place in this film.

LOOKING FOR COMEDY IN THE MUSLIM WORLD

(2005) Warner Independent; D, SP: Albert Brooks A: Albert Brooks **MAIDENS, WORST LIST**

The bad news is this tedious film features Brooks portraying an over-the-hill comedian named Albert Brooks. The good news is that Sony Pictures wisely passed on this movie, which grossed less than $1 million. Opening frames: The US government wants to "better understand the Muslim peoples of the world," and the president thinks "the only way to really understand somebody is to see what makes them laugh." So, to find out what makes Muslims laugh, officials recruit Brooks to spend 30 days in India and Pakistan. In India, Brooks never expresses real interest in any of the people. His one and only goal is to get the "Medal of Freedom." To get the award, he must complete a 500-page report. Anti-Muslim images and dialogue pollute the screen. In New Delhi, when Brooks wants to hire an assistant, he interviews and dismisses several reel dense Muslims. Finally, Brooks finds a bright, attractive woman to employ—a Hindu. Nothing wrong, here, really— except isn't his main objective to better understand Muslims? In all of India, couldn't he find a competent Muslim woman? He could have hired a clad-in-total-black Muslim applicant: she typed fast, took shorthand, and spoke six languages. But she disliked Jews. Not funny.

Consider this revised scenario. Let's put Brooks in a film where he plays a Muslim comedian who goes to Israel and tries to find a competent assistant, but all the Israeli female applicants are not qualified. Finally, he finds one competent Israeli; but she hates Muslims. Again, not funny!

Back to the Muslim world: Brooks performs his stand-up comedy routine for locals. He needs to use the bathroom but it's a long, long way off—six buildings from the auditorium. Matters get worse: his reel Indian Muslim stagehands are stupid and the Muslims watching his act are "humorless stoics." Near the end, Brooks visits al-Jazeera, the Arab TV network, where he's asked to portray a Jew in a new sitcom called "That Darn Jew," about an American Jew who lives in a Muslim apartment complex. Offended, Brooks walks away—and rightfully so. The producer panics, and shouts three times: "Get me another Jew!" It's just not funny.

A note: In reality, most of our government's PR campaigns are designed to win the hearts and minds of Arab Muslims. So, why does the action in this film take place in India?

See Deborah Young's review in *Variety* 16 December 2005.

THE LORD OF THE RINGS: RETURN OF THE KING

(2003) New Line (extended edition); D, SP: Peter Jackson SP: Fran Walsh, Philippa Boyens B: J.R.R. Tolkien A: Orlando Bloom **CAMEO, VILLAINS**

Peter Jackson's epic received eleven Academy Awards. All of Jackson's grotesque evil creatures are otherworldly—except for one group, which bears a keen resemblance to the Bedouins of our world. During the climatic ten-minute battle scene, reel evil Bedouin clones appear on battle cages and launch scores of arrows against the heroes. The cages are mounted atop huge elephants that resemble desert tents, upside down. The villains' black headscarves and other garb look exactly like the costumes reel bad Arabs wear in action films. Unlike the movie's non-human villains, the Bedouin clones possess human features. They have—boasts one member of the design team—an "exotic appearance." This reminds me that I've received a few letters saying that Watto, the vile, greedy, desert-dwelling slave trader from *Star Wars Episode I: The Phantom Menace* (1999) acted Arab. Not so. Watto may speak with a slight Arab accent, but he is definitely *not* a reel shifty Arab; he is a unique alien!

THE MAJESTIC (2001) WB; D: Frank Darabont SP: Michael Sloane A: Jim Carrey, Cliff Curtis CAMEOS, SHEIKHS

Inside California's Majestic Theater, a 1950s audience views—twice—the black-and-white B-film *Sand Pirates of the Sahara*. The movie screen displays a dark desert temple, home of "Horus, the Falcon-Headed God." Cut to the villain, Prince Khalid (Curtis), sneaking up behind an elderly American explorer and knocking him unconscious. Next, Khalid goes to take the blonde heroine, "his desert dove." Suddenly, the Western "infidel" hero enters the frame, sword in hand, and declares: "Taste my steel, you dog!" Khalid pulls his sword. Blades clash! The dashing hero kills the Arab and gets the blonde.

Reel Arabs lusting after blondes are sometimes mistaken for reel Turks, and vice versa. In *Secret of Stamboul* (1936), the villain is a Turkish ruler. But Nostalgia Video promotes the film by calling him a "lascivious Arab Prince" who imprisons and tries to "seduce" the blonde heroine.

MALIBU'S MOST WANTED (2003) WB; D: John Whitesell SP: Fax Bahr, Adam Small, Jamie Kennedy, Nick Swardson A: Kal Penn CAMEO, ARAB AMERICAN

In this Malibu, California buddy flick, the protagonist counts among his three loyal friends an Arab American named Hadji (Penn). His pals jokingly call Hadji "the beast from the Middle East." When the protagonist gets in trouble with some reel tough guys, his teenage friends are ready to help him out. To fend off the antagonists, they acquire an assortment of weapons: a spear, a musket, and—thanks to Hadji—a "rocket-propelled grenade launcher, a Christmas gift from Uncle Ahmet."

THE MANCHURIAN CANDIDATE (2004) PAR; D: Jonathan Demme SP: George Axelrod, Daniel Pyne, Dean Georgaris B: Richard Condon A: Denzel Washington, Sakina Jaffrey CAMEO, MAIDENS

This remake of John Frankenheimer's 1962 film is set in Kuwait in 1991, just before Desert Storm. Iraqis attack Captain Ben Marco's (Washington) patrol. Marco retaliates, blowing up an Iraqi helicopter and machine-gunning several Iraqis. (US soldiers similarly gun down Iraqis in *Courage under Fire* [1996].) After the "war," veterans tell Marco that they are suffering from haunting nightmares. Cut to several extreme close-ups of a grim, silent, clad-in-black, threatening-looking "mysterious Arabic woman" (Jaffrey). This insertion makes no sense—Arab women are not part of this film, and Ms. Mysterious is never seen again. Suave capitalists are the villains here, because, as director Jonathan Demme says, "Corporate totalitarianism is scary," and "multinational firms such as my movie's corrupt firm, 'Manchurian Global,' profit from war and chaos. Look at Bosnia and Iraq."

Film critic Robert Sklar takes issue with Demme, disapproving of Demme's decision to portray Halliburton clones as "nasty bad people trying to take over the country." "The most logical demons should have been al-Qaeda Muslims," Sklar argued. They are the proper equivalent to the earlier *Candidate's* "big bad Reds conspiring to take over the White House." Sklar accuses Demme of not projecting Arabs as heavies because "it's politically incorrect [in Hollywood] to offend Muslim religious and ethnic sensibilities."

That's a new one! Since when has it been "politically incorrect" to vilify Arabs? Decades before US incursions into Iraq, Hollywood was demeaning all things Arab and Muslim in hundreds of movies.

John Frankenheimer's original film was released several years after the Korean conflict. In it, evil Asian commies are the antagonists who kill and brainwash US prisoners-of-war. Yet, a puzzling two-liner in the 1962 film refers to Arabs. Aboard a train, the protagonist, Major Marco (Frank Sinatra), befriends the lovely blonde, Eugenie (Janet Leigh). Marco asks her, "You Arabic?" Says Eugenie: "No." Marco puts out his cigarette, then says: "My name's Ben." Then Eugenie asks him, "Are you Arabic?... Let me put it another way, are you married?"

See Sklar's review of *The Manchurian Candidate* in *Cineaste* Winter 2004.

THE MARINE *(2006) TCF; D: John Bonito SP: Michelle Gallagher, Alan B. McElroy A: John Cena, Firass Dirani* **CAMEO, VILLAINS**
The action in this movie takes place in the US—except for about 90 seconds. Before credits roll the opening frames reveal "Iraq—an al-Qaeda terror base 100 miles from Tikrit." It is the evening, and Arab music is heard in the background; a banner written in Arabic is on

display. Cut to several Arabic-speaking insurgents wearing fatigues; dark stocking-cap ski masks cover their faces. They brutally beat American POWs. Enter the reel hero, played by WWE wrestling star Cena. Singlehandedly, he machine-guns the baddies.

Islam is linked to violence when the main al-Qaeda guy (Dirani) shouts "Allahu akbar" (God is great) as he moves to behead the US prisoner. Cena shoots him dead and goes on to blow up the camp. As he and the three rescued US prisoners head for safety, he guns down more insurgents. And more. When one US soldier asks, "How do we get around them?" Cena smiles: "We don't. We go through them." And they do—BAM, BAM, BAM, finish! *The Marine* may attract young viewers when it comes out on DVD. But when I saw the film I was the only person in the theater.

MERCHANT OF VENICE *(2004) Sony; D, SP: Michael Radford B: William Shakespeare A: David Harewood, Lynn Collins* **SHEIKHS**

Venice 1576. Portia's (Collins) first suitor is the robed, dark-complexioned prince of Morocco (Harewood). The smiling, anxious prince appears at Portia's residence with about a dozen of his mostly silent aides. When something startles the prince, he and his Moroccans brandish their curved blades, frightening Portia and her entourage. Much to Portia's relief, the pleasant Moroccan ruler, who is sincerely smitten by her beauty, fails to win Portia's hand, and other suitors have a chance in the competition. In Shakespeare's play, writes Conrad Geller in *Cineaste* (Spring 2005), the prince greets Portia, saying: "Mislike me not by my complexion." The film version omits her reply: "Let all of his complexion choose me so."

MUMMY RAIDER *(2001) Seduction Cinema; D: Brian Paulin SP: Bruce G. Hallenbeck A: Misty Mundae* **EGYPTIANS**

The Arab–Nazi connection: In this X-Rated film, the antagonist and a revived rampaging Egyptian mummy try to bring back "Hitler's Legions" from the dead. Thanks to the heroic Misty, they fail. There are more Arab X-rated films out there, but after seeing this one, I am not sorry I didn't seek them out.

THE MUMMY'S KISS *(2002) Seduction Cinema; D, SP: Daniel F. Glut A: Mia Zottori* **MAIDENS, EGYPTIANS**

This X-rated film features Hor-Shep-Sut, a reincarnated Egyptian sorceress. When an American coed makes the deadly mistake of removing a golden death mask from an Egyptian mummy, Hor-Shep-Sut springs to life and begins terrorizing college students. She seduces some female students and kills a security guard and a professor. In a flashback to Egypt 3,000 years ago, we see Nubian slaves moving to kill the Egyptian sorceress because she was engaging in too many lesbian affairs.

In the 2005 TV movie *The Fallen Ones*, a rampaging 20-ton, 42-foot-tall mummy and his mummy offspring try to terminate Americans. An Egyptian antagonist tries to rape the blond heroine. When it comes to reel Arabs and blondes, not much has changed in 70 years. In *Fallen*, for example, there's an "unholy" seduction scene that resembles the near-rape scene from Boris Karloff's 1932 thriller, *The Mummy*.

MUNICH *(2005) DreamWorks; D: Steven Spielberg SP: Tony Kushner, Eric Roth B: George Jonas A: Eric Bana, Geoffrey Rush, Daniel Craig* **PALESTINIANS**

Hollywood has a history of demonizing all things Palestinian, and Spielberg, one of the world's most powerful and influential filmmakers, has not always been balanced in his portrayal of Arabs, so I initially balked at seeing *Munich*. But Spielberg avoids damaging stereotypes here—*Munich* is his "prayer for peace" film, a skillful, albeit fictional "inspired-by-real-events" drama that focuses on the actions of an undercover Israeli hit team trying to assassinate the masterminds of the 1972 Olympic killings. Spielberg does not present the Palestinian–Israeli conflict as a clash of cultures or religions, or sanity versus insanity, or civilization versus barbarism, or West versus East, or Islam versus Judaism, "but rather as a struggle over territory, over geography, over home." He portrays most Palestinians not as demons but as thoughtful, ordinary human beings. Palestinians are not painted in black, and Israelis are not white knights. Both articulate thoughtful arguments about what it means to be a displaced people. One telling scene depicts Ali, a Palestinian, with Avner, his Israeli counterpart, making an eloquent case for his homeland, Palestine. Avner, too, brings up ownership of the Holy Land. The men debate whether the soil belongs to Israelis or Palestinians. As describe in Richard Schickel's interview with Spielberg in *Time*, *Munich* avoids "the staples of propaganda" by dramatizing the toll violence takes. The film "refuses to reduce the Middle East controversy, and the problematics of terrorism and counterterrorism, to soundbites and spin." In the same interview Spielberg says, "The biggest enemy is not the Palestinians or the Israelis. The biggest enemy... is intransigence.... There aren't that many differences that divide Israelis from Palestinians—not as human beings, anyway.... There's been a quagmire of blood for blood for many decades in that region. Where does it end? How can it end?"

Premiere's Glenn Kenny affirms Spielberg's intentions, reminding us: "The purpose of narrative art is to ask questions, not to pronounce answers." *Munich* "never once attacks Israel. It simply asks a plethora of questions." Yet, Spielberg and screenwriter Tony Kushner were "accused of being apologists for the Palestinians, apologists for Israel, defamers of Palestinians and of Israel... even of being anti-Semitic or self-loathing." Conservative Jewish-American commentators such as Leon Wieseltier, Charles Krauthammer, Andrea Poyser, and others attacked the film; the Zionist Organization of America even called for a boycott. Writing in the *Washington Post*, Krauthammer lambasted the film because a few scenes "evoke [our] sympathy" for Palestinians. He tagged *Munich* "vicious propaganda," adding, "Never [before] have four little words 'inspired by real events'—been so appalling." In Israel, however, *Munich* went straight to the top at the box office, earning more than double its nearest rival, reports *Variety*'s Ali Jaafar. Spielberg told *Newsweek*'s David Ansen that regrettably, here in the United States, "many fundamentalists" in his own Jewish community were angry with him "for allowing the Palestinians simply to have a dialogue." The Arab press was mostly positive in its coverage. Al-Jazeera ran a special on the film, praising it.

But *Munich* should have included scenes that show the Israeli hit team killing innocent Arabs, ordinary men who had nothing to do with the Munich attack, such as the real-life assassination in 1973 of a Moroccan waiter living in Lillehammer, Norway. He was shot dead by Israelis. Opening and closing frames of the movie project reel ugly Palestinian terrorists holding hostage and killing the Israeli athletes—as a result, says Uri Avnery, in the Olympic Village and airport terrorist scenes "the Palestinians appear as miserable, ugly, unkempt, cowardly creatures, the very opposite of the film's Israelis."

Spielberg's *Munich*, like Gaghan's *Syriana*, demands our attention. Both intelligent thrillers pose incisive questions applicable to today's quest for Middle East peace: Are political objectives achieved by acts of revenge? What has the occupation and the use of force accomplished? The inventive visions of Spielberg and Gaghan allow us to better debate whether violence has brought us any closer to peace. Tony Kushner told *Entertainment Weekly* (23 December 2005) that "One of the things that people make a terrible mistake with in terms of thinking about the Middle East conflict is to think about it in terms of a clash of religions.... Behind Muslim fundamentalism, there's a history of colonialism and oppression that needs to be thought about intelligently." Spielberg, who is a principal supporter of the Steven Spielberg Jewish Film Archive at Hebrew University, reportedly brought on several advisors such as Rabbi Levi Meier and former Middle East envoy Dennis Ross to employ intelligent thinking and to smooth over possible controversies. To my knowledge, the director did not seek out or consult with any Palestinian Americans. He should have.

Munich is Hollywood's third fictional movie to dramatize events surrounding the eleven tragic deaths of Israeli athletes that took place during and after the 1972 Summer Olympics. Two compelling TV movies, ABC's *21 Hours at Munich* (1976) and HBO's *Sword of Gideon* (1986), focused on the Israeli hit team tracking down Palestinians. The TV movies reveal the humanity of Palestinian victims, and the varied motives and emotions of Israeli assassins as they go about killing, one by one, Palestinians responsible for the Israeli deaths. But both films are seldom telecast on any network and both are difficult to find, even in well-stocked video stores.

For a more accurate assessment at what took place in 1972 in Munich, I recommend the book *Striking Back*, by Aaron J. Klein. He painstakingly documents the tragedy, which includes pointing out that the Israeli hit team killed Palestinians who were not involved in the Munich attack.

See "Spielberg Takes on Terror," *Time* 12 December 2005; Glenn Kenny's review of *Munich, Premiere* 22 December 2005; "Israel LA Envoy Criticizes New Spielberg Film *Munich,*" *Haaretz* service, 12 November 2005; Kushner's op-ed, "Defending 'Munich' to My Mishpocheh," in the *Los Angeles Times* 22 January 2005; Ali Jaafar, "Arabs Get Fair Play" *Variety* 5 February 2005; and David Ansen, "Heaviness for the Holidays," *Newsweek* 14 December 2005.

NIGHT AT THE MUSEUM *(2006) TCF; D: Shawn Levy SP: Robert Ben Garant, Thomas Lennon A: Ben Stiller, Rami Malek* EGYPTIANS, EVENHANDED

Producer-director Shawn Levy's family comedy stars Ben Stiller as Larry Daly, a night guard at New York City's Natural History Museum. Larry's new job is not what it seems. After the museum ushers out all its visitors and the sun sets, all of the displays—a giant Tyrannosaurus rex, charging lions and monkeys, Attila and his marauding Huns, cowboys, Civil War combatants, Octavius and his Roman soldiers—come to life and start partying, doing the "Jumanji" thing. Eventually, Larry discovers what, exactly, brings the display figures back to life each and every night—King Ahkmenrah's (Malek) golden Egyptian tablet. When the mummified king is awakened, it isn't a reel prowling bandaged villain that pops out of the ancient tomb, but a young, handsome, and articulate Egyptian who speaks with a British accent. For years the reawakened king was "on display at Cambridge University's Egyptology department." From here on Ahkmenrah is at Larry's side assisting him. First, the king calms the angry Attila by speaking Hun; then he helps Larry retrieve the stolen golden tablet. Without the tablet, the display figures would remain immobile—permanently. But thanks to the king, Larry restores order and the tablet is tucked safely away. All the display characters manage to return safely back into the museum. Midnight partying begins at sunset!

ONLY HUMAN *(2004) Madragoa Filmes; D, SP: Dominic Harari, Teresa Pelegri A: Guillermo Toledo, Marián Aguilera, Norma Aleandro* PALESTINIANS, RECOMMENDED

This enjoyable Spanish screwball comedy brings Semites together. Using real-life material from their own families, married writer-directors Dominic Harari and Teresa Pelegri present a humorous, warm-hearted film similar to *Guess Who's Coming to Dinner* and *Meet the Parents*. In the opening frames, a Palestinian academic Rafi (Toledo) and Leni (Aguilera), his bright Jewish fiancée, prepare to meet Leni's family in Madrid. But not before they make love inside an elevator. "Remind me why we are together," purrs Leni. "We love each other and we don't care what people think," Rafi answers. Still, he wants to impress Leni's mother, but his suitcase is a mess because at the airport in Tel Aviv he was harassed by an Israeli security guard.

Cut to Leni introducing Rafi to her loveable, loony family; they reminded me of the likeable Arab-American family in *American Dreamz*. Her mother's unhappy because Leni's sister sleeps around and her brother is a religious zealot. Unbeknownst to Rafi, the family thinks he's a nice Jewish boy—Leni didn't warn her parents that Rafi is Palestinian. "I wanted them to judge you without prejudice," she says. But when Leni's mother (Aleandro) finds out Rafi's real roots, she goes into shock and chaos ensues. "The Palestinians kill the Jews." "The Jews kill the Palestinians." Their relationship will never work. Mother warns daughter: "Any baby you have will have to blow itself up." Leni's brother suspects Rafi is a terrorist; her grandfather boasts about killing Arabs. Anxious Rafi's a mess. He accidentally drops a brick of frozen soup out of the flat's seventh-story window, injuring Leni's father down below. Next, Rafi and Leni's sister dance seductively to the music of Amr Diab. Jealous, Leni becomes furious and she and Rafi argue. They decide the marriage won't work; they go their separate ways. Not for long. Seconds later, they laugh, kiss and make up. Will their wedding take place in a mosque or a synagogue? Does it matter?

Rafi reminds me of *Party Girl's* (1995) Mustafa, the Lebanese teacher-lover. And in *Casino Royale* (2006), the offscreen boyfriend of the British protagonist (Eva Green) is a "French-Algerian."

OUT OF REACH *(2004) Franchise; D: Po-Chih Leong SP: Trevor Miller A: Steven Seagal, Matt Schulze, Murat Yilmaz* **CAMEO, TURKS-AS-SHEIKHS**
Seagal crushes an Eastern European human-trafficking network in Poland. Who's in charge of this slavery operation? Who gives orders to kidnap, hold hostage, and sell young girls to high bidders? Two Arabic-speaking Turks (Schulze, Yilmaz), that's who.

PARADISE NOW *(2005) Augustus Film, dis. by Warner Independent; D, SP: Hany Abu-Assad SP: Bero Beyer, Pierre Hodgson A: Kais Nashef, Ali Suliman* PALESTINIANS, CHAMPIONS, RECOMMENDED

In 2002, the Academy of Motion Picture Arts and Sciences would not accept the nomination of Elia Suleiman's compelling film *Divine Intervention* for its Best Foreign Film award. Although *Intervention* had received several overseas awards, the Academy refused to consider it because it originated from a country not formally recognized by the United Nations. Four years later, Hany Abu-Assad's *Paradise Now* (winner of the Golden Globe Award and Independent Spirit Award for Best Foreign Film), a movie that also highlights the plight of Palestinians living under Israeli occupation, received a green light for an Oscar nomination. Thanks to an excellent cast and the fine co-writing and direction of Abu-Assad, this made-in-Nablus film makes visible the humanity of Palestinians. His Palestinian suicide bombers are flesh-and-blood human beings. As *New York Times* critic Stephen Holden explains, these humane images may "offend some viewers [because] demons make more convenient villains than complicated people with their complicated motives... Especially after 9/11, it is easier for some in the United States to imagine a suicide bomber as a soulless, robotic shell of a person programmed to wreak destruction." *Los Angeles Times* critic Kenneth Turan agrees: "We care about these two men. Even though we disagree with their motives, we understand the hopelessness of their lives." *Paradise Now* is all the more powerful, says Rob Lowman, because the director presents the two men as "products of the tragedy of the Middle East. That they are shown to be human doesn't make their intended act less horrific." The film refuses "to take sides, not even by as much as a wink." By refusing to advance Hollywood's "demon" stereotypes of Palestinians the film helps illuminate the darkness.

The Israeli-born Palestinian director told *Cineaste*: "The majority of people have one or two views on the suicide bombers: either the bombers are criminals or super-heroes. My film is about destroying those prevailing perceptions, [and] building new perceptions." Which he does: He shows us that there are no "typical suicide bombers. They can be poor, rich, educated, and illiterate. They can be anything." Set in Nablus, the West Bank, this taut drama traces 48 hours in the lives of two men, Said (Nashef) and

Khaled (Suliman). They behave and react as ordinary young people. Often, their radical political beliefs and their humanity collide. One may die, the other may not. These Palestinian young men, best friends since childhood, are not religious fanatics. We see them hanging out together, praying devoutly. They work in an auto repair shop, smoke a water pipe, enjoy home-cooked meals, drink Turkish coffee, place too many spoons of sugar into a cup of tea (a Nablus custom), tell jokes, flirt with women, and enjoy Arab music. Both men have doubts about killing themselves and Israelis; they seriously question whether they'll be "heroes in heaven," whether virgins and angels will really be greeting them in the "glorious hereafter."

The story unfolds at the auto shop where the two men work. Said meets the attractive peacenik Suha (Azabal), who has only recently returned to Nablus, and falls in love. She and Said drive into town to get Said's watch fixed. At the shop, scores of videos fill the shelves—videos of Palestinian martyrs and of collaborators. Said, whose father was executed as an Israeli collaborator, is shocked by the crude, commercial display of death-for-sale videos. Later Suha argues passionately against Said and Khaled going on a suicide mission: "There are other ways to keep the cause alive." Said objects: "You [only] feel the occupation. We sense the oppression... Life here is like life imprisonment... life without dignity is worthless." Said's despair is echoed by Abu-Assad, who told *Cineaste*: "To live as a Palestinian is to live in constant humiliation. Daily life is miserable." Suha continues to counter Said's arguments, and her passionate voice serves as the director's moral and emotional grounding wire. "Women," says Abu-Assad, "have more reasonable thoughts about killing. In matters of life and death, women are more compassionate. They care more about life; they have made life. They have carried life inside them." Suha, who is linked with a human rights organization, continues to argue that terrorism and suicide bombing are immoral. "What happens to those left behind?" she asks. Her probing questions point to the sorrow of the survivors and the violent fallout that always follows the suicide bombings: "Revenge begetting revenge that will further oppress Palestinians...Don't give the Israelis an excuse to keep on killing us," pleads Suha.

In the end, Khaled tries to stop Said from carrying out his attack. "Suha was right," argues Khaled, "we won't win this way." Said ignores his friend's impassioned plea and, armed with explosives, he crosses the border from the West Bank into Israel. He sits passively on a crowded Tel Aviv bus. Several close-ups reveal Said's friends and family. Cut to Said on the bus, which is filled with soldiers and civilians. The camera's lens tightens on Said's eyes. Silence. A white flash. And the credits roll.

Initially, *Paradise* was ignored by commercial Israeli distributors and its reception among Palestinians was equally lukewarm. Some Palestinians were unhappy because the film offered a less than valedictory portrayal of suicide bombers. Israeli critics disagreed on the movie's message and impact. Yossi Zur, whose 16-year-old son Asaf was killed by a suicide bomber, wrote: The film is a "dangerous piece of work. Awarding a [Golden Globe to] a movie such as *Paradise Now* only implicates Hollywood... in the evil chain of terror that attempts to justify those horrific acts." Journalist Uri Avnery counters that what should be remembered about this film is that everything "begins with the [Israeli] occupation, everything ends with the occupation... the film prompts us to think about a solution that will cause the youths to turn in a different direction." We need, writes Avnery, "a solution that will put an end to the humiliation, to the crushing of personal and national dignity, to the destitution and hopelessness."

Abu-Assad's three Palestinian protagonists (as well as the film's other Palestinians) are different from each other, and they are not primarily freedom fighters or pacifists or terrorists: they are human beings, with all the faults, excesses, ideals, and pain people carry. This compelling film enables us to see the tragedy and violence of Palestinian humanity under occupation. Viewers are not asked to choose sides, but rather to choose humanity.

Two other must-see movies showing how Palestinians cope with the Israeli occupation are Abu-Assad's *Rana's Wedding* (2002) and the powerful *Private* (2004), a brilliant Italian independent film by Saverio Costanzo (see their listings). Also of interest is the the British TV docudrama *Hamburg Cell* (2004), about the events leading up to the 9/11 attacks. The action focuses on a cell of Muslim revolutionaries in Germany a few years before the Twin Towers are brought down. "Told with objectivity and unrelenting tension," the film does not "demonize the men who committed this most heinous crime," in the words of critic Ray Bennet. Viewers see the attackers at the airports, but the camera never shows them on the planes, killing crew members and passengers. Several key scenes remind us of "how evidence of the impending assault was overlooked and how warnings of the dangers were not heeded." To date, *Hamburg Cell* is not available on DVD.

See "An Interview with Hany Abu-Assad," by Dan Georgakas and Barbara Saltz in *Cineaste* Winter 2005; Rob Lowman's review in Ventura's *Daily News* 21 March 2006; Stephen Holden's *New York Times* review, 28 October 2005; Uri Avnery's op-ed on *Munich* and *Paradise Now*, "Shall We Not Revenge," 4 February 2006 (bestcyrano.org/avneryParadiseNow.htm); Yossi Zur's op-ed, "Award for Film Implicates Hollywood in Killing," *Arkansas Democrat Gazette* 29 January 2006. *See also* Ray Bennett's review of *Hamburg Cell* in the *Hollywood Reporter* 31 August 2004.

PARIS, JE T'AIME *(2006) Victories International; D: Gurinder Chadha (and others) SP: Paul Mayeda Berges, Gurinder Chadha; A: Leila Bekhdi, Salah Teskouk, Cyril Descours* **CHAMPIONS, RECOMMENDED**

This romantic French movie contains segments by 21 different filmmakers. My comments focus on Gurinder Chadha's "Quais de Seine." Chadha is the Indian–British director of *Bend It Like Beckham* (2002), so not surprisingly, her pitch-perfect lighthearted segment reveals and debunks the idiocy of religious and racial stereotyping. Opening frames show three young men lounging on a park bench, harassing several attractive girls who wear revealing garb as they walk by. Observing the boys' offensive behavior is Zarka (Bekhdi), a nice-looking Arab Muslim girl in jeans and a black head scarf. When Zarka trips and falls to the ground, two boys laugh. But François (Descours), the quiet youth, rushes to her side, picks up her books and helps her put her head scarf back on. Note their dialogue:

> FRANÇOIS: You have beautiful hair. Why do you have to cover it up?
> ZARKA: I don't have to—I chose to.
> FRANÇOIS: Too bad; you're so pretty.

ZARKA: You mean I'm not beautiful in my hijab....When I wear this I feel a part of a faith, an identity. I feel good. That's what beauty is.

Zarka excuses herself and heads toward the neighborhood mosque. When François follows her, the others shout, "You into brown girls, now?" And "Fool, you touch her and Osama will personally bomb your ass."

Nevertheless, outside the mosque, François patiently waits for Zarka. She appears with her grandfather (Teskouk) at her side. Zarka introduces her grandfather to François: "This is the boy who helped me." When the grandfather walks off with Zarka, it seems François has struck out. But then the grandfather looks back and asks François to walk with them. He decides the boy, who is a history student, might be an acceptable friend, after all. "Learning history is very important," he says. "My Zarka wants to be a journalist, for *Le Monde*. She wants to write about France, her France. God willing, Inshallah!" Repeats Zarka, "Inshallah!" The movie's final frames offer fleeting images of all segments: the smiling Zarka, another girl, and François are together.
Note: Throughout, Zarka and her grandfather speak perfect French.

THE POINT MEN *(2001) Carousel Pictures; D: John Glen SP: Steven Hartov, Ripley Highsmith A: Vincent Regan* **PALESTINIANS, WORST LIST**
This made-in-Israel film was released in the US three weeks before 9/11. It shows heroic Israelis bringing down Palestinian "terrorists." The main villain is a Palestinian, Amar Kamil (Regan); he shoots dead Israeli agents and Americans, and after seducing a kind blond woman, kills her. Kamil goes on to murder his nurse and a plastic surgeon. At the end, just as Kamil is about to kill his half-brother, an Israeli agent appears and kills Kamil instead.

PRETTY PERSUASION *(2005) Samuel Goldwyn; D: Marcos Siega SP: Skander Halim A: Adi Schnall, Evan Rachel Wood, Ron Livingston* **MAIDENS, PALESTINIANS, WORST LIST**
At a posh private high school in Beverly Hills, the lying and conniving 15-year-old sophomore Kimberly (Wood) manipulates classmates, one of whom is the new student, Randa (Schnall), a

mostly silent and not-so-bright Palestinian girl who wears the hijab. Kimberly demeans all things Arab, telling Randa: There are just too many "worthless, annoying people on this planet... I have respect for all races but I'm very glad I was born white because as a woman it's the very best race." And, when it comes to ranking races "my very last choice would be an Arab... what's that thing on your head? You haven't tried to bomb anybody, have you?" Next, Kimberly tells Randa this filthy "joke," twice:

KIMBERLY: How does an Arab man get his wife pregnant?
RANDA: (*Looks confused.*)
KIMBERLY: She gets naked and lies down on the bed. He jerks off on the wall and they let the flies do the rest.
RANDA: (*Laughs.*)
KIMBERLY: Don't laugh—it's insulting to your people.

When Kimberly asks Randa what the greatest thing is about America, Randa says, "Sylvester Stallone!" Next, Kimberly's male friend mocks Randa: You're "the Arab [terrorist] chick... you want to buy a gun?" Says Kimberly: "Randa's from the Middle East. She doesn't say much, though." In spite of all Kimberly's slurs, Randa tells her: "I am most fortunate to have met you." Later, Kimberly teaches Randa all about lesbians and pornography and persuades Randa to lodge false complaints of sexual abuse against their English teacher, Percy Anderson (Livingston). Early on, the teacher vowed to fail Randa unless her compositions improved; he also complained that she and other teens, the children of wealthy immigrants, were infiltrating the school. He especially objected to those wearing "a piece of cloth" on their heads. Josh, a Jewish student, also belittles Randa. "Show me where Palestine is," he says to her, holding open a reference book. "There never has been and there never will be a country called Palestine." No one ever defends Randa or contests Josh's lie.

School officials eventually find out that the girls lied about being sexualy abused. Randa's father screams: "You've brought shame on this family." Her mother is silent. Randa returns to the school, enters a room, and writes in Arabic on the blackboard: "We are all sinners." Then she takes out a gun and commits suicide. The tragedy of the film is that instead of portraying Randa as a victim, the producers present her as a shallow, dense Muslim teenager not deserving of our sympathy—a reel stereotypical suicidal Palestinian Muslim. Film critic Scott Weinberg mistakenly referred to Randa as a shy "Hindu" girl.

PRIVATE *(2004) Istituto Luce; D, SP: Saverio Costanzo SP: Camilla Costanzo A: Mohammed Bakri* **PALESTINIANS, CHAMPIONS, RECOMMENDED**

This brilliant and compelling Italian independent film about the Palestinian–Israeli conflict is directed and scripted by Saverio Costanzo and co-written by his wife Camilla. The film projects images that viewers almost never see—the suffering and pain of decent Palestinian civilians who are forced to live under occupation. In the opening frames, Israeli soldiers invade and occupy the home of the Palestinian protagonist, Mohammad (Bakri). Without warning, gruff, armed soldiers barge into Mohammad's house and terrorize and threaten him and his family. Next, they take over the entire second floor. They force the family to live downstairs, in cramped quarters without adequate bedding. Should the Palestinians dare venture upstairs, they'll be punished, severely.

Not all the soldiers are one-dimensional villains; some question whether their ruthless actions are necessary. Both Israelis and Palestinians are presented as victims of fixed, preestablished stereotypes. Several night scenes are especially moving and, at times, uncomfortable to watch. Mohammad, his wife, and five children must sleep in a small, single room without electricity. Frightened, they huddle together, trying to rest on the floor. Israeli soldiers repeatedly threaten to evict Mohammad and his loved ones, but he will not leave. Credit Saverio and Camilla Costanzo for showing that both reel Israelis and reel Palestinians are victims of stereotyping, viewing one another through clouded lenses. *Private* is also an uplifting drama that tenderly and compassionately projects Palestinian love: love of land, love between husband and wife, love that binds parents and children. Unfortunately, *Private* has received limited distribution in the US.

PROMISED LAND *(2004) Agav Hafakot (Israeli); D, SP: Amos Gitai SP: Marie-Jose Sanselme A: Rosamund Pike, Anne Parillaud, Hanna Schygulla* **BEDOUIN, VILLAINS, NS**

Arabs as slavers, again: Amos Gitai's film projects crude Bedouin baddies kidnapping eight Estonian women whom they smuggle across the Sinai desert with their camel caravan. The Bedouin intend to sell the women to an international network engaged in prostitute trafficking. As the women cling together for sanity and survival, the Russians and Arabs chitchat. Not surprisingly, there's a rape scene. And the Estonian women are sold on the auction block. When a van unloads the captive women at what looks like a brothel, for some inexplicable reason terrorists suddenly attack.

See the IMDB review by butchins1, 31 October 2004.

RANA'S WEDDING *(Another Day in Jerusalem) (2002) Palestine Film Foundation; D: Hany Abu-Assad SP: Liana Badr, Ihab Lamey A: Clara Khoury, Khalifa Natour* **PALESTINIANS, CHAMPIONS, RECOMMENDED**
Hany Abu-Assad's *Wedding* is one of my favorite movies. It was filmed on location, on both sides of the armed border separating Jerusalem and Ramallah. The story begins one morning when an independent, spunky seventeen-year-old, Rana (Khoury) suddenly decides she wants to marry Khalil (Natour), a theater director. But Rana has only several hours in which to find Khalil, get his approval (this, she quickly does), and then pull off the wedding. Rana and Khalil speed off in a yellow VW in search of the other key players. But several border roadblocks stop them cold. The border scenes, especially, show the distrust and hostility with which Israeli guards view Palestinians. When Rana's cell phone beeps, Israeli soldiers point their guns at her. They think she's hidden a bomb inside her bag, so they bring in a remote-controlled device to blow it up. Their search takes time, and Rana's time is running out—she has only a few hours before the 4 o'clock deadline. Can she manage to locate the registrar and her father, find a wedding dress, get her hair fixed, and then gather all the family together to celebrate the wedding? Throughout, we witness scenes of the Palestinian dilemma, the state of siege Palestinians daily endure: military checkpoints; security cameras; uniformed, armed soldiers; a sad, silent Palestinian funeral procession; boys throwing rocks and firebombs; an Israeli soldier wounding, perhaps killing, a boy; a bulldozer demolishing a home. At the same time, Rana is a typical love-struck teenager—mature at times, pouting like a child at others. Eventually, Rana's wedding does

take place—next to a roadblock, inside an orange mini-van. No matter. She, Khalil, and the wedding guests dance to upbeat Arab music.

Abu-Assad's film "doesn't preach; it simply observes," writes critic Roger Ebert. "It gives a more complete visual picture of the borders, the Palestinian settlements and the streets of Jerusalem than we ever see on the news, and we understand that the Palestinians are not all suicide bombers living in tents, as the news sometimes seems to imply." Life in the occupied territories is "like water torture," continues Ebert, "breaking down Palestinians a drop at a time, reminding them that having lived in this place for a long time, they are nevertheless homeless." Though Warner Independent distributes *Paradise Now*, no major studio has backed *Rana's Wedding*. Fortunately, Seattle's Arab Film Distribution (www.arabfilm.org) distributes the movie.

See Ebert's *Chicago Tribune* review, 30 January 2004.

THE RECRUIT *(2003) Touchstone; D: Roger Donaldson SP: Roger Towne, Kurt Wimmer, Mitch Glazer A: Bridget Moynahan* ARAB-AMERICAN, CHAMPIONS, RECOMMENDED
The female protagonist in this CIA spy thriller is a loyal, intelligent Arab American, Layla (Moynahan). Layla's heroics are displayed, especially, during final frames, when she collars a corrupt CIA agent and saves her lover-colleague's life. Still, the movie promotes a common misconception: Although Layla is said to have Algerian roots, she does not speak Arabic, but Farsi, the language of Iran.

RED MERCURY *(2005) Inspired Movies; D: Roy Battersby SP: Farrukh Dhondy A: Stockard Channing, Alex Caan, Asif Chowdry, San Sella, Shiv Grewa* VILLAINS, WORST LIST
This low-budget terrorist drama—the first British feature film about a fictional Islamic terrorist attack on London—was released soon after the city's tragic July 7, 2005 bombings, which caused the deaths of 52 commuters and 4 suicide bombers. Screenwriter Farrukh Dhondy fails to offer complex portraits of his Muslim characters; though they have diverse backgrounds, he projects them as one-dimensional villains. In the movie's opening frames, the film's dark-complexioned villains Asif (Chowdry), Shahid (Sella), and their leader, Mushtaq, examine a powerful Russian-

produced explosive element—Red Mercury. Suddenly, the police arrive and the men rush out the door. They move to a central London restaurant, the Olympus Grill. Here, they hold hostage and harass the patrons and the restaurant owner, Penelope (Channing). They threaten to unleash their dirty bomb which would kill scores of civilians. Outside, the police discuss how best to go about freeing the hostages without casualties. At the end, the dark-complexioned evildoers are brought down and the hostages freed.

See "Born on the Seventh of July," *Times* (London) 25 August 2005.

RENDITION *(2007) New Line Cinema; D: Gavin Hood SP: Kelley Sane A: Reese Witherspoon, Meryl Streep, Omar Metwally, Alan Arkin, Jake Gyllenhaal, Igal Naor, Peter Sarsgaard, Zineb Oukach, Moa Khouas*

CHAMPIONS, VILLAINS, ARAB-AS-VICTIM, RECOMMENDED

This timely, evenhanded, and honorable movie shows what happens when governments kidnap and abuse innocent people. The film reflects what Army Brigadier General Patrick Finnegan said to producers of the TV series *24*: In real life, "torture backfires." Opening frames of *Rendition* reveal the bright, American-educated Anwar el-Ibrahimi (Metwally) about to depart Cape Town for his Chicago home. As the Egyptian-born chemical engineer leaves to board his plane, his hosts compliment him: "It was an honor to have you, Anwar. Your presentation was outstanding."

Back in Chicago, Anwar's pregnant American wife, Isabella (Witherspoon), plays soccer with their son while Anwar's mother sits nearby, watching. This is a reel happy family.

Cut to a busy square in a mythical Arab country, where a suicide bomber attacks, with explosion that kills one CIA agent and nearly 100 Arabs, mostly "women and children." Acting on a hunch, CIA head Corrinne Whitman (Streep) has Anwar kidnapped when his plane stops in Washington, DC. His name is deleted from the plane's passenger list. He has become a victim of "extraordinary rendition," the government's moving of suspected terrorists to undisclosed foreign locations, where they can be tortured. Whitman doesn't care about hard evidence, or that Anwar passed the polygraph test; she wants vengeance, not justice—Anwar is guilty until proved innocent.

Anwar's torturer is Abasi (Naor), an Arab official who cooperates with Whitman. Frames reveal bloodied, naked, gagged, hooded Anwar being abused, brutally, again and again. The torture images are frighteningly realistic and can't help but trigger associations with Abu Ghraib and Gitmo. Anwar insists he is innocent, saying: "I have lived in the states for 20 years; I graduated from NYU; please let me call my wife." Enter the "good" CIA agent, Douglas Freeman (Gyllenhaal). He tells Whitman to stop the torture. "You're new at this," she says. "This is my first time," admits Freeman. "The United States does not torture," purrs Whitman. Later, Freeman, reflecting the movie's theme, tells an official, "The more people you torture the more enemies you create." But no government official—Whitman or Abasi—wants Anwar to be tried in a American court of law.

Throughout, the camera cuts back and forth to related story lines: We see Abasi with his wife and family; he is a strict, but caring, parent. He loves his runaway daughter, Fatima (Oukach), who unbeknownst to him is having a secret love affair with Khalid (Khouas), an Islamic radical. Khalid has become a reel terrorist because the police, under Abasi's supervision, tortured and then killed his brother.

Back in the states, Isabella seeks help from her political friend in DC, Alan Smith (Sarsgaard), who arranges a meeting for her with US Senator Hawkins (Arkin). But both men refuse to assist her. Why? They fear their political careers will end if they are perceived as being being soft on terrorism; they don't want to be known as "bin Laden lovers."

In the end, the film provides answers to several key issues: What happens to Isabella, her children, and Anwar? Is Anwar a real victim, or do we doubt his innocence as we doubt Gabe Hassan's innocence in *Civic Duty* (2006)? What about Freeman and Whitman—who wins the ideological struggle? Does Abasi find and rescue Fatima from the radicals? And what happens to Khalid and his fellow terrorists?

Rendition is another important post–9/11 movie to offer evenhanded portraits of Americans and Arabs, especially the film's Arab women. This must-see movie warns that fear and the war on terror have changed governments and human behavior worldwide, whether we live in Chicago or Cairo—and not for the better.

SAHARA *(2005) PAR; D: Breck Eisner SP: Thomas Dean Donnelly, Joshua Oppenheimer, John C. Richards, James V. Hart B: Clive Cussler A: Matthew McConoughey, Lambert Wilson* **CHAMPIONS**

In this movie, which was filmed in Morocco, the protagonist, Pitt (McConoughey), comes across a missing Civil War battleship, the lost "Ship of Death." He uncovers a gold mine manned by slaves, and he prevents a worldwide plague. And, he brings down a blood-thirsty West African dictator and a French industrialist (Wilson) whose nuclear waste plant is poisoning the planet's ecosystem. Surprisingly, in the end, desert nomads rescue the protagonists. Explains director Breck Eisner: "I didn't want it to be that Americans come in and simply save the day." In Clive Cussler's book, *Sahara*, American, and UN troops help the heroes.

SCARY MOVIE 4 *(2006) Miramax; D: David Zucker SP: Craig Mazins, Jim Abrahams, Pat Proft A: Tony Al, Leslie Nielsen* **CAMEO, VILLAINS**

Midway into the film the producers spoof a scene from Spielberg's *War of the Worlds*. Evil Martians invade earth and everything electronic stops working. Cut to an auto garage: A swarthy, big, bearded, black-haired, wild-eyed Ali (Al) charges into innocent bystanders. Dynamite is strapped all over his torso. He shouts with a thick Arab accent, "Death to America!" The crazed Arab goes to push the detonator button—but it's electronic, so it doesn't work. Cut to the crowd of red-blooded Americans. They pummel Ali to the ground. The scene lasts thirteen seconds. Viewers may leave the theater believing everything movies and TV newscasts told them about Arabs is true: They're dangerous, they're insane, they're stupid, they're ultimately pathetic and laughable, and they're everywhere. And we Americans can easily put them out of business. That's a lot to accomplish in thirteen seconds of screen time.

Closing frames reveal the US president (Nielsen) at the UN. Cut to several Arab diplomats with huge red fezzes and large multicolored head dresses. Cut to two bearded Iranian diplomats in gray turbans. The camera closes in on a silent woman clad in black, sitting behind the Iranians. Suddenly—the diplomats are naked! Two Arabs and one Iranian rush toward the exit. The US president throws a punch, flooring the turbaned Iranian.

SECONDHAND LIONS *(2004) Touchstone; D, SP: Tim McCanlies; A: Michael Caine, Robert Duvall, Haley Joel Osment, Emmanuelle Vaugier, Adam Ozturk,* **CAMEOS, SHEIKHS, MAIDENS, WORST LIST**
In *Lions*, desert dwellers appear as buffoonish villains. Filmed in swashbuckling comic-book style, this is a warm-hearted family film. The action occurs in a 1960s Texas farmhouse. An unwanted boy, Walter (Osment), is taken in by his Uncles Garth (Caine) and Hub (Duvall). Suddenly, midway through this tale the plot shifts from Texas to far-off Arabia. Walter finds out that way back in 1914 his great uncles were shanghaied into the French Foreign Legion. Cut to the North African desert. When nasty Arabs surface, the uncles bring down the "Arab horde," slicing up and shooting dead scores of dark-skinned, mustached Moroccans. Uncle Hub fights "like 20 men" and also liberates captive veiled women, notably the lovely, silent Yasmine (Vaugier), "the most beautiful woman he had ever seen." But Yasmine has been promised to a stupid, lecherous sheikh (Ozturk). She tries to escape the ruler's grasp, but he nabs and imprisons her in his harem. Desperate, Yasmine places a knife to her throat: she would rather die than wed the sheikh. In time, Hub rescues her. As Hub cuts down the sheikh's men, the harem maidens cheer him on. The angry sheikh offers a reward for Hub's head—"10,000 pieces of gold." But Hub and Garth manage to kill even more Arabs—and then they dupe the stupid sheikh into giving *them* all the reward money!

Back in Texas, Hub tells young Walter: "People are basically good. Good always triumphs over evil; remember that." In *Lions*, "good" Texans triumph over "evil" Arabs. The uncle's farm animals—an aging lion, one pig, one chicken, and four dogs—come off better than the Arabs.

THE SENTINEL *(2006) TCF; D: Clark Johnson SP: George Nolfi B: Gerald Petievich A: Raoul Braneja* **ARAB AMERICAN, RECOMMENDED**
One Secret Service agent who protects the president is an Arab American, Aziz Hassad (Braneja). Near the end, Aziz and his fellow agents shoot it out against assassins trying to kill the president. (The Aziz character reflects reality; I have an Arab-American friend whose son is a real Secret Service agent, assigned to the White House.)

SINBAD: LEGEND OF THE SEVEN SEAS *(2003) Dream-Works Animated; D: Patrick Gilmore, Tim Johnson SP: John Logan*

SINS OF OMISSION

As a child, I enjoyed going to the movies and watching 1940s *Arabian Nights* tales that featured dashing Arab heroes like Aladdin, Ali Baba, and Sinbad the Sailor. Sixty years later, DreamWorks's animated *Sinbad* should have been titled *Homer: Legend of the Seven Seas*, for all the reference it makes to Arab culture.

Before the film's animation process began I wrote several letters to producer Jeffrey Katzenberg, encouraging him to consider bringing me on as a consultant, as he had with *The Prince of Egypt*. All that came of it was that a few months before the film's release he arranged for me and my daughter Michele to view a polished rough cut at DreamWorks. Afterward in his office, he asked my opinion of the nearly finished film. All things Arab were omitted, I said—there isn't even Arab music. I expressed disappointment, because the movie had failed to project Sinbad and his crew as they are—fictional, courageous Arabian heroes. I asked Katzenberg to consider making, before the final cut, a few changes that would not take much time or cost much. Just have Sinbad utter a phrase or two in Arabic, I said. And, when Sinbad romances the heroine have him recite one brief, fitting Arab proverb. I also mentioned that the animators might place a fez or two on the heads of Sinbad's crew. Such minor modifications, I explained, might enable some young viewers to perceive Sinbad as a reel Arab champion. Katzenberg listened attentively, saying they would certainly try and do "something." The next day, Michele and I sent three Arab proverbs to Sinbad's co-producer Mireille Soria. Soria thanked us, then went on to say that she was sorry, that although my suggested changes and the proverbs were "wonderful" ideas, Sinbad's animators "were too far along in production" to add any new dialogue or red fezzes.

Katzenberg's *Sinbad* should be relegated to Ali Baba's cave, permanently. The film distorts cinema history and classic *Arabian Nights* folk tales, as well. Screenwriter John Logan, who omits all things Arab in *Sinbad* did write Arab slavers into *Gladiator*, a DreamWorks movie that has nothing to do with the Middle East.

THE SITUATION *(2006) Red Wine Pictures; D: Philip Haas SP: Wendell Steavenson A: Connie Nielsen, Damian Lewis, Mido Hamada, Said Hamada, Said Amadis, Nasser Memarzia, Mahmoud El Lozy, John Slattery, Tom McCarthy* **VILLAINS, CHAMPIONS, EVENHANDED**
Credit Philip Haas for an intelligent first-of-its-kind Iraqi war drama, shot in Morocco in 2003, as Iraq was beginning to crumble. As early as 2003, Haas knew Iraq was in constant turmoil, that the US could not win the war, and that the situation on the ground would lead to even more casualties, injuring GIs and Iraqis and other civilians alike. There are good things to say about this independent film. Director Haas utilizes the talents of several fine Arab-American actors, perhaps the most ever to appear in an American feature film. Each performer excels; speaking English and Arabic, they portray diverse, well-defined characters—from mothers to warlords to journalists. The sensitive, stark screenplay by journalist Wendell Steavenson is first-rate; she based it on her experiences in the region. Connie Nielsen and Mido Hamada deliver memorable performances as, respectively, Anna, a blond US journalist honestly concerned about the fate of decent Iraqi families, and her colleague, a talented photojournalist. The director's powerful images and Steavenson's potent dialogue—"There is no law in Iraq"—present us with stark realities about the war.

In spite of such strengths, however, *The Situation* is more noble than engaging. Made of three interrelated stories, the film tries to explore too many complex, topical issues at too fast a pace. The movie reminded me of trying to read and comprehend the meaning of a barrage of newspaper headlines, blended together in a large bundle. Important stuff, yes, but too much cutting back and forth for one sitting. I also had difficulty identifying and empathizing with the major players, as they kept coming and going so quickly. Each locale—Baghdad, Samarra, al-Tawr village, and the US embassy—presents old characters and introduces new ones. Iraqi feuds and American incompetence trigger rapid montages of murder, conflicting loyalties, cultural barriers, even love affairs. Frames confuse rather than enlighten.

For example, continuity is shattered when the camera dwells too long on Anna's unresolved personal problem: does it matter, really, whether she romances Dan (Lewis), a CIA agent, or Zaid, the handsome photographer with a US passport? Portraits—like the war itself—are mixed; many are tainted with violence. Nearly everyone in this film is ruthless, inept, ignorant, or corrupt. Dan's superior warns him: "The [Iraqi] terrorists are arming themselves with the supplies that we [the US] are sending." Yet, to appease Iraqi warlords and thieves, Dan forks over lucrative contracts and cash to Iraqi opportunists who belong in jail, not on the US embassy's payroll. A few frames show, briefly, American brutality. Our GIs beat up and toss two innocent Iraqi boys over a bridge, where one drowns. Later, at night, our troops set off an explosion, and barge into an Iraqi family's home, terrorizing the occupants. The US response to such brutality and to Iraqi infighting is oversimplified and not fair; we act like reel dolts. Often, we see unemployed Iraqi thugs and Iraqis in police uniforms killing each other; one even guns down his peace-loving relative. Mothers and daughters grieve. We see too little of innocent, moderate Iraqis, those who are forced "to choose sides." Should they be for or against the Americans? Which insurgent group should they favor? Which one will best protect them and their families? No matter the decision, the Iraqi seeking peace is the loser. Best reflecting this film's valiant thought-provoking thesis, which is even more relevant today than it was in 2003, is a reel Iraqi, asking: "Who is responsible for the crimes of the occupier?" Iraqis, Americans, or both?

See Ronnie Scheib's *Variety* review, 30 October 2006.

SOLDIER OF GOD *(2005) Anthem; D: David Hogan SP: Mir Bahmanyar, Kathryn Kuhlen A: Tim Abel, William Mendieta, Mapi Galan, Nicholas Kadi* **CHAMPIONS, VILLAINS**
The Holy Land, 1187 AD: A gory battle between Christian knights and the Saracens. Dead bodies fill the screen. From here on, this talky film dwells on three key players: Rene (Abel), a Knight Templar; Hasan (Mendieta), an Arab Muslim; and the peace-loving Soheila (Galan), who strives to alter the men's war-like behavior. Inside her tent, Soheila shows kindness to both Rene and Hasan; she provides warm hospitality to all who enter, including a Jewish merchant and several Arabs who hate Christians. At times, the protagonists set aside religious differences and bond. Rene and Hasan pray, respectfully, and they go on to save each other's lives.

Unfortunately, the script does not allow actor Tim Abel, who plays Rene, to speak; he's silent most of the time. When he does say something, I couldn't understand him.

Unexpectedly and illogically, closing frames shatter the film's thesis. Muslim no longer respects Christian, and vice versa. Rene exhibits irrational behavior. When the knight, Hasan, and Soheila are attacked, for example, Rene becomes brutally violent. In his rage, he wields his bloodied sword, over and over again, chomping his enemies to bits and accidentally killing lovely Soheila and almost killing Hasan, as well. The Arab's respect for Rene crumbles. "This land is not a paradise," says Hasan, before he rides off. "It is hell, and I fear it always will be." In spite of its promising beginning, in the end, *Soldier* makes no sense, despite the fine camera work and outstanding score.

SORRY, HATERS *(2006) IFC; D, SP: Jeff Stanzler A: Robin Wright Penn, Abdellatif Kechiche* ARAB AMERICAN, ARAB-AS-VICTIM

In a New York City mosque, devout Muslims pray and generously reach into their pockets to assist Ashade (Kechiche), a bearded, kind-hearted Syrian-born cabbie with a Ph.D. in chemistry. Ashade struggles daily to earn enough money to support his brother's wife and child. One evening, he picks up a self-loathing career woman named Philly (Penn). He tells her all about his Syrian-born brother, his wife's husband, "a doctor, a holy man," and a Canadian citizen for ten years. My brother was mistakenly placed on an FBI list, Ashade tells her. He was changing planes at JFK when the FBI "took him to Guantanamo and then deported him to Syria where he is probably being tortured, maybe even killed." Philly becomes furious; she wants revenge on the US government. She urges Ashade to work with her, "to cause a little damage." Ashade refuses. But Philly won't give up; she continually torments Ashade, his brother's wife, and child. Near the end, Philly intentionally injures Ashade and family members, one fatally. Though the ending is sad, and Ashade suffers a great deal, he is one of post–9/11's reel decent Arab Muslims, a religious man of peace with integrity.

The DVD extras merit viewing. Film star Tim Robbins, for example, says that "Ashade is a refined person… It's very rare to see an Arab Muslim man being portrayed as a hard-working person, trying to make a better life for his family." "Never," agrees *Esquire's* Lisa Hintelmann. "I've never seen that in an American film." What happens to Ashade's reel brother bears a pointed resemblance to the June 2002 nabbing and deporting by US authorities of Maher Arar, a Canadian citizen of Syrian descent.

See DeWayne Wickham's essay in *USA Today* 26 September 2006.

SOUL PLANE *(2004) MGM; D: Jessy Terrero SP: Bo Zenga, Chuck Wilson A: Sayed Badreya* **CAMEO**

This raunchy comedy presents, briefly, a bearded "Middle East passenger" (Badreya) aboard a passenger jet. The white turbaned passenger takes his seat. Immediately, two female security guards plop down next to him, warning, "Osama, you go to the bathroom, we're going with you." But there's a happy ending, in which all the passengers dance—even "Osama." When he spins around, his white turban completely unravels. "This is a ball!" he shouts. The passengers panic, because they think he said "This is a bomb!"

SPARTAN *(2004) WB; D, SP: David Mamet A: Said Taghmaoui* **VILLAINS, SHEIKHS**

The main plot concerns corrupt politicians and their cohorts. The subplot reveals an international white-slavery ring, headquartered in Dubai. Villains kidnap and whisk off to Dubai several "blond [American] girls," including the US president's daughter. One key sex slaver is Tariq Asani (Taghmaoui), a Lebanese national just released from prison. Asani boasts to the reel American protagonist: When we reach "Dubai, I will give you many nice and smooth girls... not women, girls, all young, all blondes." Bang! Bang! The blondes are safe and Asani's shot dead.

Note: One of this film's producers is Elie Samaha, a Lebanese American.

SPY GAME *(2001) UNI; D: Tony Scott SP: Michael Frost Beckner, David Arata A: Robert Redford, Brad Pitt, Omid Djalili, Amidou* **VILLAINS, EVENHANDED**

This espionage thriller focuses on Nathan and Tom (Redford, Pitt), two CIA agents. For thirty minutes or so, we view their actions in

"war-torn Beirut, 1985." The agents' objective in Beirut is to eliminate Sheikh Salameh and his thugs before they launch a "major
attack in a civilian sector in West Beirut." Cut to silent Lebanese
villains entering an apartment complex. Cut to the agents trying
to convince a peaceful Lebanese doctor, Ahmed (Amidou), to help
them assassinate the violent sheikh. Ahmed is a humanitarian who
attends the sick and injured at a refugee camp; he detests violence.
But the agents try again. This time they show Ahmed some doc-
tored-up photographs of his dead parents, telling him the sheikh's
men did the killings. The reluctant Ahmed agrees to assist them,
asking Tom: "Is it hard to take a life?" Unexpectedly, an Arab suicide bomber lets loose powerful explosives. An entire apartment
block is leveled. Among the dead victims in the rubble: Ahmed, the
sheikh, and more than a hundred Lebanese civilians.

SPYMATE *(2006) Keystone Family Pictures; D, SP: Robert Vince SP:
Anna McRoberts, Anne Vince A: Mark Acheson, Pat Morita* **CAMEO,
VILLAINS, WORST LIST**
Need a reel grabber to hold the viewer's attention? Toss in a super-
agent chimp, like Minkey—he blows up Arabs! Opening frames
reveal the "Arabian Desert 1994." A lone, robed Arab treks across
the desert. The camera zooms in—surprise! It's not an Arab. It's
Minkey wearing Arab garb! Cut to reel Arabs speaking real Arabic
and mingling about their desert tents. The robed Minkey peers
into a tent where he sees a huge missile. Pan to the film's protagonist, bound and tied. Cut to the clad-in-black Arab terrorist
(Acheson) entering the tent, chuckling: "This missile will launch
and detonate as the world leaders are meeting for their peace summit." But just in time Minkey the Chimp floors the reel terrorist.
Another bearded Arab grabs his scimitar and attacks Minkey; they
duel. Minkey kisses the Arab on the lips, and then floors him. After
the primate frees the protagonist, they re-set the missile to explode
inside the tent. As they run off to safety, the camera reveals screaming, outraged Arabs on horseback trying in vain to catch up with
them. Cut to the missile blowing up all the desert tents and flames
filling the screen.

THE STONE MERCHANT *(2006) Martinelli Films; D: Renzo Martinelli SP: Corrado Calabrò A: Harvey Keitel, F. Murray Abraham, Jordi Molla, Jane March* **VILLAINS, WORST LIST**

Merchant is a post–9/11 film that advances the dangerous myth that Islam and fascism are one and the same. During the opening frames, stock footage shows Muslims killing innocent people in Somalia, while Professor Aleco (Molla), a handicapped teacher who lost both of his legs in an Arab terrorist attack, tells his college students that the country fell apart because "the Arabs arrived in Somalia with their money, their Quran schools." Instead of teaching Islam, he says, they taught young people "to hate." Flashback to terrorists blowing up a US embassy in Kenya, where 213 people die and Aleco loses his legs. Throughout, Professor Alceo tells everyone—his reel university students, the police, even his wife—that Islam threatens civilized Westerners, that Muslims are "in a religious war to conquer the world." All Muslims believe "terrorism is a religious duty," he preaches. When someone says, "not all Muslims are terrorists," Aleco barks back: "But almost all terrorists are Muslims." He warns, "they look like ordinary people… [yet] these terrorists are hidden in our midst." They are not "crazy, underprivileged elements of society." On TV, Aleco sees terrorists flying planes into the Twin Towers. Cut to a shoot-out at Rome's Fiumicino airport. Two silent, dark-complexioned Arab Muslims gun down civilians and nearly kill Aleco's wife, Leda (March). Hoping to forget about the attack, Leda and Aleco fly off to relax in Turkey. Upon arrival, the couple meet two terrorists pretending to be helpful, an Italian-Muslim gem merchant, Ludovico (Keitel), and Shahid (Abraham), a reel radical Muslim who "rouses mosque-goers to frenzied hatred of Christians." In a typical speech, Shahid says, "We must win everywhere! We must destroy the enemies of Islam! We must annihilate the enemies of Islam." Cut to footage showing a dark-skinned Arab cutting off a Somali's hand. A reporter says, "This kind of thing makes you want to throw up." After sly Ludovico seduces Leda, two Arab terrorists sneak into Aleco's home. Though handicapped, he is clever enough to hold the Arabs off and in time the police arrive, shooting the assassins dead. Though Ludovico loves Leda, his fellow fanatics convince him she should die. He and two Arab thugs plant a radioactive bomb inside a car that's loaded onto the same ferry Leda is taking to England. Cut to the Arabs shooting Ludovico dead. News reports reveal, "In Dover Harbor, a dirty bomb aboard a ferry enriched with radioactive material has exploded." Cut to Shahid, saying "The enemies of Allah are warned."

Then we are back in the classroom with Professor Aleco showing students stock footage of the 9/11 tragedy. He tells his class there's a real Islamic threat, that "only an Army of Christians can thwart the Muslim invasion. Islam," he says, "has renewed its march toward the West... not to understand this means not to understand history."

Everyone who participated in this sick movie should be ashamed of themselves. Especially disturbing are the performances of actors Jordi Molla and F. Murray Abraham. Molla's Aleco is one of movieland's reel dangerous racists. Abraham's Shahid is the worst post–9/11 reel bad Arab ever to surface on movie screens. Director Renzo and writer Corrado Calabrò should be billed as propagandists, not as moviemakers. They project all the film's reel dark Arab Muslims as scowling, bearded cutthroats. Their *Stone* will stand the test of time as one of cinema's most despicable, racist films; it should be studied in college cinema classes, worldwide, especially those focusing on film-as-hate-propaganda.

See Deborah Young's *Variety* review, 28 September 2006.

THE SUM OF ALL FEARS (2002) PAR; D: Phil Alden Robinson SP: Paul Attanasio, Daniel Pyne B: Tom Clancy A: Ben Affleck, Stefan Kalipha
CAMEO

In Thomas Harris's book *Black Sunday* and in Paramount's 1977 film of the same name, a reel Palestinian terrorist tries to explode a nuclear bomb at Miami's Super Bowl. In Tom Clancy's book, on which *The Sum of All Fears* is based, Arab terrorists actually infiltrate the US and set off a nuclear device at Denver's Super Bowl. When critic Michael Medved found out that *Sum's* reel bad movie villains were not Arabs but neo-Nazis, he complained about the switch. The book's "Islamic terrorists are largely realistic," writes Medved. The film's German neo-Nazis are "highly unrealistic." After all, says Medved, "Our enemies are Islamic." The critic fails to mention that Clancy's book has other villains—American Indians and former East Germans. In *Sum*, unsympathetic, not-so-bright Arabs play a minor role.

The opening frames show an Israeli pilot taking off with a nuclear bomb during the 1973 Arab–Israeli war. When his jet crashes into the Syrian desert, the bomb is buried in the sand. Fast forward 29 years. A dense Arab gravedigger (Kalipha) finds the unexploded weapon. Unaware it's a nuclear bomb, the Arab and his pals carelessly dump the weapon onto the back of a truck, intending to sell it. Cut to a suave arms merchant. The bomb's worth more than $1 million, but he dupes Arabs into accepting only $400. Later, the Arab who found the bomb becomes ill, and dies of radiation poisoning.

See "War Films, Hollywood and Popular Culture," *Imprimis* 34.5 (May 2005).

THE SYRIAN BRIDE *(2004) Eran Riklis Productions; D, SP: Eran Riklis SP: Suha Arraf A: Clara Khoury, Hiam Abbass, Makram Khoury, Ashraf Barhom, Eyad Sheety* **CHAMPIONS, RECOMMENDED**

Like *Rana's Wedding* and *Paradise Now*, *The Syrian Bride* offers memorable Arab portraits. All three movies were made not by Hollywood but by both Israeli and Arab crews. The director of *Bride*, Eran Riklis, is an Israeli; the screenplay is by Suja Arraf, a Palestinian. The film is set in a Golan Heights village and a remote border crossing. The bride-to-be, Mona (Khoury), plans to wed a likeable Syrian TV soap opera star. But border politics may prevent the marriage from taking place. Will Mona get the needed permission—from both sides—to cross from her home, the occupied Golan (Israel), into Syria? It's a catch-22: Syria says she's already in Syria; Israel contends she's living in Israel. We see Mona trying to "cross from a place one side says does not exist to a place the other side says does not exist." Israeli and Syrian border guards could care less about her problem. We see the Syrian TV star and his friends waiting patiently at the Syrian side. When their bus has a flat tire, the groom-to-be promptly removes his white dress jacket and fixes it; he doesn't want to be late for his bride-to-be. Cut to Mona's frustrated family waiting on the Golan side. Cut to Israelis stamping Mona's passport; cut to Mona at the Syrian checkpoint; the Syrian guard refuses to accept the passport—it has an Israeli stamp. Eventually, he agrees to let her cross, provided there is no stamp! A kind UN worker convinces an Israeli to white out the stamp. An optimistic Mona goes back to the Syrian checkpoint. She is greeted by a new Syrian guard who knows nothing about the "white out" arrangement and refuses to let her pass. Even if Mona does manage to cross the border, as a Syrian citizen "she can't ever return to her village on the Golan; the Israelis won't let her back in; she will never see her family again." The film reflects sad realities: Real Syrian families wanting to cross the border to see their families in Syria face the same dilemma. Frames focusing on Mona and her family are heart-rending. We see her preparing for the wedding, having her hair done at "Chez George," and happily interacting with her father, Hammid (Khoury), who was recently released from prison. We see Hammid being harassed by the same Israeli officer who jailed him for protesting the occupation. Refreshingly, the camera dwells on other family members, too: Amal (Abbass) her older feminist sister, who is trapped in an unhappy marriage; Amal's two lovely daughters; her likeable, playboy brother who drives a BMW, Marwan (Barhom); and her soft-spoken brother, Hathem (Sheety), who dared to marry a Russian woman.

Bride has a flaw or two. The camera spends perhaps too much time focusing on Amal, her unhappy feminist sister; at times she appears to be the main figure. And, all the Druze religious leaders are painted as rigid zealots.

But the movie's final frames are memorable. Hammed and his son, Hattem, make peace; Amal decides to attend an Israeli university at Haifa, despite the objections of her husband; and a determined Mona begins walking across the border to meet her intended husband. Will she make it?

Both *Bride* and *Rana's Wedding* stimulate thought, illustrating how the Israeli occupation, border guards and political red tape, disrupt the personal lives of real Arabs, young and old. Though most Arabs and Israelis want to live their lives peacefully, fear and politics separate them. Still, hope exists. As actress Hiam Abbass, who portrays Amal, told her interviewer at the Hampton Film Festival: "The cinema is the tool for peace; political borders dropped down on our cinema set." Real Arabs and Israelis worked together on *Bride* and "created something humanly possible that reaches people all over the world." Clara Khoury, the actress who plays Mona, also appears as Rana in *Rana's Wedding*.

See Roger Ebert's review in the *Chicago Sun-Times* 7 April 2006.

SYRIANA *(2005) WB; D, SP: Stephen Gaghan B: Robert Baer A: George Clooney, Amanda Peet, Alexander Siddig, Mazhar Munir, Akbar Kurtha, Nadim Sawalha* **SHEIKHS, RECOMMENDED**

Arabs and Muslims are not demonized in writer-director Steven Gaghan's taut, lucid geopolitical thriller, on which I worked as a consultant. Gaghan has said of his film that he didn't "want any stereotypes; no ridiculous Arab playboys or some villainous terrorists." To his credit, he does manage this. Arabs, Pakistanis, and Americans are projected as multidimensional characters, complete with complex motives and personal experiences.

But corruption is everywhere. Money and power determine everything. Evil feeds off of itself. *Syriana* forcefully and eloquently contends that unabated power and unconstrained violence help expedite terrorism and prevent peace. Disturbing questions are probed, asking audiences to ponder the consequences of what happens when immoral, influential government officials and corporate executives mix together greed and violence in order to maintain their monopoly on Arab oil. *Syriana's* harsh world warns us to be wary of men who consider the deaths of innocent people acceptable—religious radicals, as well as oil and government moguls. In the film, American oil executives and US government officials are equally powerful and unscrupulous. Everyone else, apparently, is expendable: educated Arabs wanting democracy; desperate, unemployed Pakistani immigrants seeking a meaningful purpose to their lives, covert CIA operatives pursuing justice; even children.

The action evolves around events in Syriana, a mythical Arab state. An aging emir (Sawalha) must choose a successor. Will it be his Oxford-educated son Prince Nasir (Siddig), who wants to bring true democracy to his nation? Or, will he select his "cunning" younger son, Prince Meshal (Kurtha)? The emir decides that Meshal—"a grown-up boy afraid of his brother"—will rule. Why? He fears the power generated by both US officials and American oil barons. Thus, Meshal becomes America's ideal "finger puppet."

The film focuses on two unemployed Pakistani-Muslim oil refinery workers who are seduced by an Islamic fundamentalist and go on to become suicide bombers. Gaghan presents one boy, Wasim (Munir), as a naïve, brainwashed victim. He loves his family, plays soccer, and talks about Spiderman movies. Cut to an overweight, bearded, patriotic CIA agent named Bob Barnes (Clooney) who tries to warn his CIA superiors about a stolen weapon. But "nobody [at the agency] wants to hear about a missing missile." So the CIA ships Barnes off to Beirut. Here, a fellow operative brutally tortures him. In time, a Hezbollah leader appears, saving Barnes's life. This petro-political drama raises some telling points regarding our dependence on Arab oil. To acquire cheap oil, should the US intervene in Arab states, using whatever means necessary? To what extent does the oil industry influence Arab and US governments? Should the US continue to support unethical Arab nations? Should we torture and murder anyone who dares oppose our goals—even CIA agents? After all, contends this scenario, "corruption is why we win." Throughout, *Syriana* offers unflattering depictions of nearly everyone engaged in global power politics—Americans and Arabs. One of the movie's few decent human beings is Prince Nasir (Siddig), a bright, reform-minded Arab royal and a devoted family man. Nasir is the film's Arab visionary. He wants to liberalize his country; he insists on giving "women the right to vote." He will allow "competitive bidding" for oil; he will not, however, allow military bases in the region. In the end, Nasir's vision and Bob Barnes's ideals get them both killed—along with Nasir's wife and children.

The movie was shot, in part, in Dubai and Morocco. Some scenes accurately reflect post–9/11 anxieties and China's quest for oil. In fictional Syriana, China wants Arab oil, just as in real life the Chinese are in Arabia lobbying for oil rights. Days after *Syriana* was released I was visiting Bahrain and encountered several Chinese dignitaries visiting the main mosque. They were telling the imam how much they respected Islam, saying that he and other Arabs would be welcomed in China. In China, they said, Arabs could build mosques and worship freely without fear of harassment. "These Chinese visitors," the pleased imam told me afterward, "are good people."

Syriana captures another reality: the desperate, parched lives of Pakistani laborers in the Gulf. The major story in Bahrain's *Gulf Times* when I was there was about suffering Pakistani workers in Dubai who hadn't been paid for six months. Alexander Siddig, who plays Prince Nasir, hopes his performance will "help temper Americans' ever-worsening attitudes toward Arabs. The most important thing," he said, "was to show that Nasir has a beating heart as fragile as anybody else's. In any group of people, you're going to find two percent of them are a bit unstable. That's just the face of humanity." In his interview with *Entertainment Weekly* Siddig said that he didn't mind playing "bad Arabs"—but, "I need to play the good Arabs to make a balance." Previously, he portrayed Dr. Julian Bashir in the TV series *Star Trek: Deep Space Nine*, and he was Saladin's friend in *Kingdom of Heaven*. *Syriana* is the second George Clooney film to offer evenhanded images of Arabs and Muslims. The first was *Three Kings*, on which I also consulted, a war drama set in Iraq during the aftermath of the 1991 war.

See the October 2005 ADC press release; the *Variety* review of *Syriana*, 20 November 2005; and Neil Drumming's "Spotlight on Alexander Siddig," *Entertainment Weekly* 18 November 2005.

TEAM AMERICA: WORLD POLICE *(2004) PAR; D, SP: Trey Parker SP: Matt Stone* VILLAINS, WORST LIST

This all-puppet action movie should be called *True Lies II*. Only one thing distinguishes *Team America* from *True Lies* (1994)—*Team America* employs heroic puppets instead of live actors. Both films show reel good protagonists terminating turbaned bad guys. In America, the team prevents Arabs from launching weapons of mass destruction (WMDs). A statement that reads like a Homeland Security press release serves as the team's motivation: "Every single minute of every single day the terrorists are planning new ways to kill you and everyone else who lives in a free country."

Cut to France, where—after the team guns down Osama bin Laden look-alikes—they discover the terrorists plan to launch an attack that will be "9/11 times 200." Off they fly to Cairo, where they kill more reel bad Arabs. Supposedly, these Arabs speak Arabic. In fact, they spew garbled mumbo-jumbo like: "I've got five terrorists going southeast on Bakalakadaka Street," says media specialist Elizabeth J. Taylor. Or, "Derk-derk-Allah. Derka derka, Baka sherpa-sherpa, Abaka-la!" and "Ooooh, Derka, derka, derka!"

The second half of the film focuses on North Korean dictator Kim Jong Il. The team terminates the nuclear dictator, his Korean cronies, and some notable Hollywood pacifists—a fact that made some of my friends call *America* an "equal opportunity offender," which exaggerates all the absurdities of the war on terror by poking fun at America's arrogance and absurd "axis of evil" mentality.

Perhaps they're right, perhaps not. I doubt if they knew about the frighteningly negative influence *Team America* had on just one marine. Soon after leaving Iraq, Corporal Joshua Belile wrote and performed "Hadji Girl," a horrifically violent video that has been viewed by thousands. He was inspired, he said, by *Team America.* (For more on "Hadji Girl," see page 22.)

See: Chris Mazzolini's, "Humor Attempt Falls Flat," *Daily News* (Jacksonville)14 June 2006.

TEARS OF THE SUN *(2003) COL, in cooperation with the Department of Defense; D: Antoine Fuqua SP: Alex Lasker, Patrick Cirillo A: Bruce Willis* VILLAINS, WORST LIST

The action takes place "somewhere off the coast of Africa." There are no Arabs here. But I mention this violent film for two reasons: It's linked with our Department of Defense and it advances Islamophobia. Throughout, we see fanatical Muslims killing devout Christians and bloodied bodies of African Christians. Brutal Nigerian Muslim militiamen "kill anyone that goes to a different church." The Muslim soldiers set aflame Christian villages, murdering women and hospital patients. And, they kill Western missionaries—two nuns. The Muslim leader grabs a machete and cuts off a priest's head.

In the end, Lt. A.K. Waters (Willis) and his elite group of Navy SEALs halt the massacres by killing the Nigerian Muslim villains.

THE TERMINAL *(2004) DreamWorks; D: Steven Spielberg SP: Sacha Gervasi, Jeff Nathanson A: Tom Hanks* SINS OF OMISSION

This Steven Spielberg tale is about Victor (Hanks), a loveable Eastern European who is caught in an immigration trap at New York's JFK airport. The movie is based on a true story about an Iranian Muslim,

Merhan Karimi Nasseri. For sixteen years Nasseri was actually stuck at the Charles de Gaulle airport terminal. Spielberg was inspired by an Iranian Muslim's real immigration predicament. So, why didn't his *Terminal* focus on a loveable Iranian?

THE TIGER AND THE SNOW *(2005) Melampo Cinematografica; D, SP: Roberto Benigni SP: Vincenzo Cerami A: Roberto Benigni, Jean Reno, Amid Farid, Nicoletta Braschi* CHAMPIONS, RECOMMENDED

Roberto Benigni's antiwar film and tender love story is set in Rome and wartime Baghdad. In the early scenes in Rome, the Italian poet Professor Attilio De Giovanni (Benigni) pines to bed and wed a beautiful scholar named Vittoria (Braschi). Vittoria, however, is busy writing a book about Attilio's friend, Fuad (Reno), "the greatest living Arab poet," and to finish the manuscript Vittoria decides to join the Iraqi poet in his native Baghdad. From this point on Benigni's gentle screenplay declares itself against the US invasion of Iraq—"this senseless war."

Vittoria is seriously injured during a US bomb attack, and Fuad calls Attilio to warn him that she may die. Attilio rushes off to a Baghdad that's under siege. Scenes reveal chaos in war-torn Iraq: lootings, clashes of insurgents, missiles igniting the sky. Appearing at Vittoria's bedside, he discovers a stark reality—the hospital lacks medicine and equipment. To find the drugs needed to save Vittoria's life, he does everything humanly possible, even "saying a prayer to Allah." His lifesaving quest reflects the real frenzied struggles of the many Iraqis who have tried to save their hospitalized loved ones. Benigni fills the screen with evenhanded portraits of Italian humanitarian-aid workers, American MPs, and Iraqis. Images of Baghdad's ordinary citizens—a young girl, the hospital physician, a shoe salesmen—and others affected by the bombings are especially moving. Reno, the French star, brings humanity to Fuad, a respected Iraqi poet who loves his country, Arab culture, and his friend Attilio.

The elderly actor Amid Farid gives a dignified performance as Al Giumeil, the brilliant pharmacist-chemist; Amid's wisdom saves Vittoria's life. As of August 2007, the *Tiger* DVD is not available in the US for rent or purchase. I purchased a copy from a film buff living in Hong Kong.

See Deborah Young's review in *Variety* 12 October 2005.

TIME LAPSE *(2001) Cinetel; D: David Worth SP: Karen Kelly, David Keith Miller A: Roy Scheider, William McNamara* **VILLAINS**
A traitorous, greedy US agent named Quince (Scheider) tries to kill his colleague, Clay (McNamara). Other key villains are Faisal and his "plain mad" Iraqis. Two scenes show Faisal and his Iraqi thugs trying to get their hands on a powerful "nuclear suitcase." But American agents—both good and bad—shoot Faisal and his Iraqis dead.

TRANSFORMERS *(2007) PAR & DreamWorks; D: Michael Bay SP: Roberto Orci, Alex Kurtzman A: Ashkan Kashanchi* **CAMEO**
Brief scenes in this movie depict Qataris fighting alongside US soldiers. Superimposed on the opening screen: "Qatar; The Middle East; The Present Day." Troops mull about a US desert base. A pro-American Qatari boy, Mahfouz (Kashanchi), brings some water to a US soldier. Abruptly, evil giant robot aliens attack, downing two fighter jets and killing scores on the ground. One soldier, Mahfouz, and several troops survive the onslaught, escaping into the desert. Several quick cuts show the troops and the Qatari boy seeking a safe place. "How far do you live from here?" a soldier asks the boy. "Not far," says Mahfouz, "just up that mountain."

Now, I've traveled to Qatar many times, and there are no mountains there—just some large sand dunes. When they reach the boy's friendly mountain village, the boy is reunited with his father, and they all assist the troops.

The reel Qatari village should look like a real Qatari town, with houses, paved roads, street lights, shopping malls, and so forth. But the producers make it look exactly like yesteryear's reel backward Arabland, complete with ruins everywhere.

One out-of-place slur targets Iranians. As our specialists in DC try to discover the identity of the attackers, one quips, "This is way too smart for the Iranians."

TWO DEGREES *(2001) Bandwagon Films; D, SP: Tony Spires A: Don D.C. Curry, Jihad (Jay) Harik, Elie Masara* **VILLAINS, ARAB AMERICAN**
In this trashy film, written and directed by Tony Spires, African Americans are stereotyped as ruthless hoods and drug dealers and

Arab Americans fare not much better. Spires features damaging liquor store scenes that pit Arab Americans against African Americans. The sloppy Faisel (Harik) and his ugly, Arabic-speaking younger brother Reza (Masara) are the rude and crude owners of a liquor store. Loud, abrasive Arab music underscores their abusive behavior. Faisel refuses to give a "free loader" correct change for a dollar. When the customer protests, Feisel threatens to shoot him. Angela, a desperate, down-and-out African-American drug addict, enters the store. She asks for something to eat. Faisel offers her groceries, provided she lets him bed her. Reluctantly, Angela agrees, and in the back room, Faisel huffs and puffs for a few seconds before collapsing on the floor. The bored Angela lights a cigarette. Later, brother Reza offers Angela the same food-for-sex deal. They go to the store's back room—and Angela's boyfriend arrives, threatening to kill both Faisal and Reza. When Faisel goes for his gun, the boyfriend shoots Faisel and Reza dead. They had it coming. African-American characters call the brothers "towel-head motherfuckers," "camel-eating ass," and tell them, "You Ayrabs ain't shit."

(For more than 175 reel slurs directed at Arabs in pre–9/11 films, see the appendix in *Reel Bad Arabs*.)

UNITED 93 *(2006) UNI; D, SP: Paul Greengrass A: Jamie Harding, Omar Berdouni, Lewis Alsamari, Khaled Abdalla* **VILLAINS**
Did this first major 9/11 fiction film about the fourth hijacked plane arrive at movie theaters too soon—only five years after the actual tragedy? When the *United 93* trailers were being screened to promote the passengers' heroics some viewers were yelling "too soon." Others, notably Jeff Jacoby of the *Boston Globe*, thought Hollywood waited too long to release such a "stark and heartbreaking re-creation of what happened to that flight." Critic Mark Cousins disagrees, writing, that if Hollywood has a cycle—"a block of time in which it digests a world event and presents it as memory and myth—five years now seems to be it. It was 11 years before the first big Vietnam movie (*The Green Berets*) appeared; the first major AIDS movie came nine years after the first diagnoses; and *Hotel Rwanda* ten years after the massacres." Eventually, movies almost always catch up with and reflect real events. What impressed me about *United 93* are the fleeting glimpses of ordinary airline pas-

sengers and flight attendants, all courageous, honorable Americans who fought back against the Arab-Muslim hijackers. These Americans sacrificed their lives to save countless others on the ground. Jacoby, however, questioned whether viewers could "handle a movie that sets the murderous depravity of our enemy against the American heroism that met it in the skies over Pennsylvania on that terrible day." Of course we can. In this harrowing reenactment, the key question should be: Will this film, which reflects one person's respectful view of the tragedy, adequately honor the brave actions of the passengers and crew? According to the press kit, the film was: "Painstakingly researched… *United 93* paints an unforgettable portrait of everyday people confronted with an unthinkable situation." The kit goes on to say, writes Brandeis Professor Thomas Doherty, that "family members were kept involved at all stages of production." But can any Hollywood feature ever adequately recreate the horror of that day? Of course not. Fiction cannot duplicate the horrific, painful real realities of that crash.

So despite the director's noble intentions, *United 93* fails to offer "unforgettable portraits." Too much time is spent on air traffic control centers. The passengers function as backdrops, not as real people trapped in a death plane. I wanted to know more about the passengers and the crew. It's not enough to show brief clips of flight attendants serving meals, young and old Americans knitting, requesting water for pills, and complaining about the delayed takeoff. Like other imagemakers presenting fiction films that are based on real tragic events, producer Greengrass adds a dramatic soundtrack to heighten tension, and he makes key decisions about which facts to include and delete. (He is now adapting for Universal *Imperial Life in the Emerald City*, a book about the turmoil surrounding the fall of Baghdad.)

Writing in the Winter 2006 *Cineaste*, Dylan McGinty criticized Greengrass's research, saying that it "relied almost exclusively on official government reports and documents." McGinty contends that "serious questions remain unanswered about what really happened with Flight 93." At the time of the crash, writes McGinty, there were "several other planes in the area" and the heavily guarded crash site was "devoid of plane parts and bodies," and "the transcript of conversations by the flight-data recorder ended three minutes before the plane crashed."

On September 11, 2005 the Discovery channel telecast a compelling United 93 documentary, *The Flight that Fought Back*, attracting over 7 million viewers. On January 30, 2006, A&E's made-for-TV movie *Flight 93* drew the channel's best ever audience. Yet *United 93* did poorly at the box office. After the first four weeks it grossed only $28 million.

Some real world incidents surrounding *United 93*: Some American Arabs and American Muslims feared that after watching the film's ruthless, wide-eyed fanatics kill innocent people, their fellow moviegoers would take out their anger on them. A few viewers did just that: In Phoenix, Arizona, for example, two people who saw *United 93* confronted several young Arab-Muslim women, telling them to "take off your fucking burqas and get the fuck out of this country." The Iraq-born actor Lewis Alsamari, who plays one of the film's hijackers, has lived in the United Kingdom for a decade, but the US denied his visa request to attend the film's premiere at the Tribeca Film Festival.

For those interested in seeing an accurate historical document that reflects the human spirit of New Yorkers, I highly recommend Steven Rosenbaum's brilliant documentary, *7 Days in September* (2002). Rosenbaum's assembled footage, shot by 28 New Yorkers, will stand the test of time as a memorable, educational, and unforgettable post–9/11 documentary; it shows New Yorkers coming together after the 9/11 attacks. "Everyone in the city had one thing in common," says one New Yorker, "fear, hope, and love and comfort for one another." One woman creates a circle of prayer, reminding us of "the power we have to be transformers in the world." She and others join hands and sing "Amazing Grace."

See Mark Cousins, "Cinema Gets Real," *Prospect* (June 2006); Jeff Jacoby, "Musings, Random and Otherwise," *Boston Globe* 10 May 2006; and CAIR's Press release, 6 May 2006.

V FOR VENDETTA *(2006)* WB; D: *James McTeigue* SP: *Andy Wachowski, Larry Wachowski* A: *Natalie Portman* CAMEO, SHEIKHS, ⟩ EVENHANDED

It is the year 2020. A fascist British government rules England. They control the media, suppress free speech, and persecute dissenters. "We did what we had to do," boasts a radical conservative TV commentator. "Immigrants, Muslims, homosexuals, terrorists... they had to go."

Early on, a security guard watches a popular government propaganda TV show, *Storm Saxon*. The TV screen shows the hero and the blond heroine. Cut to the protagonist (Portman), who asks the guard, "Why do you watch shit like that?" Minutes later, when Portman's character, who is hiding from the police, looks up at the TV set, it features a fat, white-robed Arab sharpening two knives. The TV Arab noisily scrapes the blades together, laughing maniacally. The blond heroine, all tied up, shouts, "Storm, Help!" The TV scene lasts seconds.

Some viewers may think the scene criticizes the government's anti-Arab policies. Others think the TV Arab's sinister behavior enforces the stereotype. This set-in-the-future film displays discriminatory policies that are frighteningly real. Today, anti-Arab and anti-Muslim feelings abound throughout the US and Europe.

In *Vendetta*, reel police barge into a liberal TV host's home. Here, they find "a copy of the Quran, 14th century." When asked why he, a non-religious person, keeps the Quran, in defiance of the law, the TV host says: "I don't have to be Muslim to find its images, its poetry moving." Offscreen, the police execute him.

Children of Men (2006), another film set in a near-future dystopia in England, projects Muslims as victims. Near the end, we see, briefly, hundreds of imprisoned refugees, including some Muslims. Several attend a funeral procession, saying *Allahu akbar* (God is great). All the refugees are held in a large concentration camp and called "fugis," slang for refugees.

THE WAR WITHIN *(or* OVER THE MOUNTAINS*) (2005)* HDNet *Films; D, SP: Joseph Castelo SP: Ayad Akhtar, Tom Glynn A: Kamal Marayati* VILLAINS

Beware the immigrant: A young Muslim from Pakistan travels to New Jersey to live with a Muslim family. Unbeknownst to the warm-hearted, patriotic family, this Pakistani, who once attended the University of Maryland's engineering school, is intent on committing an act of terror—he's a reel ruthless terrorist. In the end, the student, who belongs to a New York–based terrorist cell, refuses to embrace the Quran's message "to forbid the wrong [and] commend the good." Instead, he sets off a deadly explosion at Grand Central Station, killing scores.

Arab-American actor Kamal Marayati, who portrays the film's devout imam, called my attention to this movie. But he refuses to watch it. He wrote to me saying: "Dr. Jack, there are two versions of the ending. In version one, the protagonist decides to spare the lives of innocent people and he blows himself up in Central Park. In version two, he kills scores of American commuters. I'm not sure which one the producers used" (10 February 2005).

WATERBORNE *(2005) Drops Entertainment; D, SP: Ben Rekhi A: Ajay Naidu* RECOMMENDED

I highly recommend this independent film, in which the protagonists are Sikhs—this time (unlike in other films featuring dark-complexioned convenience store owners) loyal, law-abiding Americans who happen to be dark-skinned, have beards, long hair, and turbans. In *Waterborne*, the Sikh protagonists are likeable three-dimensional characters—family members who bicker, love, work, study, and pray. The film shows how damaging stereotypes trigger acts of violence that seriously injure innocents. The Sikhs' convenience store is looted by a man who believes the store owners are Arab. The intruder severely injures the Sikh mother, Vikran (Naidu), who owns the store. While in the hospital, Vikran comes to recognize that America's a very nice place to live, after all. She "lets go of her prejudices" and gives her devoted son a hearty thumbs up to marry his Jewish-American girlfriend. Closing frames memorably offer hope for tolerance.

There are other exceptions to Hollywood's general rule that all Muslims are Arabs, such as *Tears of the Sun* (see page 170); *East Is East* (1999), which nevertheless refurbishes stale Arab stereotypes by projecting a Pakistani-Muslim husband as a polygamous wife-beating tyrant. On the plus side, four *Bad News Bears* baseball films show an African-American Muslim teenager, Ahmad Abdul Rahim, as "one of the boys."

WEIRDSVILLE *(2007) Darius Films; D: Allen Moyle SP: Willem Wennekers A: Raoul Bhaneja* **ARAB CANADIAN, NS**

In Weirdsville, a small Canadian town, one long-time resident is Omar (Bhaneja), the local drug king pin. Omar, a reel Maronite Catholic from Beirut, wears a cross around his neck.

YES *(2005) Greenstreet Films; D, SP: Sally Potter A: Joan Allen, Sam Neill, Simon Akbarian* **CHAMPIONS, RECOMMENDED**

This compelling film illustrates that cultures need not divide, but can connect. For the first time in cinema history we witness reel love between the American blond heroine, She (Allen), and a dark-complexioned Arab man, He (Akbarian). She, an Irish-American molecular biologist, has a torrid affair with He, a struggling Lebanese immigrant working in a London restaurant. He was once a brilliant surgeon in Beirut; during the civil war he operated on everyone, no matter what side they were on. One day, he miraculously saved a patient's life. After the operation, however, militants barged into his office and killed the man "without a thought to color and creed." So, He fled Lebanon and became a cook. Early scenes show She romancing her Lebanese lover, and vice versa. In and out of bed he treats her with respect and dignity. When he first undresses her, he sings in Arabic; later he joyously dances and cooks for her. Unexpectedly, while he is working away in the restaurant's kitchen, a young, bigoted dishwasher assaults him. The sudden attack hurts and angers the Lebanese doctor. Later when he meets up with his lover, he tells her: "You insult my people, you insult me. Islamic law is fair." He says the US views all Arabs as inferior. He then rejects her, saying, "You want me [only] as your exotic lover... You're a scientist and from the West. You think you know it all, that you're the best. One life of yours [is] worth all the rest." The dialogue—written and spoken entirely in rhymed iambic parameter—expresses clashing beliefs about Middle Eastern and Western worlds, especially the Iraq war and US involvement in the region after 9/11. A sample:

> HE: Your country want[s] our land and oil.
> SHE: You are confusing me with them.
> HE: You hear our children's screams but feel no loss because

they are not yours.

SHE: Look, I am an individual. I am me!

After the argument, they go their separate ways.

One memorable must-see scene advances religious tolerance: He appears before an outdoor nativity scene, reverently bowing his head. He could be Muslim or Christian. No matter. He respects both Islam and Christianity. Finally, the couple happily reunites. He and She appear on the beach enjoying each other's smiles, embraces. Director Sally Potter reminds us that besides the "history of conflict, there is also the history of multicultural friendship. [The creation] of an evil enemy 'Other' is to reduce people to a single cliched image of who they are—they become one homogenous thing—whereas in reality almost everyone I know is very complex with interweaving identities and histories."

See Cynthia Lucia, "An Interview with Sally Potter," *Cineaste*, Fall 2005.

YOUNG BLACK STALLION *(2003) Buena Vista; D: Simon Wincer*
SP: *Jeanne Rosenberg* B: *Walter Farley, Steven Farley* A: *Biana Tamimi, Gerald Rudolf, Ali Al Ameri, Richard Romanus* **VILLAINS, CHAMPIONS**

Before viewers could blink, Disney's *Stallion* appeared in movie theaters and then promptly disappeared. This boring, poorly written, and shabbily produced 45-minute film displays nasty Arabs ripping off a benevolent elderly Arab, Ben Ishak (Romanus). The "bad" Arabs also ridicule his granddaughter, Neera (Tamimi).

The setting is the desert, post–World War II Arabia. Arab brigands attack a friendly Arab caravan. One lecherous Arab leers at the young Neera. In time, Neera escapes, rushing off on her camel. Amazingly, we never see or find out what happens to her caravan friends again. Only the writers know their fate. Alone in the desert, Neera finds and befriends a young stallion. She returns safely home to Ben Ishak, the horse clinging to her side.

Cut to the Arabs' annual desert race. Posing as a boy (since of course no women are allowed to compete), Neera enters the race and rides her coal-black colt to victory. She defeats all the male riders, including the lecherous bandit. Neera's heroics are applauded. Her grandfather regains the community's respect, and then some.

Beginning in May 2002, my agents and I began corresponding with Disney executives, asking them to consider enlisting my services as a consultant on this movie and *Hidalgo*. Over a seven-month period, many letters were sent to Disney CEO Michael Eisner; Dick Cook, chairman of Walt Disney Motion Pictures Group; and vice presidents Karen Glass and Andrea Marozas. Finally, several weeks before *Stallion* was released, Disney made arrangements for me to screen the film in Burbank. No one from the studio, however, was there to discuss the film.

FILM CATEGORIES

In *Reel Bad Arabs* I recommend only 50 of 950+ pre-9/11 films—roughly five percent of the total. Here, I recommend about twenty percent of the total—23 out of 100+ post–9/11 films. I also list 8 films with evenhanded images and 18 worst films.

Of the recommended films, five are foreign—Spanish, Italian, French, and Tunisian. Another three are Arab–Israeli co-productions.

[1] Features Sikhs
[2] Arab–Israeli co-productions
[3] Foreign films with English subtitles

Recommended Films
And Now… Ladies and Gentlemen (2002)
Babel (2006)
The Chronicles of Riddick (2004)
Days of Glory (Indigenes) (2006)[3]
Enough (2002)
Flightplan (2005)
The Gold Bracelet (2006)[1]
Kingdom of Heaven (2005)
Only Human (2004)[3]
Paradise Now (2005)[2]
Paris, Je t'aime (2006)
Private (2004)[3]
Rana's Wedding (2002)[2]
The Recruit (2003)
Rendition (2007)
Satin Rouge (2002)[3]
The Sentinel (2006)
Sorry, Haters (2006)
The Syrian Bride (2004)[2]
Syriana (2005)
The Tiger and the Snow (2005)[3]
Yes (2005)
Waterborne (2005)[1]

Evenhanded Images
American Dreamz (2006)
Day on Fire (2006)
The Final Cut (2004)
Hidden (Caché) (2005)[3]
Night at the Museum (2006)
The Situation (2006)
Spy Game (2001)
V for Vendetta (2006)

Worst Films
Air Marshal (2003)
Black Hawk Down (2002)
District B13 (2004)
Fatwa (2006)
Four Feathers (2002)
Full Disclosure (2001)
Hidalgo (2004)
The Kingdom (2007)
Looking for Comedy in the Muslim World (2005)
The Point Men (2001)
Pretty Persuasion (2005)
Red Mercury (2005)
Secondhand Lions (2004)
Spymate (2006)
The Stone Merchant (2006)
Team America: World Police (2004)
Tears of the Sun (2003)
Two Degrees (2001)

Arab American
A Day without a Mexican (2004)
American Dreamz (2006)
Enough (2002)
The Final Cut (2004)
Flight Plan (2005)
The Kitchen (2001)
Malibu's Most Wanted (2003)

The Recruit (2001)
The Sentinel (2006)
Sorry, Haters (2006)
Two Degrees (2001)

Arab Canadian

Weirdsville (2007)

Arab Impersonators

Five Fingers (2006)

Arab-as-Iranian

The Recruit (2003)

Arab-as-Victim

Civic Duty (2006)
Crank (2006)
Hidden [Caché] (2005)
Rendition (2007)
Sorry, Haters (2006)

Bedouin

Jarhead (2005)
Promised Land (2004)

Cameos

Belly of the Beast (2003)
Borat (2006)
Click (2006)
The Condemned (2007)
Cradle 2 the Grave (2003)
Crank (2006)
Dawn of the Dead (2003)
A Day without a Mexican (2004)
The Deal (2005)
Delta Farce (2007)

Deuce Bigalow: European Gigolo (2005)
A Different Loyalty (2004)
Dreamer (2005)
Final Destination 3 (2006)
Flags of Our Fathers (2006)
Full Disclosure (2001)
Gen-Y Cops (2003)
The Hot Chick (2002)
Inside Man (2006)
Jackass Number Two (2006)
Larry the Cable Guy: Health Inspector (2006)
The Last King of Scotland (2006)
The Last Shot (2004)
The Lord of the Rings: Return of the King (2003)
The Majestic (2001)
Malibu's Most Wanted (2003)
The Manchurian Candidate (2004)
The Marine (2006)
Out of Reach (2004)
Scary Movie 4 (2006)
Secondhand Lions (2004)
Soul Plane (2004)
Spymate (2006)
The Sum of All Fears (2002)
Transformers (2007)
V for Vendetta (2006)

Champions

And Now... Ladies and Gentlemen (2002)
Babel (2006)
The Chronicles of Riddick (2004)
Day on Fire (2006)
Enough (2002)
Kingdom of Heaven (2005)
Paradise Now (2005)
Paris, Je t'aime (2006)
Private (2004)
Rana's Wedding (2002)

The Recruit (2003)
Rendition (2007)
Sahara (2005)
The Situation (2006)
Soldier of God (2005)
The Syrian Bride (2004)
The Tiger and the Snow (2005)
Yes (2005)
Young Black Stallion (2003)

Egyptians

Cradle 2 the Grave (2003)
The Hot Chick (2002)
Mummy Raider (2001)
The Mummy's Kiss (2002)
Night at the Museum (2006)

Maidens

Around the World in 80 Days (2004)
Fatwa (2006)
Hidalgo (2004)
Looking for Comedy in the Muslim World (2005)
The Manchurian Candidate (2004)
The Mummy's Kiss (2002)
Pretty Persuasion (2005)
Secondhand Lions (2004)

Palestinians

Day on Fire (2006)
Full Disclosure (2001)
Land of Plenty (2004)
The Last King of Scotland (2006)
Munich (2005)
Only Human (2004)
Paradise Now (2005)
The Point Men (2001)
Pretty Persuasion (2005)

Private (2004)
Rana's Wedding (2002)

Sheikhs

Around the World in 80 Days (2004)
Click (2006)
Delta Farce (2007)
Dreamer (2005)
Fahrenheit 9/11 (2004)
Gen-Y Cops (2003)
Hidalgo (2004)
The Majestic (2001)
Merchant of Venice (2004)
Secondhand Lions (2004)
Spartan (2004)
Syriana (2005)
V for Vendetta (2006)

Sins of Omission

Sinbad: Legend of the Seven Seas (2003)
The Terminal (2004)

Turk-as-Arab

Around the World in 80 Days (2004)

Turks-as-Sheikhs

Out of Reach (2004)

Villains

Air Marshal (2003)
American Dreamz (2006)
Belly of the Beast (2003)
Black Hawk Down (2002)
Cavite (2006)
The Condemned (2007)
Dawn of the Dead (2003)

The Deal (2005)
District B13 (2004)
Fatwa (2006)
Final Destination 3 (2006)
Fire over Afghanistan (2003)
Flight of the Phoenix (2004)
Four Feathers (2002)
Hidalgo (2004)
Home of the Brave (2006)
Inside Man (2006)
Jackass Number Two (2006)
The Kingdom (2007)
Larry the Cable Guy: Health Inspector (2006)
The Lord of the Rings: Return of the King (2003)
The Marine (2006)
Promised Land (2004)
Red Mercury (2005)
Rendition (2007)
Scary Movie 4 (2006)
The Situation (2006)
Soldier of God (2005)
Spartan (2004)
Spy Game (2001)
Spymate (2006)
The Stone Merchant (2006)
Team America: World Police (2004)
Tears of the Sun (2003)
Time Lapse (2001)
Two Degrees (2001)
United 93 (2006)
The War Within (2005)
Young Black Stallion (2003)

WORKS CITED

Adachi, Jeff, dir. *The Slanted Screen*. Asian American Media Mafia, 2006.

Advisory Group on Public Diplomacy in the Arab and Muslim World. Edward P. Djerejian, chair. *Changing Minds, Winning Peace: A New Strategic Direction for US Public Diplomacy in the Arab and Muslim World*. Washington, DC. 1 October 2003.

Akers, Paul. "Sighs and Wonders." Editorial. *Fredericksburg Free Lance-Star*. 10 June 2006.

Alsultany, Evelyn. "The Changing Profile of Race in the United States: Media Representations and Radicalization of Arab- and Muslim-Americans Post-9/11." Diss. Stanford University, 2005.

"Arabic TV Gives False Impression of US." Associated Press 7 January 2006.

Arsu, Sebnem. "If You Want a Film to Fly, Make Americans the Heavies," *New York Times* 14 February 2006.

"Attacking Mecca Effective, Tancredo Says." Associated Press 3 August 2007.

Avnery, Uri. "Shall We Not Revenge." 4 February 2006 (bestcyrano.org/avneryParadiseNow.htm).

Bart, Peter. "Mideast: The Good, the Bad and the Ugly." *Variety* 7–13 August 2006.

Bataille, Gretchen and Charles Silet. *The Pretend Indians: Images of Native Americans in the Movies*. Ames, IA: Iowa State University Press, 1980.

Belien, Paul. "Pigs to the Rescue." *Brussels Journal* 6 December 2006.

Benhorin, Yitzhak. "Hollywood Stars Blast Nasrallah." YNet News 16 August 2007.

Bennett, Ray. Review of *Hamburg Cell*. *Hollywood Reporter* 31 August 2004.

Bernstein, Richard. "Madrasa in New York? Hysteria Trumps Reason." *New York Times* 7 May 2007.

Bittner, Donald. Personal interview. 18 July 2006.

Black, Gregory D. *Hollywood Censored: Morality Codes, Catholics, and the Movies*. Cambridge, UK: Cambridge University Press, 1994.

Braude, Joseph. "The Arab World Goes to the Movies." *Los Angeles Times Magazine* 20 November 2005.

Breznican, Anthony. "Ready or Not, Terror Hits Film," *USA Today* 21 April 2006.

Burnham, Gilbert, Riyadh Lafta, Shannon Doocy, and Les Roberts. "Mortality after the 2003 Invasion of Iraq: A Cross-Sectional Cluster Sample Survey." *Lancet* 368.9545 (21 October 2006) 1421–1428.

"Bush, Hollywood, and 'The Hitcher.'" Associated Press 14 September 2000.

Bush, Jason. "Mouse Ears over Moscow." *Business Week* 11 June 2007.

Chang, Justin. Review of *Civic Duty*. *Variety* 12 June 2006.

Chopra, Deepak. "Try Listening to the Muslim World." *Baltimore Sun* 21 June 2006.

Cieply, Michael. "With Real Bullets Still Flying, Hollywood Brings War Home." *New York Times* 26 August 2007.

"Cinema Urged to Uphold Humans' Dignity." ZENIT News Agency 15 November 2006.

Clinton, Hillary. Comments on Arab Americans. Associated Press 21 March 1999.

Cole, Juan. "Combating Muslim Extremism." *Nation* 19 November 2007.

Collins, Scott. "The Network Tries to Revive the Sitcom Format with an Injection of—Gasp!—Politics." *Los Angeles Times* 20 August 2007.

Council on American-Islamic Relations (CAIR). Action alert. 19 July 2007.

———. "American Muslim Voters: A Demographic Profile and Survey of Attitudes. Washington, DC: CAIR, 2006.

———. Press release on *United 93.* 6 May 2006.

Cousins, Mark. "Cinema Gets Real." *Prospect* June 2006.

Crowdus, Gary and Dan Georgakas. "Interview with Spike Lee." *Cineaste* Spring 2001.

"Cuban Filmgoers." CNN International 23 May 2007.

"Danger Lurks in Use of Term 'Islamofascism.'" Editorial. *Boston Globe* 8 November 2007.

"Debating Politics at the Movies." Editorial. *Cineaste* Spring 2006.

De Los Santos, Nancy, Alberto Dominguez, and Susan Racho, dirs. *The Bronze Screen: 100 Years of the Latino Image in American Cinema,* 2002.

D'Hoop, Phyllis, ed. "An Initiative: Strengthening US–Muslim Communications." Washington, DC: Center for the Study of the Presidency, 2003.

DiCaprio, Leonardo. Interview by Dotson Rader. *Parade* 12 December 2004.

Dodds, Paisley. "Gitmo Prisoners Told Panel about Abuse." Associated Press 31 May 2005.

Doherty, Thomas. Review of *United 93. Cineaste* Fall 2006.

Drumming, Neil. "Spotlight on Alexander Siddig." *Entertainment Weekly* 18 November 2005.

Ebert, Roger. Review of *Not Without My Daughter. Chicago Sun-Times* 11 January 1986.

———. Review of *Rana's Wedding. Chicago Sun-Times* 30 January 2004.

———. Review of *The Syrian Bride. Chicago Sun-Times* 7 April 2006.

Eck, Diana. *Encountering God.* Boston: Beacon Press, 1993.

Elliott, Andrea. "After 9/11, Arab-Americans Fear Police Acts, Study Finds." *New York Times* 12 June 2006.

Eliot, Marc. *Jimmy Stewart: A Biography.* New York: Random House, 2006.

Elon, Amos. *The Pity of it All: A History of the Jews in Germany 1743–1933.* New York: Henry Holt, 2002.

Engelen, Leen. "History on Film? What Belgian Fiction Films (1918–1924) Tell Us about the Great War and Its Aftermath." *History in Words and*

Images. Ed. Hannu Salmi. Turku: University of Turku, 2005.

Epstein, Edward Jay. *Agency of Fear.* New York: G.P. Putnam, 1977.

———. *The Big Picture: Money and Power in Hollywood.* New York: Random House, 2005.

Epstein, Rob and Jeffrey Friedman, dirs. *The Celluloid Closet.* Sony Pictures Classics, 1995.

Erens, Patricia. *The Jew in American Cinema.* Bloomington, IN: Indiana University Press, 1988.

Ervin, Clark Ken. "The Usual Suspects." *New York Times* 27 June 2006.

Esposito, John L. "Islam FAQs—The 2004 World Almanac." *ARAMCO World* September/October 2003.

"FBI: Hate Crimes Escalate." *USA Today* 20 November 2007.

"Facing East." Editorial. *Cineaste* Summer 2006.

Fairness and Accuracy in Reporting (FAIR). "This Isn't Discrimination, This Is Necessary." *Extra!* November/December 2001.

Fallaci, Oriana. *The Rage and the Pride.* New York: Rizzoli International Publications, 2002. To see other anti-Arab, anti-Muslim statements made by Fallaci, go to www.brainyquote.com.

Fallows, James. "Declaring Victory." *Atlantic Monthly* September 2006: 60–73.

Farber, Stephen. "The Kingdom." *Hollywood Reporter* 12 September 2007.

Felperin, Leslie. Review of *Borat. Variety* 10 September 2006.

Featherstone, Liza. "Flying While Arab." *Nation* 22 November 2006.

Finke, Nikki. "The Mysteries of Munich." *LA Weekly* 5 December 2005.

Fischler, Steven, dir. *Beyond Wiseguys: Italian Americans & the Movies.* Pacific Street Films, 2007.

Fisk, Robert. "Why Ridley Scott's Story of the Crusades Struck Such a Chord in a Lebanese Cinema." *Independent* 4 June 2005.

Ford, Peter. "Europe Cringes at Bush 'Crusade' against Terrorists." *Christian Science Monitor* 19 September 2001.

Forman, Jim. "Store Owner Fights Back after Attack." *Washington News* 22 February 2007.

Freedman, Samuel G. "Critics Ignored Record of a Muslim Principal." *New York Times* 29 August 2007.

Freeh, Louis J. *My FBI: Bringing Down the Mafia, Investigating Bill Clinton and Fighting the War on Terror.* New York: St. Martins Press, 2005. See Freeh's opening chapter, "Khobar Towers," about Saudi cooperation with the FBI.

Friedman, Thomas. "The Best PR: Straight Talk." *New York Times* 20 May 2005.

Fumento, Michael. "Hollywood Goes to War." *New York Daily Sun* 25 October 2007.

Gabler, Neal. "The World Still Watches America." *New York Times* 9 January 2003.

Gavlak, Dale. "Ben and Izzy Cartoon Promotes Tolerance between East and

West." Associated Press 20 May 2006.

Geir, Peter. "News Bias Hurdle: Middle East Clients." *Daily Report* [Georgia Law] 1 June 2006.

Gibran, Kahlil. *The Prophet.* New York: Alfred A. Knopf, 1923.

Georgakas, Dan and Barbara Saltz. "An Interview with Hany Abu-Assad." *Cineaste* Winter 2005.

"Globalization and Film Criticism." Editorial. *Cineaste* Winter 2005.

Greiner, Robert. "Moving Beyond Stereotypes." *Creative Screenwriting* 9.2.

Gritten, David. "Politics Threaten to Upstage Films at Morocco's International Festival," *Los Angeles Times* 23 September 2002.

Gutman, Nathan. "America-Backed Arabic TV Network Comes under Fire on Capitol Hill." Forward.com 18 May 2007.

Hagberg, David. *Allah's Scorpion.* New York: Tor Books, 2006.

Hagopian Elaine C., ed. *Civil Rights in Peril: The Targeting of Arabs and Muslims.* London: Pluto Press, 2004.

Hagopian, Robert, dir. *Images of Indians, Part I: The Great Movie Massacre.* 1979.

Hamilton, Jamie. "Islam Reporting in Context and with Complexity." Harvard University Nieman Reports. Summer 2007.

Hammond, Jeffrey. "Honored by Hate: Elite Propaganda in the Middle East." Editorial. www.opednews.com 13 July 2007.

Hartl, John. "The Kingdom: Star Power, Opulent Sets, But Little Substance." *Seattle Times* 28 September 2007.

Henninger, Daniel. "Washington Defines Politics Downward." *Wall Street Journal* 24 February 2006.

Hishmeh, George. "Open the Door to a Viable Peace Plan." *Gulf News* 28 March 2007.

Holden, Stephen. Review of *Paradise Now. New York Times* 28 October 2005.

Honeycutt, Kirk. Review of *Borat. Hollywood Reporter* 12 September 2006.

Horn, John. "Playing a Terrorist: An Actor's Dilemma." *Los Angeles Times* 26 April 2006.

Hourani, Albert. *Islam in European Thought.* Cambridge: Cambridge University Press, 1991.

Hsu, Tanya and Grant F. Smith, "Of Virtue and Vice: The Saudi-American Fight Against Terror Financing." Institute for Research Middle East Policy of Saudi Arabia, 23 December 2003.

Humbert, Marc. "First Lady's Family Aids Senate Run." *Los Angeles Times* 14 August 2000.

Hudson, Michael C. "Washington vs. Al-Jazeera" in *Arab Media in the Information Age.* United Arab Emirates: Emirates Center for Strategic Studies and Research, 2006.

"Imams, Rabbis Urge Mutual Respect." Associated Press 24 March 2006.

Internet Movie Database (IMDB). News on Iraq videos. 2 August 2006.

Insdorf, Annette. "When Hollywood Ignored the Holocaust." AMC-TV 3 April 2005.

"Iraqis Say They are Worse Off as Fear Dominates Lives." *Middle East News* 19 March 2007.

Isaacs, Harold Robert. *Scratches on Our Minds: American Views of China and India.* Armonk, NY: M.E. Sharpe, 1980.

Isikoff, Michael. "Sharp New Look at 'Material Witness' Arrests," *Newsweek* 4 July 2005: 6.

"Israel LA Envoy Criticizes New Spielberg Film *Munich.*" *Haaretz* [Israel] service 12 November 2005.

Jaafar, Ali. "Arabs Get Fair Play." *Variety* 5 February 2005.

———. "Mideast Directors Offer Unique POV." *Variety* 2 April 2007.

———. "More Parts for Middle East Actors." *Variety* 31 August 2007.

———. "Saudi Pic Causes Stir." *Variety* 2 April 2006

Jackson, Joshua. Comments at the Dubai International Film Festival. Al-Jazeera International. 12 December 2006.

Jacobovici, Simcha, dir. *Hollywoodism: Jews, Movies and the American Dream.* Canadian Broadcasting Corporation (CBC), 1998.

Jacoby, Jeff. "Musings, Random and Otherwise." *Boston Globe* 10 May 2006.

al-Jadda, Souheila. "News to Bridge the Divide," *USA Today* 11 October 2006.

Jhally, Sut, dir. *Reel Bad Arabs: How Hollywood Vilifies a People.* Media Education Foundation, 2006.

Johnson, Barbara. "Hollywood's Last Taboo." *Wall Street Journal* 13 July 2005: D10.

Johnson, Ted. "War is Hell for Coalition." *Variety* 17 September 2006.

Jolie, Angelina. Interview. *Glamour* April 2007.

Joshi, Khyati Y. "Because I Had a Turban." *Teaching Tolerance* Fall 2007.

Kayyali, Randa. "The People Perceived as a Threat to Security: Arab Americans since September 11." Migration Policy Institute (migrationinformation.org). July 2006.

Keen, Sam. *Faces of the Enemy: Reflections of the Hostile Imagination.* San Francisco: Harper & Row, 1986.

Kelly, Andrew, Jeffrey Richards, and James Pepper. *Filming T. E. Lawrence: Korda's Lost Epic.* London: IB Tauris, 1997.

Khalil, Ashraf. "But Can You Play a Terrorist?" *Los Angeles Times* 14 October 2007.

Khawly, Carol. "An Arab-American Community Perspective." American-Arab Anti-Discrimination Committee. December 2004.

Kearney, John. "My God is Your God." *New York Times* 28 January 2004.

King, Rep. Peter T. Remarks discussed at the Politico blog (www.politico.com/blogs/thecrypt) 19 September 2007.

Klavan, Andrew. "The Nation Needs More Gung-ho, Patriotic War Movies That Celebrate Our Fight against Islamo-Fascists." *Los Angeles Times* 7 May 2006.

Kotler, Steven. "Hollywood Mujahideen." *Life* June/July 2005: 24.

Kristof, Nicholas D. "Homegrown Osamas." *New York Times* 9 March 2005.

Krugman, Paul. Editorial. *New York Times* 29 October 2007.

Kuruvila, Matthai Chakko. "Typecasting Muslims as a Race." *San Francisco Chronicle* 3 September 2006.

Kushner, Tony. "Defending 'Munich' to My Mishpocheh." Editorial. *Los Angeles Times* 22 January 2005.

"Lawmaker Won't Apologize for 'Islamophobic' Letter." CNN 21 December 2006.

Leab, Daniel J. *From Sambo to Superspade: The Black Experience in Motion Pictures.* Boston: Houghton Mifflin, 1976.

Lee, Felicia R. "Comedians as Activists, Challenging Prejudice." *New York Times* 10 March 2007.

Lewerenz, Spencer and Barbara Nicolosi, ed. *Behind the Screen.* Grand Rapids, MI: Baker Books, 2005.

Lobe, Jim. Special to the *Daily Star* [Beirut, Lebanon] 20 March 2004.

Lowman, Rob. Review of *Paradise Now. Daily News* [Ventura] 21 March 2006.

Lucia, Cynthia. "An Interview with Sally Potter." *Cineaste* Fall 2005.

Lyman, Rick. "Bad Guys for Bad Times." *New York Times* 3 October 2001.

Lynch, Jim. "Catholic Church Defaced with Anti-Arab Graffiti." *Detroit News* 4 April 2007.

Lynton, Michael. "Globalization and Cultural Diversity." *Wall Street Journal* 4 September 2007.

Maher, Bill. *Real Time,* HBO. 19 March 2004.

"Making an Arab-American Film in Hollywood." *Arab American News* [Dearborn] 16 February 2007.

Manzoor, Uzma. E-mail to Media Education Foundation. 17 August 2007.

Massing, Michael. "Black Hawk Downer." *Nation* 25 October 2002.

Mayer, Jane. "Whatever It Takes." *New Yorker* 12 February 2007.

Mazzolini, Chris. "Humor Attempt Falls Flat." *Daily News* [Jacksonville, NC] 14 June 2006.

McCarthy, Todd. Review of *Babel. Variety* 23 May 2006.

McDonald, Andrew and Gina. "Writing during the War: Prisoner of the Mountain, a Model," *Creative Screenwriting* 9.2.

Medved, Michael. "Hollywood's Terrorists: Mormon, not Muslim." *USA Today* 14 August 2007.

———. "War Films, Hollywood, and Popular Culture." *Imprimis* 34.5 May 2005.

Mehdi, Anisa, dir. *Inside Mecca. National Geographic* documentary. 2003.

Moaveni, Azadeh. "300 Versus 70 Million Iranians." *Time* 13 March 2007.

Morgenstern, Joe. "Kingdom Has Oil, Guns, Sheikhs, But Little Depth." *Wall Street Journal* 28 September 2007.

Moritz, Robert. "Natalie Portman: Every Bit of Good Helps." *Parade* 28 November 2004.

"Muslim Scholars Call for Peace with Christians." Reuters online 11 October 2007.

Naff, Thomas. Personal interview (about marsh Arabs). 19 March 2005.

The 9/11 Commission Report: Final Report of the National Commission on Terrorist Acts upon the United States. New York: WW Norton, 2004.

O'Brien, Chris and Jason Witmer, dirs. *Images of Indians: How Hollywood Stereotyped the Native American.* Starz! Encore Entertainment, 2003.

Oren, Michael B. *Power, Faith, and Fantasy: America in the Middle East: 1776 to the Present.* New York: WW Norton, 2007.

Ozernoy, Ilana. "Eyes Wide Shut." *Atlantic Monthly* November 2006.

Pew Research Center poll. "Muslim Americans: Middle Class and Mostly Mainstream; War on Terror Concerns." 22 May 2007.

Pope John Paul II. "To Those Responsible for Communications." Speech. 24 January 2005 (www.vatican.va/holy_father/john_paul_ii).

"Quick Takes: DePalma's Iraq Film Stuns Venice Fest." *Los Angeles Times* 1 September 2007.

Ramadan, Tariq. Op-ed. *New York Times.* 1 September 2004.

Renov, Michael. *Hollywood's Wartime Women: Representation and Idealogy.* Ann Arbor, MI: Umi Research Press, 1988.

Richardson, Joel. *Antichrist: Islam's Awaited Messiah.* Enumclaw, WA: Wine-Press Publishing, 2006.

Riding, Alan. "Islamic Art as a Mediator for Cultures." *New York Times* 6 April 2004.

Riggs, Marlon, dir. *Color Adjustment.* California Newsreel, 1992.

———. *Ethnic Notions.* California Newsreel, 1986.

Robinson, Linda. "The Propaganda War." *US News & World Report* 29 May 2006.

Rollins, Peter C., ed. *The Columbia Companion to American History in Film.* New York: Columbia University Press, 2003.

Rosenberg, Howard. "Negative Stereotyping Distorts Arabs' Image." *Los Angeles Times* 30 July 2001: F1.

Rosin, Hanna. "Can Jesus Save Hollywood?" *Atlantic Monthly* December 2005.

Roug, Louise. "Extreme Cinema Verite." *Los Angeles Times* 14 March 2005: A1+.

Rubin, Ari B. Letter. *New York Times* 9 May 2007.

Sacirbey, Omar. "TV Show Offers Positive Image." Religion News Service 8 September 2007.

St. John, Warren. "Refugees Find Hostility and Hope on Soccer Field." *New York Times* 21 January 2007.

Scheib, Ronnie. Review of *The Situation. Variety* 30 October 2006.

Schickel, Richard. "His 'Prayer for Peace.'" *Time* 12 December 2005.

Schwarzbaum, Lisa. "Mission: Implausible." *Entertainment Weekly* 5 October 2007.

Scott, A. O. "FBI Agents Solve the Terrorist Problem." *New York Times* 28 September 2007.

"Senator Conrad Burns on Terror." Associated Press 30 August 2006.

Shaheen, Jack G. "Arab Americans," in Rollins.

———. *Reel Bad Arabs.* Northampton, MA: Olive Branch Press, 2001.

Shanker, Thom. "Pop Culture Alive and Well in Iraq." *International Herald Tribune* 13 April 2004.

———. "Military to Report Marines Killed Iraqi Civilians." *New York Times* 26 May 2006.

Sorkin, Aaron. Remarks at "We Hate You But Please Send Us More Austin Powers" symposium at Norman Lear Center. December 2002.

Sklar, Robert. Review of *The Manchurian Candidate. Cineaste* Winter 2004: 43.

Soliman, Ahmed M. *Born in the USA.* New York: iUniverse, 2007.

"Spielberg Takes on Terror." *Time* 12 December 2005.

Spires, Christine. Comments on *Babel. Entertainment Weekly* 2 February 2007.

Steyn, Mark. "Post Mortem: Moustapha, Messenger of Hollywood." *Atlantic Monthly* January/February 2006.

Sterling, Douglas Walter. "Moderate Muslim Clerics in the US Tend to Their Faithful—and Help the FBI Fight Terrorists." *Time* 21 November 2005.

Stone, Oliver. Comments at panel in Dubai 15 December 2007. (Taped by Australian filmmaker Diana Ford.)

Strauss, Bob. "Authentic *Rendition* Sets Aside Arab Stereotypes." *Los Angeles Daily News* 19 October 2007.

Swofford, Anthony. *Jarhead.* New York: Scribner, 2003.

Tapper, Jake and Audrey Taylor. "Terrorist in Training." On the Rifle Fire blog (www.rifle-fire.com) 21 June 2006.

Thompson, Fred. Comments on the *Tonight Show* 12 June 2007.

Tierney, John. Review of *Borat. New York Times* 11 November 2006.

Tirman, John. "A Focus on Facts Ought to Dispel Mistrust." *Christian Science Monitor* 30 January 2005.

Toplin, Robert Brent. "An Anatomy of the Genre." *Cineaste* Spring 2004.

Townsend, Tim. "Baptist Convention Told: Muslims 'Are Here to Take over Our Country.'" *St. Louis Post Dispatch* 1 November 2006.

Twair, Pat McDonnell. "Healing South Central." *ARAMCO World* May/June 2007.

Triplett, William. "Goodwill Hunting." *Variety* 14 May 2006.

Turan, Kenneth. "The Kingdom." *Los Angeles Times* 28 September 2007.

Updike, John. *Terrorist: A Novel.* New York: Ballantine Books, 2007.

United Nations Development Programme (UNDP). *Arab Human Development Report 2002: Creating Opportunities for Future Generations.* New York: UNDP, 2002.

UNICEF. "Iraq Surveys Show 'Humanitarian Emergency.'" Study. 12 August 1999.

Vera Institute of Justice. "Law Enforcement and Arab American Community Relations after September 11, 2001: Engagement in a Time of Uncertainty." Two-year study. Findings published June 2006.

Weissberg, Jay. Review of *Five Fingers*. *Variety* 4 May 2005.

Welkos, Robert W. "Death to the US, but Not Films." *Los Angeles Times* 31 October 2001.

Whitaker, Brian. "The 'Towel-Heads' Take on Hollywood." *Guardian* 11 August 2000.

Wickham, DeWayne. Essay on *Sorry, Haters*. *USA Today* 26 September 2006.

Williams, Daniel. "In Egyptian Movies: Curses! We're the Heavies." *Washington Post* 20 March 2006.

Winik, Lyric Wallwork. "Can the US Rebuild its Image?" *Parade* 28 January 2007.

Woll, Allen and Randall Miller. *Ethnic and Racial Images in American Film and Television*. New York: Garland, 1987.

World Peace Passport. American Hospitality Academy publication, 2005.

Wright, Evan. "Dazed and Confused." *Life* December 2005.

Wright, Robin. "From the Desk of Donald Rumsfeld…" *Washington Post* 1 November 2007.

Yoffie, Rabbi Eric. Comments. *Haaretz* [Israel] 1 September 2007.

Young, Deborah. Review of *Looking for Comedy in the Muslim World*. *Variety* 16 December 2005.

———. Review of *The Stone Merchant*. *Variety* 28 September 2006.

———. Review of *The Tiger and the Snow*. *Variety* 12 October 2005.

Zahn, Paula. "Little Mosque on the Prairie." CNN 5 January 2007.

Zogby, James. "Washington Watch: The Public Diplomacy Debate, Again." Arab American Institute (www.aaiusa.org) 1 February 2004.

Zoroya, Greg. "Study Estimates 600,000 Iraqis Dead by Violence." *USA Today* 11 October 2006.

Zur, Yossi. "Award for Film Implicates Hollywood in Killing." Editorial. *Arkansas Democrat Gazette* 29 January 2006.